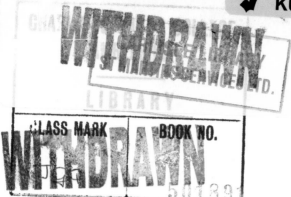

FINDING AND HELPING THE ABLE CHILD

Edited by
TREVOR KERRY

CROOM HELM
London & Canberra

© 1983 T. Kerry
Croom Helm Ltd, Provident House, Burrell Row,
Beckenham, Kent, BR3 1AT

British Library Cataloguing in Publication Data

Finding and helping the able child.
   1. Gifted children
   I. Kerry, Trevor
   371.95 '2   HQ773.5

   ISBN 0–7099–1514–4

Printed and bound in Great Britain by
Biddles Ltd, Guildford and King's Lynn

CONTENTS

ACKNOWLEDGEMENTS

The Editor wishes to thank the Director of Education of
Suffolk County Council for permission to quote from the
Authority's working party document. He is conscious, too,
of the demands he has made on the various authors in the
course of their busy professional lives. As usual, he is
indebted to Carolle Kerry for unstinting labour in checking
and proof-reading, and for being his most incisive critic.
Linda Wightman has laboured diligently over the
manuscript. Of Croom Helm staff, Peter Sowden has been
both supportive and patient.

LIST OF FIGURES

Introduction

Trevor Kerry

This is a book about the bright, able or gifted child. Able children vary widely in ability and in the scope of that ability. Some have IQ scores of around 130; others range up to 170. There is a considerable intellectual gap between these two groups. Yet others may have relatively low IQs but have specific and precocious skills or talents, for example in music.

Interest in the more able child has been stimulated in recent years by the move to comprehensive schooling, the widespread experiment with mixed ability teaching, and the work of a growing number of specialized centres for gifted child education. Nevertheless, research suggests that many teachers are still unaware of the underlying issues, the size and scope of the problem, and the classroom procedures which they might adopt to help their ablest youngsters.

This collection of papers draws together some of the thoughts and expertise of five teachers experienced in handling the problems associated with educating the able pupils in our schools. It is intended to start the reader thinking seriously about provision in his or her own school and Local Education Authority. It suggests some criteria for identification, and then goes on to examine a selection of approaches to improving provision and teaching method.

The collection is not simply a manual of skills for teachers, but such material of this kind as exists is referenced in the text. Nor does it claim to be a detached theoretical statement about the nature of intelligence; but again theory is implicit and is referenced.

These papers are designed to help teachers working alone on their professional skills, course organizers and those with responsibility for initial and in-service education to re-think some of their approaches and priorities in this field

Introduction

Joan Freeman clears the ground by discussing the identification of gifted pupils. Dr Freeman was a senior lecturer at Preston Polytechnic, and recently gained her PhD for work in this field. Her contribution emphasizes the individuality of able youngsters and their individual needs.

The Advisory Teacher for Gifted Education in Essex, Belle Wallace, takes up the identification theme by following the history of one able pupil in a detailed case study before turning her attention to the principles of curriculum development. She suggests that in curriculum the key-note is quality: of provision, of teachers and of learning experiences. However, this quality is, she urges, beneficial to all pupils in a class or school, not just an élite handful of the more able.

In the fourth chapter Trevor Kerry, formerly Co-ordinator of the DES-financed Teacher Education Project, and author of Teaching Bright Pupils in Macmillan's Focus series, takes an overall view of teacher training in Britain. His argument is that, however effective initial training may be, it is inadequate to prepare the student to cope with all the demands of a budding professional career. Trevor Kerry advocates a compulsory element of continuing professional training and development throughout each teacher's career.

The fifth and sixth chapters are concerned with specific classroom skills. Chris Burke talks about the kinds of strategies she uses to help the more able pupils she encounters in her mixed ability primary class at a school in the East Midlands. Trevor Kerry reviews a range of possible tactics open to teachers in secondary comprehensive schools. These two chapters are essentially concerned with what can be done on a daily basis by teachers in their own classrooms.

Chapters 7, 8 and 9 have broader concerns than those of the individual classroom because they deal with in-service initiatives.

Chapter 7 is an account by Roderick Thompson, an experienced deputy head, of how an individual school can scrutinize its own practice and make improvements. He describes the events, over the course of about two years, through which staff have been encouraged to heighten their awareness of able pupils, enrich their curriculum provision, and sharpen up specific aspects of their own teaching skills.

Belle Wallace returns in Chapter 8 to give an account of innovation at Local Authority level. Essex is one of the most active authorities in catering for its able pupil population; and this account might well serve as a stimulus to advisers and education officers to grasp the nettle of able child provision.

While not all LEAs are as conscientious as Essex has been, nevertheless there is a hopeful increase in awareness of the problem of the able child in the non-selective school. Following a letter to one hundred LEAs in England giving information about this book some thirty responses were received describing what, if any, provisions were made for the able. Carolle Kerry, who has worked on the administrative side of special educational provision, has compiled these responses, and examines their effectiveness and flexibility for others to follow.

The book ends with a brief review of problems and aspirations which ought to be taken into account by educational planners and teachers in the run-up to the end of the second millenium.

Each contributor to this volume is expressing his or her own private views on education for the able. Nevertheless, their concerns often overlap. Appropriate cross-referencing will help the reader to pursue ideas from chapter to chapter. At the same time it was felt to be less confusing to list each author's references at the end of his or her chapter rather than in a bibliography at the end of the book. Our hope is that this is a book which teachers and advisers will find readable from cover to cover; but ideally we would like to find them dipping back into its pages many times to pursue one good idea after another. The remainder of this Introduction paints a backdrop to the whole subject by examining some of the issues in the literature of the able; and it casts a rapid glance at gifted child provision in other countries and at why such special provision is desirable here.

Much of the literature of the able child is concerned with identification, and while this subject is more fully discussed by Joan Freeman in the next chapter, some reference to the broad issues is desirable from the outset. But identification cannot proceed until some definition of intelligence is adopted. Even this is rather more complicated than one would wish.

A somewhat dated, but still useful, way of thinking of intelligence in individuals is to suggest that each has a general intelligence factor ('g') which is basic to any intellectual operation; while other more specialized abilities (verbal, spatial-mechanical) are also present in varying degrees in each person. This theory traces its origins to Spearman (1927) and has been adopted, with variations, by many workers since. Thurstone (1938), for example, listed eight "primary factors" in intelligence which operated alongside a general factor. These factors were: verbal, number, spatial, rote memory, perceptual speed, word fluency, inductive reasoning and deductive reasoning.

A widely adopted model nowadays is that of Guilford (1959) - see Figure 1.1. From a theoretical point of view this three dimensional model is excellent; but given that any single intellectual act may be plotted to one of 120 cells it

PRODUCTS

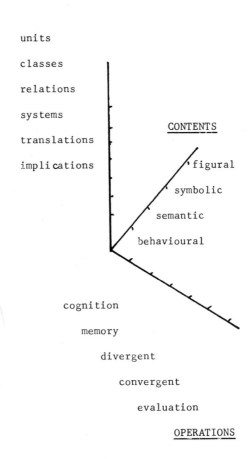

units

classes

relations

systems

translations

implications

CONTENTS

figural

symbolic

semantic

behavioural

cognition

memory

divergent

convergent

evaluation

OPERATIONS

Figure 1.1   A structure of the intellect

/Based on the ideas of Guilford; diagram adapted./

4

is a difficult model to use in experimental situations. For example, it could be argued that to obtain a rounded picture of a person's intelligence level one would need to devise and administer an appropriate test to measure performance on each individual cell of the model.

Some other definitions of intelligence are simpler, though not necessarily more helpful. Those which are commonly quoted are as follows:

... the ability to think in abstract terms (Terman 1916)
... the aggregate or global capacity of the individual to act purposefully, to think rationally, and to deal effectively with his environment (Wechsler, 1944)
... the ability to undertake activities that are characterized by difficulty, complexity, abstractness, economy, adaptiveness to a goal, social value, emergence of originals, and to maintain such activities under conditions that demand a concentration of energy and a resistance to emotional forces (Stoddard, 1945)

The classroom teacher could do worse than conceive of intelligence in Spearman's manner, as a 'g' factor plus a mix of special abilities: this accords with the way in which pupils actually perform, even if the picture is over-generalized and crude. But Stoddard's definition would repay re-reading and reflection. Classroom activities should be reviewed to discover to what extent they are likely to tax the able by providing difficulty, complexity, abstractness, economy of thought, goal-relatedness, social value, originality, the need for concentrated effort and persistence. However, Stoddard's definition is rather clinical and leaves out of account one important factor in this taxing process - excitement. So a last word on the issue of definition might be left to Hersey (1952) who, in a flight of almost poetic fancy, maintained:

> Intelligence of a high order is mysterious, manifold, fast-moving, luminous, tantalizing and incredibly beautiful, like aurora borealis on a cool September night.

Once one has some notion of what intelligence is the temptation is to construct some means of assessing or measuring it. The pioneer work of intelligence testing, Binet's 1905 test, was designed to identify the severely below average for treatment. But since the various revisions of this test (Stanford-Binet, 1937) the emphasis has changed. For over fifty years the work of Sir Cyril Burt was central to intelligence testing in England; and the emergence of a tri-partite system of education with its selection procedures at eleven plus was a legacy of his work.

Introduction

Regrettably, a high amount of doubt has now been shed on Burt's honesty and reliability as a researcher (eg Kamin, 1977). Since at least some of this criticism appears to be justified it may well be necessary for many widely-accepted views about intelligence and its manifestations to be questioned and re-tested by researchers in the next two decades. One is left with a lingering suspicion that while many of Burt's experimental results may now be legitimately regarded as methodologically unsound, his conclusions may well have been reasonable, but the problems will need to be reworked.

The most widely used individual measure of intelligence is the revised Wechsler scale (WISC- R) for children, which differs from Stanford-Binet in including performance tasks as well as verbal ones. This is an important advance because one of the most serious criticisms of intelligence testing is that the results are biased towards the culturally advantaged. In its simplest form this argument maintains that, since most tests rely heavily on verbal items, children from culturally deprived homes will tend to score badly, not from low intelligence, but simply because of their restricted language skills. Worse, some tests include general knowledge items: and these may well be less relevant in some cultures, or sub-cultures, than others. These arguments have led to a proliferation of literature in two important fields.

First, these criticisms of cultural bias of intelligence tests have raised the whole nature-nurture problem in a specific form. Some psychologists (Eysenck, 1973) have maintained that test results show intelligence differences between races; and they have drawn the conclusion that these differences have a genetic cause. Others have seen the dangers of this potentially racialist view, and have argued vehemently that it is the cultural bias in inadequate tests which discriminates against racial minorities tested by means of instruments validated for use in a western, white community. Hundreds of articles have been generated by this explosive subject; and a collection of some 520 pages of them can be found in Block and Dworkin (1977). Much of the controversy surrounding the comparative influence of genetic factors over environmental ones centres around studies of identical twins who, through force of circumstances, have been separated at birth. In ideal conditions, if the geneticists are right, these studies ought to show close correlations in IQ between pairs of identical twins even when the two individuals are reared in widely differing environmental circumstances. Some of the studies purport to do just this (Burt, 1966). Kamin (1977), however, reveals sizeable flaws in Burt's data and methodology. He goes on to examine three other twin studies (Newman, 1937; Shields 1962; Juel-Nielson, 1965) and makes a fascinating discovery. He lists all the twin pairs in age order thus: A^1A^2, B^1B^2,

C^1C^2 etc. He then takes the two pairs of twins nearest in age (A^1A^2, B^1B^2 and so on) and swaps the partners (A^1B^1, A^2B^2). Then Kamin correlates the IQs of the newly created pairs, and he is led to conclude that while the observed IQ correlation between the male pairs (in Newman's study) is 0.58, the pseudo-pairing procedure produces a correlation of 0.67; so "for the males, at least, we can predict an individual's IQ just as well from knowing his age as from knowing his twin's IQ".

A second area of proliferation in the literature resulting from the controversy over cultural bias in intelligence testing has been that which seeks to advocate or establish the culture-fair intelligence test. These tests contain non-verbal items or rote-learning of nonsense syllables. Thus Hegarty and Lucas (1978) set out some requirements for such a test. It must provide activities which are equally unfamiliar to all respondents; contain items related to school work but which are also unfamiliar to all respondents; and ensure that in learning tasks such as memorizing nonsense syllables, the syllables are really nonsense to children of all linguistic backgrounds. The instructions to the individual tasks in the test must be totally clear to the respondent before he begins to perform them. Emphasis in these tests may shift to assessing learning ability rather than measuring some ill-defined quality in the respondent called intelligence. There is still a great deal of progress which needs to be made before existing culture-free tests can be regarded as valid and generally useful.

To sum up the nature-nurture and culture-fair debate it is, perhaps, reasonable to quote Mehrans and Lehmann (1975):

> If there were really no genetic differences between people and if we used a measuring instrument that ruled out (or equated) environmental effects, then everyone would get exactly the same score on the test.

To reinforce this line of argument one might point to two very recent pieces of evidence. A BBC series on 'The Human Brain' has demonstrated that a variety of intellectual, linguistic and physical abilities depend upon the cells and nerve-fibres of the brain. These cells and nerves are created genetically: therefore it cannot be in any way unlikely that our genes affect our basic innate potential to perform a whole variety of tasks. However, it is also likely that few of us are taxed to the limit of potential in our daily lives: so there is room for improvement. Therefore, practice and external circumstances may conspire to bring about change. In a recent paper in Nature, Anderson (1982) has argued that the average IQ of the Japanese has risen sizeably in recent years, and he attributes the major causal factor to improved diet.

Whatever IQ tests measure, and whether they measure effectively all that we call intelligence is doubtful, IQ is clearly not fixed. Pupils can be coached to do better on tests; but then it also appears probable that they can, by learning, extend their 'intelligence' when this is defined as improved facility to think rationally or abstractly, tackle complex issues and deal more effectively with the environment. This observation applies to all children and adults, otherwise education would be a waste of time. The thesis of this book is that it may apply especially to the able, since they are less stretched than others by standard educational procedures.

So far in these opening remarks we have looked at some definitions of intelligence, some IQ tests, and the controversies which rage around these. It should be noticed that these tests are of the kind which are generally administered to individual pupils by specially trained personnel. Teachers need to be able to interpret the results of these tests on their pupils when they are known; they should also be aware that there are group tests of intelligence which can be administered by teachers in their own classrooms. It is beyond the scope of this book to describe these, and their limitations; but this is usefully done in Jackson (1974).

Some teachers will find the whole subject of IQ testing divorced from the classroom; but, it may become important where an able child is referred for more specialist assessment. There are two other important considerations in a background study of the able which have a more direct bearing on classroom work. These are the part played by creativity in intelligence; and the problems of the bright child who fails to reach his potential. To these two topics we now turn.

The widely-read work of Getzels and Jackson (1963) established beyond reasonable doubt that some able youngsters were distinguished from other high IQ pupils by a quality which the researchers labelled 'creativity'. Given a series of tasks to perform or pictures to respond to, the verbal and non-verbal productions of these creative pupils showed more examples of stimulus-free themes, unexpected endings, humour, incongruities, playfulness and violence, as well as a tendency to mock conventional attitudes. Getzels and Jackson concluded that intelligence is a component of creativity but not synonymous with it. Their highly creative pupils, in comparison with the high IQ group, showed individuality, a healthy solitude, intuition, and evaluative abilities. For the classroom the implications of this study were that the possession of many isolated facts should not be confused with education: teachers need to set demanding but not impossible tasks which would replace the factual curriculum by an evaluation 'of the quality of wisdom'. They needed to signal that they valued creative responses, and should not be put off by the independence of the creative pupil, confusing it with rebelliousness.

In Britain, Liam Hudson (1966) carried out an investigation into convergent and divergent thinking. Divergent thinking corresponds approximately to creative thought in the American study; convergent thinking confines itself to logical progress along traditional paths. Hudson suggested that there were deep-rooted variations in personality between convergers and divergers; and he found that divergers preferred arts subjects while convergers tended to favour the sciences.

Both Getzels and Jackson's work and Hudson's are open to criticism: in both cases the samples were drawn from schools in the private sector or in areas of selection, for example. Nevertheless, some replication studies have been carried out and the concept of creativity is now widely accepted.

Creative pupils are those who devize problems not just solve them. But they do appear to have some problems in educational settings. Snyder (1967) suggested that certain institutions may stifle creative approaches and so produce 'drop-outs'. Several such studies have pointed to the frustration and disenchantment which such students come to feel. There was evidence that emotional and cultural barriers are erected to prevent the potential non-conformity of these youngsters' deliberations from materializing (Osborn, 1957). Edward de Bono's (1975) work on thinking skills is used in some British schools as a way of helping pupils and teachers of all abilities to overcome their blockages to creative problem-solving. Nevertheless, these creative pupils may have to face a good deal of prejudice in school from all levels of the school community.

Prejudice is almost certainly a factor, too, in underachievement by able pupils. Little is known about underachievers: they have the strong motivation of peer-group pressure to hide their talents and they become skilled at deception. Persecution of able youngsters by their classmates is sometimes powerful enough to reach the national press (March 1977). Often it is covert. But recent pronouncements by HMI (1978) leave little doubt that underachievement is widespread, and the blame should be laid directly at the door of teachers who underestimate the quality of thought pupils can achieve, hold back the general pace of work to the pace of the average or below, fail to deal adequately with conceptual material, and rely overmuch

on worksheets. The whole concept of mixed ability classes
may need to be rethought. For the underachiever is the able
pupil whose work is of quality, but who finds it under-
valued or rejected and his visions under social threat. Nor
is it a new problem, for Shaffer wrote of it in 1936:

> The pupil of superior intelligence is also
> educationally maladjusted in the conventional school,
> for he is kept from progressing up to the potentialities
> of his ability ... Compelled to sit through lessons
> which are boresome (sic) to him, the gifted pupil may
> resort to daydreaming and slipshod habits of work ...

Studies of quite extensive samples beginning from
Terman's classic works have documented what Newland (1976)
has come to call 'the near-typical underachievement of the
gifted'. Newland himself makes three valuable points:

> ... some underachievement has its roots in social
>   disadvantage
> ... habits of non-work are learned in school
> ... underachievement is often reinforced by teachers.

Here, then, we have them: the intelligent, the
creative, the under-achiever. All of them are able pupils
from the standpoint of this book. What kind of solutions
are offered to meet their particular needs?

There can be little doubt that the teacher is the single
most powerful influence over a child's progress in learning;
this was the outstanding discovery (if it needed discovery)
of the Banbury Report (Newbold 1977). In the previous decade
Rosenthal and Jacobson (1968) had caused a major stir by
trying to show that teachers were suggestible: that if they
were told they should expect a low performance from a pupil,
or a high one, that behaviour and judgements would become
examples of the self-fulfilling prophecy. These efforts met
with vitriolic scorn (Thorndike, in Sperry, 1972). But
despite doubts cast on the validity of this piece of
research it remains true that most educators do accept that
the self-fulfilling prophecy operates in the classroom:
tell a child he is incompetent and he becomes unable to
perform the task (Nash, 1976).
    One method, therefore, of coping with able pupils is to
depress their abilities to the point where they are no
longer a threat to personal self-confidence or professional
competence. Thus the editor once knew a headteacher of a
middle school who regularly tested the pupils' reading.
Using the Holborn reading scale he made sure that even his
slowest learners kept abreast of chronological age in

reading ability: no effort was spared. But he maintained staunchly, in a large school in a mixed catchment area, that he needed no provision for outstandingly able readers. There were none: not a single pupil had ever scored a reading age above 13.9.

But the test ceiling is 13.9.

This kind of spurious self-congratulation and avoidance of the issue may mollify a few parents of able children who are unfamiliar with the world of education. It is professionally dishonest. So what are the alternatives? The two most commonly adopted are acceleration and curriculum enrichment.

Acceleration means that a pupil is promoted beyond his or her year-group in order to be stretched by 'harder' work. In extreme cases acceleration results in grossly premature sitting of '0' or 'A' level examinations and entry to a university by a very young teenager. There are some obvious dangers in acceleration: the most important is the resulting mis-match between intellectual development on the one hand, and social/emotional development on the other. Acceleration in anything other than its most limited form is not advocated by the contributors to this volume. Case studies of accelerated pupils such as those collected by Povey (1980) are usually of too short a duration for the long-term effects of this method to be critically examined; though Painter, in the same book, argues that since able pupils often prefer the company of older peers the social/ emotional arguments may deserve less weight than is sometimes accorded them.

The process of curriculum enrichment is ably described by Belle Wallace in Chapter 3 of this book. A major problem is that much so-called curriculum enrichment consists simply of extra work of exactly the same kind as before: practice not progression (Kerry, 1978). Bridges (1975) described some early attempts, and the tradition has been continued by Ogilvie (1980) with the Schools Council Curriculum Enrichment Project.

Another possible approach to catering for the most able is that of special provision. Nationally there is a wide variety of special provision including

- ... Saturday morning clubs,
- ... summer schools,
- ... specialist musical tuition, and
- ... selective schooling.

The range of LEA provision is described in the concluding chapter by Carolle Kerry. Problems here are the localized nature of these provisions, the élitist charges they have to counter, and their (sometimes) inefficient nature which is born of their essential state of divorce from the rest of the pupil's educational experience.

A central message of this book would be the following statement: the best way to stimulate an able pupil is through raising the quality of thinking which takes place in classrooms; the most efficient means to this end is to improve the teaching skills of classroom practitioners. The case is pursued throughout these pages; but before we turn our attention to it we should cast a swift glance at able child education in other countries, and ask ourselves why this subject ought to occupy a significant place in our thinking.

Mallinson (1980) reviews educational provision for the able in Western Europe. Belgium, he claims, accomplishes its aims for this group through 'complicated systems of option electives which can fully stretch the brightest', though there is no attempt to bring forward any evidence that they do. In Holland the system is academically geared to university entrance through a series of examination hurdles. France has developed a curricular-controlled system which, for the most able, assures a <u>culture générale</u> of considerable academic demand.

From personal experience it would appear that the Swedes value a particular view of democracy above any attempt to help the most able. They take the view that the under-privileged must be given extra chances and facilities, but the "already privileged" should not be rewarded with still more special attention and resources. Their system works well in training specialist remedial teachers; but differential provision for the able is a deeply offensive concept.

Oddly enough, it is Russia which puts most emphasis on fostering talent. The Russians acknowledge the socio-economic importance of skills in any field: academic, aesthetic, physical. The need to make a good show in the world is a spur to provision of special schools and training experiences for the specially talented in almost any field. Teaching methods might be considered to veer towards cramming, but lessons do not lack variety, activity or pupil participation. In a study of modern language lessons Muckle (1981) noted the high standards demanded of average pupils /one education official is quoted as saying "Ninety-nine per cent of the normal population can master a foreign language. We have proved this in practice and no longer discuss the matter."/. He also found a greater degree of high level cognitive demand than is typical of many modern language lessons in this country. He attributes the purposefulness of modern language teaching to five factors which would probably be equally true across the curriculum:

... course aims are clearly delineated
... methodology and materials are well organized to a
   set pattern
... professional monitoring by heads and inspectors is
   continuous
... syllabuses are not deflected from central issues
   into turgid background studies
... children's time is not wasted by long periods of
   undemanding activity.

Most well-known and well-documented of gifted child
programmes abroad come from the United States. Here, there
is a greater readiness to accept that giftedness comes in
many forms, social giftedness for example may compare
alongside academic ability (Pegnato and Birch, 1975). The
Americans are not as afraid as we are of the rise of the
meritocracy (Perritt and Mertens, 1979). Research and
government reports are more readily commissioned (U.S.
Commission of Education, 1971). Federal initiatives are
undertaken (Bartolini, 1979). Writers such as Newland
(1976) give detailed consideration to devising programmes
for the gifted, staffing them, financing them and
evaluating them.

To temper the picture, it still remains true that the
US Commission found that 57½% of school principals
questioned claimed they had no gifted pupils in their
schools; and Vernon et al (1977) introduced their work with
the statement that:

It is surely ironic that the most able and talented
children in western societies, such as Britain, the
United States and Canada, by and large receive the
worst education.

Despite this gloomy Canadian perspective, however, the
authors are able to include a proforma compiled by one
School Board which solicits parental involvement in
identifying their able pupils. Such a thing would
certainly not be countenanced in Britain, so perhaps the
conclusion we should draw is that we fare worst of all in
this country. But does it matter? Why bother? Why show
a concern, as the Swedes put it, for the already privileged?

Whenever I am asked to justify a concern for the able I have
in my mind a picture of a black-coated clergyman pottering
about the Hampshire lanes sometime early in the last
century. His name was Gilbert White. To the little
parish of Selborne he is twentieth century life:
naturalists still flock to his little parish church, the
house which now serves as a museum, and to the hangar above

Selborne   village which White helped cut, a zig-zag path to take him on his wildlife walks. Leaving aside preferment, this highly educated country parson spent almost every year of his long adult life poking his nose into the now taken-for-granted mysteries of nature. Long before the television fame and the fortune of a million copies of Life on Earth, White speculated about migration, weighed dormice, correlated events in nature with his log of the weather and recorded the sleeping habits of his tortoise. He distinguished for the first time in science the little greenish songsters of the woods: goldcrests, willow warblers, chiffchaffs and wood warblers. His diary, in some two hundred and fifty posthumous editions, has been translated into almost every civilised language. He is my picture of a self-fulfilled man. No-one could doubt his curiosity, creative thought, flair and scientific doggedness. He must have been an archetypal bright pupil - creative even, for he wrote a little poetry! For most of us we lack that sparkle: but for all of us, the key to real fulfilment is to live up to our potential, however limited. Somewhere, perhaps, in the underachieving mixed ability class is a Gilbert White looking for his Selborne. What a privilege if you or I were the fortunate anonymous teacher to link one with the other.

White was fulfilled, and from his diaries we have every reason to suspect him happy. Not all talented people are happy in that way. Darwin lived with the heavy burden of his knowledge, Barnes Wallis regretted that others could not see his crystal visions, Churchill had his ups and downs. Perhaps these, and   others like them, have been lonely men. The able have their needs, weaknesses, emotions. Because they are intellectually privileged, who are we to deny them the fulfilment of those needs by refusing to recognize their special qualities?

But let us be more selfish, think only of our mediocre selves. Can any of us doubt that in scientific discovery, technological advance, commercial success, ecological survival, we can dispense with the able, still less with the creative thinkers? In socio-economic terms the talents and abilities of such people are vital to our future success and prosperity. Even if we can't contribute to that prosperity most of us would prefer to bask in its sunshine.

We live in a world of change, and change has the property of accelerating at an ever increasing pace. To keep up with and ahead of change we need visions. And the men and women of vision will, hopefully, improve the quality of our lives. Take one obvious example: would you prefer to visit your dentist fifty years ago or tomorrow? Technological advance has everything to do with quality of life.

Then there is the fostering of individual skill. When I

visited Sweden I heard the argument advanced that society was undemocratic while ever we have 'underprivileged' elements in our society: dustmen, sewage workers and so on. It was suggested that unpleasant jobs should be shared around the community so that we took our turn at emptying bins. For my own part I would have no strong objection to emptying bins; but I hope when it comes to the brain surgeon's turn for bin duty, I don't get the dustman on exchange at the hospital! What errant nonsense! Rare and socially valuable skill should be rewarded - and I shan't lose any sleep when I park my ten-year-old mini next to the surgeon's new XJS.

Finally, there is an educational reason for coping with bright pupils in the way this book suggests: through the improvement of teaching skills leading to a greater cognitive demand in classrooms. This improvement in teaching skills is going to benefit every single pupil, without exception.

Bright pupil education should be aimed at creating and conveying to the pupil a sense of adventure. While I was trying to sum up what education should mean to a bright pupil, the ethos I should (as a teacher) pass on, I wandered into a shop which sold cards for various occasions. There, on the shelf in front of me, unacknowledged, was the sentiment I was looking for. It read:

> Do not follow where the path may lead -
> Go instead where there is no path and leave a trail.

FOR FURTHER STUDY

ANDERSON, A (1982). 'The great Japanese IQ increase', Nature, vol 297, 20.5.82.

BARTOLINI, L. A. (1979). 'Survey of Provisions for Gifted
          Children in Illinois', Mimeograph paper,
          AREA Conference, April 1979.

BLOCK, N., DWORKIN, G. (1977). The IQ Controversy, Quartet.

BRIDGES, S. A. (1975). Gifted Children and the Millfield
          Experiment, Pitman.

BURT, C. (1966). 'The Genetic Determination of Differences
          in Intelligence : a study of monosygotic twins
          reared together and apart', British Journal of
          Psychology, Vol. 57.

DE BONO, E. (1976). Teaching Thinking, Temple Smith.

EYSENCK, H. J. (1973). The Inequality of Man, Temple Smith.

GETZELS, J. W. and JACKSON, P. W. (1963). Creativity and
          Intelligence, Wiley.

GUILFORD, J. P. (1959). 'The three faces of intellect',
          American Psychologist, Vol. 5.

HEGARTY, S. and LUCAS, D. (1978). Able to learn? The
          Pursuit of Culture-Fair Assessment, NFER.

HERSEY, J. (1959). Intelligence, Choice and Consent,
          Woodrow Wilson Foundation.

HMI (1978). Mixed ability teaching in Comprehensive Schools,
          HMSO.

HUDSON, L. (1966). Contrary Imaginations, Methuen.

JACKSON, S. (1974). A teacher's guide to tests and testing,
          Longman.

JUEL-NIELSON, N. (1965). 'Individual and environment: a
          psychiatric-psychological investigation of
          monozygotic twins reared apart', Acta
          Psychiatrica et Neurologica Scandinavica,
          Monograph Supplement.

KAMIN, L. J. (1977). The Science and Politics of IQ,
          Penguin.

KERRY, T. (1978). 'Bright Pupils in Mixed Ability Classes',
          Brit. Educ. Res. Jnl., Vol. 4.2, pp 103-111.

MALLINSON, V. (1980). 'Educating the Gifted Child: A Comparative View' in R. Povey (ed.) Educating the Gifted Child, Harper & Row.

MARCH, R. (1977). 'Too bright for their own comfort', Guardian, 11th October.

MEHRENS, W. A. and LEHMANN, I. J. (1973). Standardized Tests in Education (2nd ed.), Holt, Rinehart & Winston.

MUCKLE, J. (1981). 'The foreign language lesson in the Soviet Union: observing teachers at work', Modern Languages, Vol. 62.3, pp 153-163.

NASH, R. (1976). Teacher Expectations and Pupil Learning, Routledge & Kegan Paul.

NEWBOLD, D. (1977). Ability Grouping, NFER.

NEWLAND, T. E. (1976). The gifted in socio-educational perspective, Prentice-Hall.

NEWMAN, H., FREEMAN, F. and HOLZINGER, K. (1937). Twins: a study of heredity and environment, University of Chicago Press.

OGILVIE, E. (1980). 'The Schools Council Curriculum Enrichment Project' in R. Povey (ed.) Educating the Gifted Child, Harper & Row.

OSBORN, A. F. (1957). Applied Imagination, Scribner.

PEGNATO, C and BIRCH, J (1975). 'Locating gifted children junior high schools' in W Barbe & J Renzulli Psychology and Education of Gifted Children, Wiley.

PERRIT, L. J., MERTENS, D. M. (1979). 'Gifted Education: Teacher and Community Attitudes', Mimeograph paper, AREA Conference, April 1979.

POVEY, R. (1980). Educating the Gifted Child, Harper & Row.

ROSENTHAL, R., JACOBSON, L. (1968). Pygmalion in the Classroom, Holt, Rinehart & Winston.

SHAFFER, L. F. (1936). The Psychology of Adjustment, Houghton Mifflin.

SHIELDS, J. (1962). Monozygotic twins brought up apart and brought up together, O.U.P.

SNYDER, B. (1967). 'Creative Students in Science and Engineering', Universities Quarterly, Vol. 21.2, pp. 205-218.

SPEARMAN, C. (1927). The abilities of Man, Macmillan.

STODDARD (1945). The meaning of intelligence, Macmillan.

TERMAN, L. M. (1916). The measurement of intelligence, Houghton Mifflin.

THORNDYKE, R. L. (1972). Review of 'Pygmalion in the Classroom' in L. Sperry, 1972 Learning Performances and Individual Differences, Scott, Foreman.

THURSTONE, L. L. (1938). Primary Mental Abilities, University of Chicago Press.

U.S. COMMISSION OF EDUCATION (1971). Education of the Gifted and Talented, Washington DC: Report to the Congress of the United States.

VERNON, P. E., ADAMSON, G. and VERNON, D. (1977). The psychology and education of gifted children, Methuen.

WECHSLER, D. (1944). The measurement of adult intelligence, Williams & Wilkins.

Chapter 1

IDENTIFYING THE ABLE CHILD

Joan Freeman

Annette, Michael, Robert, Janet, Mark, Howard and Fiona all attend Anywhere Comprehensive School.

Annette is an accomplished pianist, and reached grade VII this year, though she is only eleven years old.

Michael has been involved at the local children's hospital for two years, and as part of a sixth form project has just invented a device to help a handicapped youngster feed himself more effectively.

Robert shows no special talent at any one subject, but has just passed in nine GCE 'O' level subjects.

Janet is thirteen, and has just won a national competition to design a dress for a special occasion.

Eleven-year-old Mark is obsessive about cricket and collects everything to do with the game: autographs, photographs, books. He has just been a panelist on a local radio sports quiz game.

Howard has been awarded an Open Scholarship in mathematics and wants to become an accountant.

Fiona had one of her paintings selected for hanging by the County Society of Arts annual exhibition committee.

All of these children exhibit sizeable talent in one field or another, or simply a good all round academic ability. They are all able pupils, despite the diversity of their talents.

This book is about these pupils, and tens of thousands of others like them.

We begin, however, by looking more specifically at ways in which children with talents and abilities may be recognized. The literature of this subject has traditionally spoken of these children as gifted. This is slightly unfortunate, perhaps, because the general public tends to confuse giftedness with genius. The latter is a rare individual, a Darwin or a Churchill; but we meet the able and the gifted every day of our lives. Except perhaps in the smallest and remotest rural communities or the most desperate of Educational Priority Areas, each year group in every school will encompass a few.

So let us begin by asking two questions: What is giftedness? Who are the gifted?

Giftedness, like beauty, is in the eye of the beholder. Throughout history, the meaning of giftedness has varied, as it still does between different societies, according to the conceptions of the people who use the term. This means that giftedness cannot be viewed as excellence per se, but is always a relative matter - a function of circumstance, time and culture.

It is important, too, in identifying intellectually gifted children, to recognize that the motives which may underlie the choice of this description are not always conscious or given recognition. The label is not always complimentary and the motives and beliefs behind its use may come from a variety of sources which may appear as honourable, selfish or simply mistaken, according to personal points of view. Sometimes they lead to prejudice against those who are so described.

In practice the term 'gifted' is always used in a comparative manner. It can be a description of outstanding ability in either a general or specific sense, indicating superiority over others. As a basis for comparison, it is always relative. Even in the same field of activity, children are called gifted at varying levels of achievement, depending on the comparison being assumed. For example, children with identical achievement attending different schools may be termed dull, average or gifted, depending on the outlook and expectations of the school.

In an attempt to rectify this discrepancy, in some American States children are being assessed in terms relative to their immediate social environments. Thus, an attempt is being made to avoid comparing the achievements and abilities of children from poor educational environments with those of children from good educational environments (Mercer, 1975). However socially justified, this adjusted measurement does add to the complication of defining giftedness. A child who might score badly on an intelligence test or a test of mathematics, which has been standardised nationally, may now be identified as gifted in terms of the local population. Alternatively a special test may be devised to take account of social factors such as housing or poor dietary habits and children scoring highly on it will be termed gifted. The proliferation in America of these parochial tests of ability makes statistical comparison between them impossible.

Probably the most reliable measure of educational potential to date is the intelligence test. A baseline IQ measure has been used in definitions of giftedness since Terman (1925) first employed it in California. In the United

States, gifted children are often described as those who score over 130 IQ, though in Britain the baseline for giftedness in terms of intelligence is more often 140 IQ. Though the concept of intelligence is never all-embracing in the description of giftedness, it often appears to be a crucial thread. Considerable information has been amassed about the origins and development of intelligence; and whatever it is that intelligence tests measure, however questionable its validity, the measure of IQ is reliable and is thus amenable to research. It is also by far the most frequently used indication, whether measured or judged, of intellectual giftedness in children by parents and educators.

The definition of giftedness used by Eric Ogilvie (1973) in his survey of facilities for gifted children in Britain epitomised the difficulties of presenting a precise guide for identification:

> the term 'gifted' is used to indicate any child who is
> outstanding in either a general or specific ability,
> in a relatively broad or narrow field of endeavour ...
> Where generally recognised tests exist as (say) in the
> case of 'intelligence' then giftedness would be defined
> by test scores. Where no recognised tests exist it can
> be assumed that the subjective opinions of 'experts' in
> the various fields on the creative qualities of
> originality and imagination displayed would be the
> criteria we have in mind.

This definition is open-ended and could not be called either rigorous or precise, though it is a fair summary of our present knowledge about gifted children. However, there is a real need for some more rigorous definition and, above all, one which has predictive value.

The results of a six-year research project, carried out across the North West of England - the Gulbenkian Research Project on Gifted Children - were described in "Gifted Children" (Freeman, 1979). Considerations and further findings from the research since that publication, which are specific to problems of identification, are presented here.

THE RECOGNITION OF GIFTED CHILDREN

Even before considering the problems of hard-and-fast identification procedures for gifted children, one needs to consider whether such children are even recognized. It cannot be taken for granted that the gifted child is recognized as a special category of child at all, much less that such a child might have needs or problems. It can be argued that what some may consider to be the problems of giftedness are so insignificant, if not illusory, that they are not worthy of either consideration or action. In addition, since these so-called problems are not as obvious as, for instance, those of mongolism, and may even be construed as advantages, they are sometimes said to be not worth searching out. Why should help be given to the already advantaged, one is asked?

Headteachers in Britain are not, on the whole, in favour of recognizing the presence of giftedness as a phenomenon. Teachers in some schools see the term gifted as synonymous with demanding parents and difficult children, as I discovered during my research. When a child bears the label of gifted in a school with that outlook it will probably not be to his advantage. Where the phenomenon of giftedness is recognized to exist it is usual for a teacher to see any resulting needs or problems in terms of the individual child, rather than as impinging on all gifted children (Ogilvie, 1973; D.E.S., 1977; Freeman, 1979). Perhaps in the present state of incomplete and ambiguous evidence, this is the safest, if not the most constructive approach.

Labelling

A general theory of how labelling affects a person's behaviour has been the concern of social psychologists for some years (Becker, 1963). The effect of labelling a child as gifted is very likely to alter the child's self-concept and possibly his actual physical circumstances - he may be put into a special school or class. Whether this is good or bad for the individual, it will certainly influence his whole life.

Expectancy

Allied to the effects of labelling are those of expectancy - the self-fulfilling prophecy. The influence of expectation on the part of parents and teachers has now entered the folklore of education through the work of Rosenthal and Jacobson (1968). Educational literature abounds with accounts of how pupils' performance is depressed or elevated by the way in which their teachers see them (Goodacre, 1968; Pigeon, 1970). The information, which is slowly accumulating, about teachers' influence on pupils (Rutter et al, 1979) shows how considerable this effect is, occurring for several hours each day in term-time and accentuated by informal staffroom policy-making towards children. Labelling a child as gifted could be expected to improve academic performance, if not social behaviour.

Attention

The Hawthorne effect is a commonly used phrase from the social sciences to indicate that increased attention to an individual increases his achievement or efficiency as he responds to being the centre of interest. It is the most frequently offered explanation as to why children in any kind of specialized education course do better than those in the general class. The argument is that increased attention to any child will improve that child's performance - no matter what is taught. In the case of a gifted child, for instance, extra lessons on computer technology might be quite irrelevant to his general development as they stand; but their attention value is considerable, and improved school performance can be attributed to this Hawthorne effect. The argument seems to presuppose that not enough attention is given to individuals in the usual course of events, so that the extra is bound to have an effect. No doubt many educationalists would agree. But it is possible that enough attention could never be paid to _every_ child, so that the Hawthorne effect could never be eliminated.

Categorizing

It is of essential importance, particularly if lessons from research results are to be translated into practice, to know exactly _how_ gifted children come to be assigned to that category by teachers, psychologists and others. Conclusions which may be drawn from the study of labelled groups of gifted children can be quite irrelevant to the unlabelled, but equally gifted children, as the writer discovered when she compared children labelled as gifted with an intellectually matched but unlabelled group (Freeman, 1979). A unified approach to the subject of giftedness in children suggests that both sociological and psychological aspects of behaviour should be taken into account, allowing a variety of factors in the designation of children as gifted to be recognized and evaluated. Thus in the United States children are sometimes labelled as socially gifted quite apart from intellectual qualities. Such social giftedness is deemed to consist of such characteristics as popularity with peers, leadership skills, tact and humour.

SOCIAL IDENTIFICATION

Simply on the criterion of numbers, gifted children are abnormal: they are a small percentage of any child population. The higher up an ability range a gifted child is rated, the less statistically normal his position in society. It is in question how recognition of this high position on an ability spectrum affects behaviour - both of the child and of the people around. If the social behaviour of gifted children is seen as different or deviant from that of less able children, it may indeed be due to their abnormality per se. But it may also be due to the reaction of society to the idea of that abnormality and the label of giftedness.

In popular mythology the concept of the gifted child is one which lends itself to unfounded stereotypes. In spite of well established research evidence to the contrary (Terman, 1925), gifted children are most often visualized as physically underdeveloped, mentally distressed, absent-minded and unable to manage healthy relationships in a normal day-to-day life. P E Vernon made the same point:

> The very bright child, according to traditional lore, is poorly developed physically, short-sighted, no good at athletics; also precocity is flash-in-the-pan and doesn't last. (Vernon et al, 1977)

The earlier a child is identified as gifted the more likely he is to adapt to this popular prescription of stereotyped giftedness which is imposed upon him. It is often described as a 'problem' of giftedness that it results in 'unacceptable' antisocial behaviour, for example, that such children are "prone to sudden bursts or rage resulting from frustration", (Hopkinson, 1978). Some of the children's behaviour is likely to be the direct result of the adult's communicated belief that they are reacting to the stress of the mediocrity around them; for it is part of the mythology of gifted children that they should do so.

It is not difficult to imagine a family group imposing the mythic mantle of giftedness on a bright child. Every sign of even normal ability would be applauded as though it were exceptional and even indications of disturbance are welcomed, for they appear to add to the evidence that theirs is a gifted child who has the mythical difficulty of living in a mediocre world. Giftedness, real or imagined, can sometimes be made the excuse or give a child licence for bad behaviour.

BEHAVIOURAL IDENTIFICATION

A well-favoured method of recognizing and identifying gifted children is to draw up a list of their "characteristics". The lists begin with a small selection of characteristics, such as intense curiosity, independence of mind or early reading; but there are always children who are exceptions to each of these categories. A particular child will not always fit exactly, so the lists grow in order to accommodate the exceptions. As they grow longer and more detailed over the passage of time, they also become more all-embracing, until

some of them would describe almost any child! Where a list
might say, for example, that a characteristic of a gifted
child is that he asks a lot of questions it would tell us
little about an average individual brought up in a home
atmosphere which encourages such behaviour. Children from
such backgrounds will be more likely to ask questions than an
equally or more gifted child for whom parents signal that such
behaviour is unacceptable, and who thus take pains to control
the flow of enquiry. Other characteristics and abilities may
also be concealed if children find them disapproved of by
people they value; whether these people are adults or other
children. Fashion, too, is important; the primary
characteristic described for a socially gifted child in
America in the 1950s was general physical attractiveness
combined with neatness in appearance; and even today the
Stanford-Binet intelligence test uses aesthetic appearance as
a component of the IQ score.

The makers of lists usually suggest that they are
presenting some characteristics frequently found in gifted
children and hope only to stimulate a parent or teacher's
awareness that a child might be gifted: the next move would
be to approach an "authority" on the subject. Unfortunately,
lists themselves are not entirely successful as
identification tools because they have no predictive or
definitive value, and the "authority" may not have access to
information that is omitted from the list. The following
list from the Department of Education and Science (UK) is
typical; the starred items are the particularly important
indicators.

GIFTED CHILDREN: A TEACHER'S CHECKLIST

(Exceptionally able children are likely to show the following
characteristics. A child showing most characteristics on the
checklist, but not those starred, is likely to be a gifted
child who is under-achieving educationally.) Such children:

1. Possess superior powers of reasoning, of dealing
   with abstractions, of generalizing from specific
   facts, of understanding meanings, and of seeing
   into relationships.
2. Have great intellectual curiosity.
*3. Learn easily and readily.
4. Have a wide range of interests.
5. Have a broad attention-span that enables them to
   concentrate on, and persevere in, solving problems
   and pursuing interests.
6. Are superior in the quantity and quality of
   vocabulary as compared with other children of their
   own age.

   7. Have ability to do effective work independently.
* 8. Have learned to read early (often well before school age).
   9. Exhibit keen powers of observation.
  10. Show initiative and originality of intellectual work.
  11. Show alertness and quick response to new ideas.
  12. Are able to memorize quickly.
  13. Have great interest in the nature of man and the universe (problems of origins and destiny, etc).
  14. Possess unusual imagination.
  15. Follow complex directions easily.
  16. Are rapid readers.
  17. Have several hobbies.
*18. Have reading interests which cover a wide range of subjects.
*19. Make frequent and effective use of the library.
*20. Are superior in mathematics, particularly in problem solving.

                                   (Hoyle and Wilks, 1975)

In a study of East Midlands teachers, Kerry (1981) found that teachers had their own checklists of characteristics. They thought of able youngsters in the following ways:

PROFILE OF THE BRIGHT PUPIL
Teachers recognize bright pupils as those who ...

Grasp concepts or experiments readily
Think out problems for themselves
Show above average intellectual ability
Think and understand quickly
Ask intelligent questions
Use their initiative
Make connections back to previous knowledge
Draw conclusions
Assimilate facts quickly
Have lively and enquiring minds

Such checklists are often useful pointers to a hard-pressed parent or teacher with little time or opportunity for objective testing. However, although we have now accumulated some descriptive signs of giftedness, we still need more assurance of their validity. A further requirement is a knowledge as to which of these discriminating signs may be accompanied by others, which are not in themselves discriminating. For example, a high IQ may in itself be a discriminatory and even measurable sign, but we cannot say for certain whether this intellectual potential is accompanied by any linked behaviour. There is also the problem of specific gifts, which appear to come in pairs or groups. For example, skills in mathematics and music are commonly considered, even by specialist teachers in these subjects, to be related to one another; though there is little evidence to support this assumption, and there has in fact been evidence against it. In her study of the inheritance of musical ability, Shuter (1968) found that music is most frequently a singular specific gift. She concluded that any connection that musical talent might have with mathematical or scientific ability was due to an all-round "integrated intellect", but could not otherwise be accepted as an established pairing. Revesz (1953) found that only 9% of professional musicians had mathematical talent or interest in mathematics. Unfortunately, the large investigation at John Hopkins University, (Stanley, Keating and Fox, 1974) on mathematically gifted children did not investigate the possibility of a musical link.

The distinction between potential and achievement, relative to other children, is extremely important in identifying giftedness. However, the writer's research has shown that children whose home backgrounds have enabled them to exercise their abilities and to achieve more highly are far more likely to be identified as gifted than children from culturally poorer homes (Freeman, 1981). When children of equal intellectual ability but from different educational environments were compared in terms of their identification by intelligence, those with superior facilities were found to be more likely to be selected as gifted. This is a considerable problem, particularly for a school serving a poor community, where there is some tendency for teachers to lose heart over their unprepossessing charges. A headteacher once told the writer "You won't find any gifted children here: they're all 'Council' children", and another wrote "In my list of priorities gifted children come very low. We've got more important things to concern ourselves about in this area". Both statements were understandable in their contexts, but they both, perhaps, fell somewhat short of the ideals of child-centred education.

Naturally, there is a direct connection between the kind of measure of giftedness used and the characteristics of the gifted children defined by it. Each measure will contain an interest bias. There may be a bias in the judgement of the tester. Where parents believe their children to be gifted, it cannot be said that they will show the same characteristics as children identified by IQ test. Human judgement must always involve a personal perspective, which takes into account the meaning of the event to the person concerned. This applies to teachers, of course, as well as to parents in their identification of gifted children.

DEVELOPMENTAL SIGNS OF GIFTEDNESS INVESTIGATED BY THE GULBENKIAN RESEARCH PROJECT

The Gulbenkian Research Project looked in detail at some alleged determinants of giftedness. The rest of this chapter goes on to review the usefulness of some of the determinants in helping the classroom teacher decide whether or not to consider a child as gifted and in need of special help or attention.

PHYSICAL DEVELOPMENT

There is no proven relationship between giftedness and physical development, either for weedy or powerful children. But, the higher up the socio-economic scale a child is, the physically healthier he is likely to be (Tanner, 1978; Davie et al, 1972) and, because of the cultural bias of intelligence tests, the higher his IQ score is likely to be too. But gifted children who are measured on non-verbal, culture-free tests of intellectual ability (which do not result in an IQ score) show no significant difference when compared for their physical development. Nor do intellectually gifted children have a different pattern of health from other children; though the research showed that children who were subjectively identified as gifted by their parents had more ailments such as asthma, clumsiness and poor sleep.

Eyesight

According to the stereotype, gifted children are likely to be short-sighted and to wear glasses, and for once the popular image seems to be correct. Several studies have found that highly achieving children who are harder working, more attentive and have more academic-style hobbies are also more likely to wear glasses. They also receive more encouragement from home and may thus spend longer at these tasks.

There is the possibility that when children have to peer more closely at their books, the side-effect is an increase in concentration. This seemingly greater effort to learn on the part of the children then positively reinforces the parents to greater encouragement. A positive cycle is thus set up whereby children and parents (as well as teachers) reinforce each other to produce the best school results of which the child is capable.

Coordination

Dexterity in physically normal children is most likely to be associated with general psychological adjustment rather

than with intelligence as such. However, boys do have more
difficulty with fine motor control than girls, which is most
likely to show up in their handwriting. Indeed, gifted
children of both sexes tend to be messy in their handwriting,
a feature which is usually considered to be due to their very
rapid thinking abilities which are far in advance of their
writing skills. This could be a cause of teachers
underestimating their pupils' intellectual ability,
especially in the early school years, by putting too much
emphasis on this relatively physical aspect of communication.

CONCLUSIONS: PHYSICAL SIGNS OF GIFTEDNESS

Physical development and health in gifted children appear to
be most closely related to socio-economic level and
psychological adjustment. It is not advisable to use
physical development as a sign in the judgement of
intellectual giftedness.

EMOTIONAL DEVELOPMENT

In her study of "Able Misfits", Mia Kellmer Pringle (1970)
found that the misbehaviour of the able boys she studied was
not due to their giftedness, but to their unhappy homes,
illogical parental discipline and "inconsistent handling".
Other studies have shown that gifted children, as measured by
high IQ, are in fact better adjusted in the classroom than
less able children (Gallagher, 1975; Terman, 1925; see also
Chapter 5).
    It was demonstrated in the Gulbenkian research project
that very high intellectual ability is not directly related
to emotional adjustment. Nor were intellectually gifted
children in normal classrooms and among mixed-ability
children found to be suffering from emotional frustration.
However, it is possible that where giftedness and
maladjustment are combined in a child, the mixture is liable
to cause considerable problems. The popular stereotype of
emotional disturbance being related with giftedness can serve
only to impede the identification of gifted children as
teachers may be on the lookout for odd behaviour, whereas
most gifted children are at least as conforming as any others.
Nice, quiet little gifted girls, who do what they're told to -
and no more - are probably the most likely to be missed, and
among such pupils the teacher should seek out the
underachievers.

Feeling different
Gifted children do feel themselves to be different from other

children, largely in respect of their enhanced intellectual
abilities. They are often more sensitive to others than less
gifted children, and can empathise more readily with other
people. But gifted children are unlikely to have
distinguishable personality traits. Some traits which are
often described for gifted children, like ambition or
curiosity, may, in fact, be attributes of their upbringing,
and not of their intellect. Belle Wallace describes in
Chapter 8, the relief some bright youngsters feel when they
discover they are not unique in behaviour or interests.

Sleep

Most lists of characteristics by which a gifted child might
be identified contain a reference to the idea that the gifted
child needs less sleep than other children. But this alleged
characteristic has never been shown to be valid in a research
study. Quantity of sleep depends on what parents expect and
on the children's psychological adjustment. For example,
working-class children are usually put to bed later than
middle-class children and so are less frequently described as
having sleep problems by their parents, whatever their
intellectual ability. As identified gifted children are most
frequently middle-class they often appear to have sleep
problems, though this is not an indication of giftedness but
of parental attitudes.

Children's friends

Part of the stereotype of a gifted child is that he is a
loner. This is true only to the extent that he is likely to
be more self-sufficient and to have less need of friends'
support. At school, gifted children mingle as freely as
others with their class-mates. At home, however, gifted
children are more likely to get on with their own affairs
and like music practice or hobbies which don't usually
involve others. Intellectually gifted children are often not
very keen on team games either; if they're sporty, they're
more likely to prefer athletics.

When children are physically separated from others of
their age-group by virtue of their ability, say in a special
class, it can put up a barrier to the development of normal
social relationships. This process can be harmful to the
child and, in effect, turn him into something of a social
isolate. But, of course, every child is an individual and a
gifted child may prefer to work hard at school. If this is
not acceptable behaviour to the rest of the class, of any
ability, it may isolate him from them through his failure to
conform to the school or class mores. Teachers should
always keep an eye out for the signs of such problems
developing in their classes.

Boredom

It is often considered that if a gifted child is not intellectually stretched, he will be bored and get up to mischief. There is little documented research evidence for this, but perhaps a considerable fellow-feeling from educationalists. This feeling was not expressed by the gifted children of the research project in England, though that does not imply that they were fully active educationally. Most schoolchildren, it is sad to say, are subject to boredom at some time or another, both in school and out. This theme is taken up again in Chapters 5 and 6.

CONCLUSIONS: EMOTIONAL SIGNS OF GIFTEDNESS

Gifted children are as emotionally well balanced as other children, but their popular image as oddities does affect other people's expectations and interpretations of their behaviour. Repeated research studies have shown that disturbed emotional behaviour is not a feature of gifted children.

MENTAL DEVELOPMENT

Because mental development is measured in a variety of ways, the results of the measurements are just as varied. Teachers need to be aware of how to interpret the measures. Many educationalists prefer to measure giftedness by IQ alone (Bridges, 1973; Callow, 1980; Painter, 1980). Others have supplemented the IQ with other tests (Pringle, 1970; Hitchfield, 1973; Tempest, 1974), while some prefer to do without tests altogether (Guilford, 1967; Torrance, 1975; Gallagher, 1975). The Gulbenkian research approach has been to regard IQ as a measure of realized potential, i.e. largely of achievement. This is because it has been found to be cumulatively affected by home-background, particularly at its highest levels (Freeman, 1981). It is important, when identifying gifted children, to be aware of how different types of measurement or judgement select out specific groups of children as gifted which another test may reject.

Verbal development

Although verbal development is clearly an ability which is susceptible to influence by social class - the higher up the scale, the more complex and fluent language is likely to be used at home - even children measured as gifted on non-verbal tests of intelligence were often found to be verbally precocious. This applies to the three skills of talking, reading and writing.

As they become older, children who had such an early start usually become much more avid and wider readers than is usual and reading is still a passport to knowledge and a key to educational and vocational opportunities. The relationship between verbal ability and IQ is strong even for children as early as three-years-old.

Leisure activities

Gifted children tend to have a very wide variety of interests: but these do not appear to follow a pattern. They are not, for example, keener on jigsaws or collections than other children: the Newsoms (1979) in their study of seven hundred 7-year-olds, found that 73% of them had specific collections, not counting the eclectic ones. Gifted children are more discriminating in their television watching, but enjoy most of what is shown; they have comics (sometimes surreptitiously), music, encyclopaedias and almost anything interesting that comes by. Range of interest may be a feature of these youngsters.

Curiosity

It's not the quantity, but the quality of their curiosity which distinguishes the gifted. Children's questions can arise from a variety of causes, such as attention-seeking, and teachers have to be careful not to miss the intellectual potential of gifted children who only speak or ask questions occasionally.

An unfortunate feature of gifted children in this respect is that sometimes inquisitiveness is seen as smugness by adults. In certain circumstances these children may not seem curious, but rather "know-all". In these cases they may possibly be trying to live up to their label of cleverness, even if this is self-imposed. In this respect, the occasional exclusive company of other gifted children can be a boon to them.

Concentration

The ability to concentrate, and to derive great benefit from it, is a notable feature of a fine intellect. It shows itself from a very early age, and does not seem to be an aspect of home-background. Not surprisingly, this facility usually enables gifted children to make excellent academic progress, although the exclusivity of the concentration may sometimes irritate other children and adults.

Memory

The gifted child usually has an exceptional memory from a

very early age and uses it in gathering his great store of
general knowledge. Teachers aren't always sufficiently aware
of this feature of very high intelligence (Ogilvie, 1973),
but it is worth watching for and is commoner than is
sometimes supposed.

Sense of humour

Gifted children have often been described as being
particularly witty. They are supposed to see and to
emphasise absurdities in everyday situations, to enjoy
playing with words and making up nonsense, limericks and so
on. However, in the Gulbenkian research project it seemed,
to the contrary, that gifted children were particularly
serious. When they did show a sense of humour, it was often
wry. Perhaps in our case it is a feature of the "Lancashire"
outlook of the research subjects, as American studies have
had different results.

Achievement

All children's achievements, including their IQ scores, are
affected by their home backgrounds. When children are
selected as gifted by virtue of their IQs, it must be
supposed that the results contain an effective measure of
their environment and its influence.

This effect was seen very clearly in my research. The
parents of the very high IQ children (IQ 141 or more)
showed very much higher levels of educational achievement
and of involvement in cultural activities than the parents
of the moderate IQ children (IQ between 100 and 140). This
difference even extended to the grandparents. The high IQ
children enjoyed a particularly high level of educational
help in the home. It is still not known, however, the extent
to which achievement of IQ potential is dependent on
environmental factors.

However, for the children who were measured as gifted
on a non-verbal test (the top 1% on the Raven's Matrices)
the only effective home influences were the cultural milieu
of the home and the facilities provided for the children's
educational progress.

It appeared that at the very highest levels of ability,
children's all-round achievement (even including teachers'
reports) was heavily influenced by home background. After
all, gifted children can only work with what they have -
Yehudi Menhuin would not have become a great violinist had
he not had access to a violin.

The gifted children who had had the best resources were
found to be much better able to make beneficial use of them
than less able children. They shot ahead. The gifted
child's considerable potential to gain from input would be

expected to widen the achievement gap between gifted children from good and poor environments respectively. Hence gifted children identified by IQ alone are almost inevitably from excellent home backgrounds.

Intelligence Quotient

Evidence from my study has shown that at IQ 130-135, the environmental effects begin to be particularly potent. It is therefore suggested that the lower level of IQ 130 be used as a base measurement from which giftedness might be further judged. This would involve about 3% of the child population. IQ points measured above that would then be considered as achievement for purposes of identification.

It is also suggested that where an IQ test is used as a measure of giftedness, then some other form of non-verbal or specific ability measure be used in parallel. Although it is impossible to measure a child's intellectual ability independently of environmental influences, it is possible to minimise their effects.

Teacher selection of children as gifted is, not unnaturally, influenced by the pupils' measureable achievement; a judgement of what children do do rather than what they can do. Achievement itself, however, depends at least in part on outside factors such as opportunity or quality of teachers. Those who dispense with other forms of measurement than a child's attainment are possibly throwing out the baby with the bathwater, as they then have to rely on the child's overt behaviour, such as his achievement, and on their own subjective interpretations. Kerry (1978) found that teachers often identified the brightest pupils in their classes by "instinct". The answer to identification is - as always - a compromise.

CONCLUSIONS FROM THE RESEARCH

Children who are intellectually gifted, as measured on a culture-free, non-verbal test (in the top 1%) are most likely to

... derive greater benefit from education provision; and
... be physically,
     emotionally,
     socio-economically, and
     in personality, normal youngsters.

Children who have realised their potentials at IQ 141 or more (the top 1%) are likely in addition to

... have had considerable educational support,

... be from a fairly high socio-economic environment,
... feel "different" and independent,
... be exceptional in intellectual ways:

    1) Concentration
    2) Memory
    3) Multi-attentiveness
    4) Empathy
    5) Speed of perception
    6) Depth of thought,

... be exceptional in span of ability:

    1) Verbal ability
    2) School progress
    3) Perseverence
    4) Variety of interests
    5) Occupational aspirations
    6) Musical ability
    7) Poor handwriting,

... have good physical development,
... have a normal emotional development,
... be more likely to be first born or only children.

About identification in general we can say that children who are identified as gifted by non-test means are unlikely to be typical of gifted children identified by testing. Behavioural indices such as questioning, sleep habits, etc. may not be valid indications of giftedness. The IQ measure is heavily contaminated with accumulative home environment effects, particularly in its higher ranges, beginning at IQ 130. Non-verbal tests are the best measures of intellectual potential and should always be used along with an IQ test. The proportion of gifted children in the national population is unsure, but it is probable that we should be casting our net wider than we do at present.

As far as the educational system goes teachers can work on the premise that gifted children function at a superior intellectual level to other children, but are in all other respects normal. Gifted children can obtain greater benefit than other children from the educational environment, from a very early age, and can therefore benefit more from educational provision. Gifted children, who are separated from other children for their education over appreciable lengths of time, would find it harder to make normal social relationships. Non-specialist teaching does not bring about emotional disturbance in gifted children. Flexibility in education is probably the key, with an ideal situation one in which teachers respond to individual needs in a child-centred context.

Identification

The majority of gifted children co-exist happily and prosperously alongside children of moderate ability, though whether more of them could go further in realising their potentials is a matter for debate. This book suggests that they could, and aims to help teachers, advisers and LEA officers provide more effectively for them.

For further study:

BECKER, Howard S. (1963). <u>Outsiders</u> . Glencoe, New York: Free Press.

BRIDGES, S. (1973). <u>IQ - 150</u> . London: Priory Press.

CALLOW, R. (1980). 'Recognising the Gifted Child'. In R. Povey (ed.) "Educating the Gifted Child", London: Harper and Row.

DAVIE, R., BUTLER, N., GOLDSTEIN, J. (1972). <u>From Birth to Seven</u> . A report of the National Child Development Study", London: Longmans.

DES (1977). <u>Gifted Children in Middle and Comprehensive Schools</u> , London: HMSO.

FREEMAN, Joan (1979). <u>Gifted Children: Their Identification and Development in a Social Context</u> , Lancaster: MTP Press.

FREEMAN, Joan (1981). 'The intellectually gifted'. In K. I. Abroms and J. W. Bennett (eds.) "Primer in Genetics and Exceptional Children", San Francisco: Jossey Bass.

GALLAGHER, J. J. (1975). 'Research summary of characteristics of the gifted'. In W. B. Barbe and J. S. Renzulli (eds.) "Psychology and Education of the Gifted", New York: Wiley.

GOODACRE, E. J. (1968). <u>Teachers and their pupils' home background</u> , Slough: NFER.

GUILFORD, J. P. (1967). <u>The Nature of Human Intelligence</u> , New York: McGraw Hill.

HITCHFIELD, E. M. (1973). <u>In Search of Promise</u> , London: Longman.

HOPKINSON, D. (1978). <u>The Education of Gifted Children</u> , London: Woburn Press.

HOYLE, E. and WILKS, J. (1975). <u>Gifted Children and their Education</u> , London: DES.

KERRY, T. (1978). 'Bright pupils in mixed ability classes', Brit. Educ. Research J., 4, 103-111.

Identification

KERRY, T. (1981). Teaching bright pupils , Basingstoke: Macmillan.

MERCER, J. R. (1975). 'Psychological assessment and the rights of children', In N. Hobbs (ed.) "The Classification of Children", Vol. 1. San Francisco: Jossey-Bass.

OGILVIE, Eric (1973). Gifted Children in Primary Schools , London: Macmillan.

PAINTER, F. (1980). 'Gifted children at home and school'. In R. Povey (ed.) "Educating the Gifted Child". London: Harper and Row.

PIGEON, D. A. (1970). Expectation and pupil performance , Slough: NFER.

PRINGLE, M. K. (1970). Able Misfits , London: Longman.

PRINGLE, M. K. (1970). 'Bristol Social Adjustment Guides'. In O. K. Buros (ed.) "Sixth Mental Measurements Year Book", Highland Park, N.J.: The Gryphon Press.

REVESZ, G. (1953). An Introduction to the Psychology of Music , London: Longman.

ROSENTAL, R. and JACOBSON, L. (1968). Pygmalion in the Classroom , New York: Holt.

RUTTER, M., MAUGHAN, B., MORTIMORE P. and OUSTON, J. (1979). Fifteen Thousand Hours , London: Open Books.

SHUTER, Rosamund (1968). The Psychology of Musical Ability , London: Methuen.

STANLEY, Julian C., KEATING, Daniel P. and FOX, Lynn H. (1974). Mathematical Talent: Discovery, Description and Development , Baltimore and London: John Hopkins University Press.

TANNER, J. M. (1978). Foetus into Man , London: Open Books.

TEMPEST, N. R. (1974). Teaching Clever Children , London: Routledge and Kegan Paul.

TERMAN, L. M. et al (1925). Mental and Physical Traits of a Thousand Gifted Children , California: Stanford University Press.

TORRANCE, E. P. (1975). 'Emerging concepts of giftedness'. In W. B. Barbe and J. S. Renzulli (eds.) "Psychology and Education of the Gifted", New York: Irvington.

VERNON, P. E., ADAMSON, G. and VERNON, D. (1977). The Psychology and Education of Gifted Children , London: Methuen.

Chapter 2

Belle Wallace

Both the Introduction to this book, and the first chapter on
identification, have been at pains to be inclusive, ie to
suggest that many children should be regarded as able: those
with high IQs, those who show creative flair, those who have
special talents in a single field, those who do well at
attainment tests or public examinations, those who would
have been in the upper échelons of the selective school
system. Both writers have also, quite correctly, laboured
the point that most able children are normal children: happy,
secure and well-adjusted. But there are exceptions.
Ability may be, if not a handicap, at least a social
embarrassment; and more able children begin with social or
economic disadvantages.

This chapter aims to redress the balance so far
established by looking at a case study of one able pupil who
needed more than intellectual stimulation. The story of
John may one day have a happy ending: but one is left
wondering how many Local Education Authorities are equipped
to deal with similar problems, how many would have been
fortunate enough to have managed so much co-operation
between the educational and welfare agencies.

But let this account tell its own story.

John: a child at risk

John was referred to the educational psychologist at the end
of the spring term of the first year of his junior school.
His teacher recognized his obvious ability but John was
reluctant to write anything down, was inattentive yet very
demanding, was overflowing with general knowledge and
creative ideas but disorganised, seldom completing work or
concentrating on an activity for any length of time.

He was totally rejected by the rest of the class.
Firstly, this was because he appeared to them to be a very
naughty boy with odd ideas they frequently failed to
understand. Secondly, he was often physically aggressive:
when they would not let him play, or became angry at his
interference in their affairs, he would retaliate by pushing
or kicking or bursting into tears. Moreover, he constantly
smelled of urine, his clothes and his person were grubby and
unwashed and he seemed to have a permanent cold. He was
desperate to communicate and would cling to any adult who
paused to listen to his monologue: the school caretaker, the
domestic staff, the traffic warden, the local shopkeepers.
He had developed the habit of rummaging through a number of
secondhand junk shops finding odd bits of machinery and
bargaining with the shopkeeper to sell them for a few pence
so that he could build his inventions. He was interested in
the intricacies of telephone communication so had personally
sought out a senior officer at the local telephone exchange
and had bombarded him with questions. The school had
endeavoured to cope with him but a crisis had occurred
because John was truanting regularly, missing school two or
three days each week.

The teachers in John's infant school had recognized his
exceptional ability and had endeavoured to provide an
individualized programme of work; he had open access to all
reading books which were available and staff had built up a
personal library for him. Special arrangements had been
made so that he could range widely and deeply in mathematics
but he had always tried to avoid writing. He began to
stutter because he had so much to express and was impatient
even with his speed of speaking, and words would cascade in
torrents. Social problems arose very early as the other
children avoided him and he never had a close friend. He
soiled himself as a "pay-back" mechanism whenever he felt
thwarted or frustrated and his outbursts of anger stemmed
from an unusual degree of determined self-will.

The educational psychologist assessed John's ability on
the Weschler Intelligence Scale for children as being over
160 ; with a chronological age of 7:10 years, his reading age
was 15+ years. The report confirmed that he was a child
possessing an exceptionally high intelligence with a quality
of thinking which isolated him from other children. He had
particular social and emotional problems since he was
naturally very affectionate and could not understand why
other children did not like him.

Obviously John needed greater challenge and the chance
to communicate and work with intellectual peers. His parents
also needed support and guidance; they were loving, but the
home was rather disorganized and John tended to live so much
in a world of fantasy that basic hygiene never intruded into
his preoccupation with his world of ideas.

When I met John in school for the first time, I was presented with a slight, pale, fair-haired untidy child who needed only the <u>slightest</u> encouragement to talk to me about his latest interest which was 'explosions'. He assured me that one could make a powerful bomb using cigarette tobacco, sodium and alcohol and when I asked why he was interested in explosives, from a wisdom of eight years of age he told me that much of the world was a junk-heap and he intended to destroy some of it and then to design and rebuild a more exciting world.

It seemed that the first priority was to provide John with opportunities for meaningful communication. It was inappropriate merely to present him with a series of individual 'intellectual challenges' since he was very reluctant to record, had already developed the habit of minimal written effort and was obviously very lonely. He had retreated from the real world and told everyone that he thought he had been born out of time and really belonged to the twenty-first century.

Accordingly, to ease John's sense of intellectual isolation and to relieve the class teacher from his constant questioning, we decided to try to provide him with tutorial sessions when <u>his</u> ideas could provide the central theme for discussion. Contact was made with a local college which has a large science/technology department. It was hoped that one or two of the lecturers or senior students could perhaps spare an hour each week to listen to John and to guide and question his scientific theories and fantasies. John and his father were invited to the college Open Day to meet the staff informally so that they could talk to the child and possibly assess the level of his knowledge and interest. Predictably, John did not manifest himself as a studious young professor but as a rather disorganized, inattentive over-active eight year old. His attention flitted rapidly from one display to the next; when he asked questions, he appeared not to listen to the answer, he merged fact and fantasy and hardly stood still but twisted and turned, constantly scanning the large hall filled with fascinating displays.

A few days later when a meeting was held to discuss the possibility of some help for John, the college staff felt that they lacked the expertise and experience of dealing with young children, particularly in the case of a somewhat eccentric, atypical eight-year-old, and felt that although they might have the scientific and technical background, they did not have the skills of a good primary teacher.

A second approach was made to a local secondary school where one of the teachers, Mr Martin, had participated in local and countywide In-service Education courses on the 'Needs of Exceptionally Able Children'. Mr Martin had also taught on curriculum extension courses for primary pupils and so understood the problems and had personal experience in

dealing with exceptionally able young pupils. Mr Martin's
specialist subject was not science but we felt that perhaps
he could provide John with opportunities to discuss his
extensive reading, particularly in the area of science
fiction where John's appetite was insatiable and his recall
of accumulated knowledge seemingly inexhaustible.

Mr Martin knew of a group of very able sixth formers
who met regularly to discuss aspects of science fiction.
John's dilemma was discussed with the group and a few boys
offered to give up a lunch hour each week to talk with John.
Their initial impression was of a child who was a careless
and disorganized thinker, who was interested in everything,
who talked incessantly and who desperately wanted their
friendship. After several weeks Mr Martin and the students,
in assessing the success of the lunch-time sessions, said that
John often knew more about the latest theories in science and
engineering research than they did. He asked very
provocative and searching questions and, although he
fantasized, his ideas were based on accurate knowledge, he
merely developed them in highly original ways. He was
particularly keen to apply his theories to the production of
a working model and was more interested in the functioning
than in a smart design. The students felt that they had
derived more benefit from the meetings with John than
perhaps John had derived from meeting them; but Mr Martin
assured them that their interest, friendship and acceptance
of John had helped him enormously. They might not have
extended his knowledge but they had given him the
opportunity to communicate and exchange ideas and had, by
their questioning, encouraged him to present his thoughts
coherently and logically.

An effective and real source of help and support came
from Mrs Smith, a retired primary teacher who was very active
in all aspects of work with exceptionally able children. In
co-operation with the Headteacher and class teacher, Mrs
Smith undertook to work with John on a regular weekly basis,
and the following account is an extract from her report
written after two terms.

I first met John at an Enrichment Day course for
Juniors at our local Teachers' Centre in June 1980.
At breaktimes he wandered round all the topic tables
on his own. He asked me a few questions, but as the
topic of 'The History of Transport since 1900 and its
effect on the development of our Town' obviously did
not appeal to him, he wandered off again. That which
interested him most appeared to be: Byzantine chess,
geology (because they were smashing rocks), and
skeletal structure. All the teachers that day noted
his restlessness, his constant interruptions and
inability to listen.

In December 1980, the County Advisory Teacher for
Gifted Children asked me if I could perhaps help John on
an individual basis by going into his school once a
week. The headmistress was very willing, although at
first she did wonder about him getting too much
attention; but at least the class teacher would be able
to help the other children uninterrupted for a while.

His class teacher, very concerned and experienced, had
realized John's potential and had done all she could to
encourage his scientific interests, even starting a
lunch-hour 'Electronics Club'. His apparent inability,
or unwillingness, to concentrate on any other aspect of
the school curriculum, maths, English, topics of
nature, history, etc, was obvious by the poor state of
his exercise books. Work was untidy, unfinished, and
at about the level of an average seven-year-old. The
headmistress said I could have John one whole afternoon
a week and do what I liked.

My first aim was to establish a relationship, and so
for the first two weeks he did nearly all the talking
and I mostly listened. He poured out words non-stop
as though a dam had burst, he seemed so relieved to
have a listener. Topics ranged, with startling
rapidity, from lasers, repeating photography, traffic
lights controlled by an individual whilst walking,
Chinese language, Bristol and Brunel, volcanoes and
the origins of diseases, to anagrams, palindromes, codes
and ciphers, even the invention of a fairy postman who
could deliver Christmas presents by remote control!

My role was to query those of his statements which
seemed particularly 'way out', generally trying to find
out where he had got his ideas from and why he thought
it a good or bad idea. Most conversation turned to
electronic devices and machines, but there was a fair
sprinkling of ideas from films and television ('in
'Sapphire and Steel' they do ...' or in 'Diamonds are
Forever' James Bond did ...') and I felt that there was
much Science Fiction and fantasy mixed with his facts.
John read voluminously, had a photographic memory, but
(I suspect) read so quickly that he didn't always read
correctly, and it was interesting to notice how adroit
he was in changing the subject if (a) he did not know
the answer to a question, or (b) one could prove him
wrong!

At the third visit we looked at, and talked about, his
class books, and I asked if he would like to make a
special book with a gold card cover called 'The findings

of John' - the topics to be of his choosing, but work had to be in good English and best writing. That idea did appeal, and he asked to find out about 'Fire' - we were to look up in books, jot down headings in his notebook which he would work on for the next week.

That was the idea, one we endeavoured to adhere to over the next three weeks, but while he had obviously glanced at some of the books, remembered one or two unusual facts, he had not done any real work on his topic at home or in school, although time had been allowed for it. Eventually we agreed that the first fifty minutes of the afternoon should be discussion and research, the next half-hour collating and writing in rough, and the last forty minutes used to produce a finished piece of work.

This arrangement seemed to work, there was time for some of his ideas to come tumbling out, for us to analyze and classify them, to find the best way to express them, and at the end of the period to have produced a piece of work that was at least legible and complete. At first there was preoccupation with things that kill or destroy, special disabling bombs, killer satellites, fire machines, lasers, though he was quick to point out to me that his ioniser 'could help people with asthma and other things'. Later a short history of the area where he lived he found interesting.

When John got excited he talked very badly, taking breath in the middle of his words and gabbling, so for a few minutes each session we did some exercises in breath control. He thought this great fun, and his eventual rendering of 'Hissing Sid' showed that he could read poetry with expression and feeling. He has a great sense of humour, and a teasing remark often produced better work. His writing, though somewhat laboured, was quite correctly formed and written, his vocabulary was extensive, far wider than his 'creative writing' would lead one to believe.

Progress was not even, sometimes I felt I had not achieved anything, he seemed so pre-occupied, but he seemed to enjoy our sessions, was always waiting at 1.30 pm and reluctant to go at home-time.

Since going into the top junior class, he seems to have matured in several ways, he is more open to suggestions in checking his ideas and is quicker in his written work. As we only have one-hour sessions now, we have tried various games and exercises that require

quick thought but careful logical answers, and then we
talk of anything he has read about, seen on television,
or would like to do or make. He would obviously love to
haunt science and other museums, but at present they are
too distant for us to visit. In the Christmas holidays,
John spent nearly two hours with a friend of mine who is
a Physics graduate discussing his 'gravity powered
vehicle' and the friend's comment was that much of
John's thinking and reasoning was 'certainly beyond
O-level standard'. Hopefully in the coming year we
can continue to help him so that his written skills
will be commensurate with his ideas.

While trying to meet John's intellectual needs it was
equally necessary to try and meet his emotional and social
needs. He seemed to crave affection and physical contact.
His physical appearance suggested lack of care and his
enuresis exacerbated the problem of his isolation within the
classroom. On one occasion he had come to school in a wet
shirt because he had washed it himself that morning.

A case conference was held involving the educational
psychologist, the medical officer, the school nurse, a health
visitor, the class teacher, the headmistress, Mrs Smith and
myself.

Subsequently, the educational psychologist interviewed
John's parents and discussed their problems and his special
needs. The health visitor was to visit the home regularly
to help mother in organizing and coping with the demands of
a very active family. Problems were discussed and the
mother felt that she had some support and guidance in trying
to understand and satisfy some of John's seemingly insatiable
demands. Both parents undertook to listen to him more often,
encouraging him to talk about his interests and ideas. They
tried to manage some time to visit museums and exhibitions
and he was introduced to the librarian in the local adult
library so that he could borrow the books he really wanted.
He began to attend school cleanly and tidily dressed
responding very well to the 'gold star and chart' régime.
The school nurse saw him regularly to praise and encourage
and she also visited the home to provide the same support
for the mother.

Since 1970, Essex Education Authority has provided
opportunities for groups of exceptionally able children to
work together for short periods. The courses are called
'Curriculum Extension Courses' and are seen as an essential
part of an In-Service Education programme. Teachers meet
regularly to explore problems of the definition and
identification of exceptionally able pupils. The principles
which should underlie curriculum extension and teaching
methods are discussed and alternative strategies of
organization explored. After the initial introductory

series of workshops, teachers are invited to continue into
the second stage where they prepare a curriculum extension
project in co-operation with colleagues. Projects are then
tried out on a curriculum extension course for pupils. This
allows the teacher to evaluate the project, to gain
experience of working with exceptionally able pupils and it
also enables pupils to work together with their intellectual
peers.

John was invited to attend a residential five-day course
in the summer term of 1981. He arrived, looking unusually
clean and tidy and in the very first session was immediately
distinguishable by his rapid high-powered delivery of
idiosyncratic fact and fantasy. The theme for the week was
'Space and Time' and so John was overjoyed to pour out his
wealth of ideas. He was outstanding even in a group of
exceptionally able pupils and at first reluctant to listen
to the others' opinions until the teacher insisted that
everyone had a right to speak and should be heard. Groups
are fortunately very small to allow each child to
participate fully and John began to realize that <u>other
children could challenge his ideas and offer exciting ideas
of their own.</u> Nevertheless, often he was functioning at a
level way beyond them, leaping to a conclusion while they
were still analyzing the problem. He was unused to working
with others and tended at first to pursue his activities
regardless of other people. However, towards the end of the
week, he was noticeably different, he had made friends and
was especially protective of another boy who was a little
shy. His greatest triumph was that two little girls actually
invited him to play 'Tag'. John was also pleased because he
was clean and did not smell and glowed at compliments about
his appearance.

One teacher had offered to supervise unobtrusively
John's personal hygiene, since he would neglect to visit the
lavatory if he was engrossed in what he was doing. Even so,
there were a few accidents and he needed to shower during
the day and his clothes had to be washed.

After each curriculum extension course parents are given
a questionnaire which invited them to comment on their
child's reaction to the course. John's parents described
his reaction to the course as 'ecstatic'. He talked about
it constantly and they felt he was more relaxed and amenable
within the family. He was so pleased to have made some
friends and had gained in self-confidence and self-assurance.
For the first time he had met children who had accepted him
and with whom he could discuss and exchange ideas. His eyes
certainly had a brighter glow by the end of the week.

John is approaching the end of his junior school phase
and his headteacher feels that he is happier and better
organized but, while there has been considerable alleviation,
the fundamental problems of loneliness and insecurity amongst

his classmates remain. His written work has improved, although his speed of thinking still outstrips his writing skills. In a report written at the end of the spring term of his fourth junior year, the headteacher wrote:

> Unfortunately, John is still prone to defiant or anti-social behaviour if he becomes frustrated. John's teachers feel threatened by this and also find it difficult to accept a feeling of personal failure even though there is reassurance that they have tried their best to meet John's needs. A common defence has been to be hyper-critical of him so that even mild deviations of behaviour which would be tolerated in other children are not considered acceptable in a child who is 'exceptionally able'.

As John approaches the secondary phase of his education, his progress will be carefully monitored. It is hoped that it will be possible to provide the individual programme he so obviously needs and that the examination success he requires to progress into higher academic fields will not be the straight-jacket it unfortunately so often is.

Appendix 1. Case-note comments, made by John's parents, on his pre-school years

John's arrival was planned in the most definite way. We had wanted another child very much for a considerable time, but waited until we both felt we were as ready as we could be, emotionally, financially and in the home we had ready. His arrival, he being our first child together, completed our joy in each other in a very real way, this being our second marriage.

Pregnancy was normal in every way, happy, a time of 'glowing health' for Mum, and went full-term. It was perhaps one of the most fulfilling periods of our marriage so far.

It was a home birth with midwife and father in attendance. Delivery was normal, fairly rapid, and without complications. The rest of the family were all overjoyed with the new arrival. His older brother and sister were very proud of him and there were almost no jealousy dramas at all.

The first 3-4 months were quite normal as far as can be remembered - eating, sleeping, crying, etc - nothing unusual.

From the time he began to 'sit up and take notice', although his behaviour and growth were quite normal, John did begin to exhibit a marked dislike for being left alone when awake. It was often necessary to carry him around whilst doing housework, to keep him happy. In this and in his general alertness, particularly at the latter end of this period, John showed a distinct difference from his older brother who had been far more placid as a baby.

He began to crawl and walk at normal times as far as we can remember (walked about 11 months). Still very alert, he showed increasing signs of curiosity as his ability to move around increased. Although perhaps not abnormally curious for his age, he did frequently exhibit a noticeable single-mindedness and impatience towards the object of his curiosity, by which he appeared oblivious of anything else, such as things in his path, even walking off steps as if they weren't there.

At about 18 months old, John began to become 'difficult' at bed-time, not with tantrums but he was obviously not at all ready for sleep. As soon as he was able, he would repeatedly climb out of his cot to carry on what he had been doing or to come to us. His younger brother, Simon, born when John was 16 months old, developed the same 'game' as he grew older.

This activity became so intense at times, we had to use a pram harness clipped to prevent them turning over or climbing out, often coupled with sitting and reading to them to discourage it and give us a measure of peace (dreamers that we were!).

John did not really have many children in our area to play with at this time, but as far as we can remember, he showed no difficulty relating to his peers at this age. He did, however, begin to show an inclination to prefer the company of adults.

In the main, during this period, John appeared normally happy and well-adjusted. Some signs of the introspection he was to show more as he grew older appeared, as did his sensitivity to failure and criticism. Toilet training was difficult, with frequent failures.

Intellectual development at first seemed apparently normal. No real pre-school encouragement in reading and writing was given. He did not attend a nursery school (none was available). At about 4 years old, John's aversion to (or lack of need for) sleep did produce one interesting phenomenon. He often awoke, or being already awake, left his bed and came and climbed into ours with us, invariably as we went to bed (waiting for us?). Although he liked a cuddle at these times, it quickly became evident that comfort or reassurance was not all he wanted. He wanted to TALK. This is one of his great passions in life. It often happened that John and Dad would sit, or lie, and talk on and on, sometimes for well over an hour. Subjects discussed were varied - the day's happenings, a comic, a TV programme or anything which came into our, or usually John's, minds. Simon also joined in this activity for quite a while. As time went on, and particularly after John went to school and began to read, these discussions became more involved and covered more advanced topics - space machines, stars, science. Looking back, it is perhaps worthy of note that it was seldom a case of holding a discussion with a child, it was usually more like talking normally to an adult, except that John's need to interject frequently his own thoughts, move several steps ahead of the point before it was fully covered and go off at tangents, was almost obsessive.

From the time he began school, John's ability to relate
to children of his own age has been spasmodic to say the
least. At times he has been happy playing and working
with them, at others he has not only felt 'different'
and isolated, but has been made painfully aware of it
by other children. This situation now seems to be
improving steadily as he grows older. It has, at times,
created considerable emotional difficulties for him and
has, we think, played a large part in his lack of toilet
control (although this is now almost completely cleared
up).

Intellectually, going to school, learning to read,
write(!) and reason opened up a real wonderland for
John. His plunge into the new world of words and ideas,
new concepts and new possibilities, was rapid,
fundamental and is today unabated; although it seems
that only now is he beginning to understand the need
for the formal work and the disciplines necessary to
pursue these. Almost as soon as he could read a few
words, his appetite for magazines, books, almost any
written material, became insatiable. He often
preferred reading cereal packets to eating his
breakfast. We soon got into the habit of getting books
on odd subjects, particularly scientific ones, and
leaving them around for him to pick up, which he did.
Whilst the range of his probings widened steadily, his
main interest always seemed to be scientific, and still
is. He also seemed to move easily and quickly into the
Christian faith, which we are sure has, at times, been
of considerable support to him. Quite early on, we
bought an illustrated (comic-strip) version of the
Bible in 6 volumes, which he read almost completely in
one sitting! His ability to absorb what he reads seems
enormous - we have lost count of the number of times we
say: 'Where on earth did he get that from?'. As early
as the first year of his infant schooling, he was able
to regale an assembly one morning with the detailed
functioning of the element of an electric kettle.

The vistas opened up to John by such things as your
and Mrs Smith's contact with him, the visit to
Brooklands* etc, continue to inspire and delight him.

* The centre where curriculum extension courses are held.

Appendix 2. Comments made by the School Nurse.

John was brought to my attention during the second term
of his third year in the junior School.

Both Class and Head Teacher were concerned about his
general hygiene and lack of adequate clothing. He
presented himself as a sullen, poorly clad, pathetic
child, his face and hands were dirty, his clothing
soiled and torn and his shoes needed repair. He was
obviously rejected by his fellows. The combination of
body odour, soiling, stale urine and dirty clothing was
overpowering.

Once on his own, John wanted to talk and he enjoyed the
individual approach. I learned from this and
subsequent interviews that there was little supervision
at home in the morning or in the evening. His mother
left home at about 8.00 am and John and his younger
brother were constant late attenders, often arriving in
school having had no breakfast.

I spent many hours trying to contact Mother but home
visits were unsuccessful. I continued weekly visits
to the school and saw him in the classroom and also on
a one-to-one basis. We tackled basic hygiene first and
John tried really hard to cope with this situation.
Mother continually broke appointments and refused to
answer the door. Finally, I rang her place of work and
made contact with her. Many of John's problems may be
due to lack of parental support. He had never been
trained to clean himself after going to the lavatory,
the daily routine of washing, cleaning teeth or feeding
himself properly was not insisted upon and there seemed
to be a lack of 'mothering'. Clean clothing was rarely
available and consequently John dressed himself in any
underpants and top clothing which came to hand.

Throughout the school year, I monitored John's progress
but I saw little improvement in his physical well-being.
The pattern of being clean for two days after I had seen
him, but gradual reversion to soiled clothing and an
unwashed boy in four or five days, continued. He
remained socially unacceptable and unable to make any
lasting relationships with his peers or his teachers.
His class teacher labelled him as an egocentric and
disruptive and I can appreciate that, in a class of
thirty, John's constant inventive activities would
indeed by very disruptive.

I encouraged John to read books about body development.

We talked about the bone structure, muscle development and structure of vital organs but these left him uninterested. We then discussed brain development and the nervous system and this so stimulated him that I had difficulty in keeping him supplied with books. Cell development also interested him.

I discovered that he had poor muscular co-ordination and would destroy a physical game in the playground by disrupting the players rather than attempt to join in. At this stage, aged 9+, he ran almost like a toddler and was unable to ride a bicycle.

He spoke about his interest in the church choir and looked forward to choir practice and learning to read music. Both parents are committed to church work and sing in the choir but John was removed for disruptive behaviour. However, he does go out to a church club and Sunday School with his father.

During the period from September 1981, with support from the social worker and educational agencies, there has been considerable improvement. John is beginning to have some self respect and is appearing in school wearing clean clothes, his face and hands clean. There are occasional lapses with soiling, but on the whole John is not the disruptive influence he had been previously.

Chapter 3

PRINCIPLES OF CURRICULUM BUILDING
FOR THE ABLE CHILD

Belle Wallace

Characteristics and problems of the able child

This chapter looks at some principles upon which it is
possible and desirable to build a school curriculum for the
able child. It is not an attempt to look at the detailed
content of such a curriculum. Rather it deals with global
concerns about intentions, philosophies and underlying
structures. The chapter serves as a link between Joan
Freeman's on identification and those by Christine Burke and
Trevor Kerry which are concerned more specifically with
classroom procedures.

Let us begin by considering some of the particular
characteristics and problems of gifted children and their
teachers.

The reason for identifying a child as gifted is that he
(or she) manifests certain characteristics which are
exceptional when compared with other children. He is in a
minority group and he can be lonely because he feels
different (this is a point to which I shall return in
Chapter 8). If we nourish his gifts we increase the
difference because he learns faster and the gap widens. So,
we must also give him emotional security; and this security
must be such that it breeds the courage to accept his
difference and to stand alone. We must also help him to
develop understanding and tolerance of others who are much
less able. We hear a great deal about mixed ability
teaching's social advantages. Whether able pupils find
themselves in mixed ability, bands, sets or streamed groups
they must always learn to acquire the social graces of tact
and patience. The teacher needs to be aware that the more
we foster the gift and increase the intellectual divergence,
the greater is the problem of reconciling the gap between the

child and his peer group in social and intellectual terms.

This problem of balancing individual differences and social integration is particularly relevant in the case of those children who might be described as highly creative. Creative thinking involves risk-taking, non-conformity, stepping outside the conventional, thinking differently from the group. In order to tolerate a position of intellectual insecurity and isolation, the creative person must sometimes step out from a position of emotional security. Moreover, the extra-sensitive perception of adult issues which is so characteristic of gifted children increases the discrepancy between emotional maturity and intellectual understanding; the very act of stepping out into the unknown takes him further into adult problems of morality and compromise than most other children can delve.

Frequently such able children have advanced fluency and mastery of language which they use to refine ideas which are already more mature in concept than the ideas of their peers. If this skill is further nourished, the gap in communication levels between able and average children may be increased. Language is not simply a communication system, it is a medium through which all kinds of covert signals are sent and received. The appropriate language of the able child, rewarded by the teacher in a learning situation, may be a barrier to social intercourse in the peer-group. Hence, in the classroom, teachers frequently remark that the bright pupils form friendship pairs or groups together, regardless of any imposed social grouping the teacher may attempt to engineer.

With young children, particularly, the teacher needs to be aware too of the individual frustration of being able to conceive and perceive advanced ideas without having the appropriate advanced manual or technical skills to execute them in practice. A teacher has firstly to balance the development of manual skills against intellectual ability and secondly, to find appropriate methods for a child to express fully the advanced ideas he has. In normal schools this has to be done against a background of catering for the thirty children in the class, each of whom has individual needs and problems.

It is characteristic of these children that they have the capacity for rapid absorption and retention of ideas and knowledge so that they build up extensive general and specialist knowledge which accumulates, often taking them not just beyond other pupils but beyond their teachers. They read quickly and absorb, having voracious appetites, so that even the school library is often inadequate and quickly exhausted. This has several implications for teachers. First, that the teacher's attitude must be moulded to allow that degree of humility which can accept and foster the pupil's expertise. Secondly, the teacher needs to encourage these magpie-like enthusiasms by showing an appropriate interest and encouragement. Thirdly, the teacher may need to educate himself in the topic simply in order to converse with the pupil - and not all such enthusiasms by able pupils are in the most obvious subjects! Finally, the teacher must become a collector, too: of resources of every kind, so that he can feed and nurture the young enthusiast.

But the able are not hide-bound by facts and information - however absorbing. They have quick perception of the sequential stages in concept mastery, needing the minimum of practice and reinforcement. They apparently leapfrog through the normal logical series of concepts and can often operate with advanced concepts, even without having the formal language to explain. They move forward in a linear sense and although the teacher tries to give breadth of experience, the linear advance cannot be prevented. To hold back such youngsters is to bore them, so individualization of learning is important so that they can proceed in ways commensurate with their abilities.

What are the implications of this lightning review of the classroom characteristics of the able child? Clearly, if we provide for these individual needs then not only are we increasing diversity of both teaching method and learning experiences but we must accept that we need to provide a continuous systematic programme which is fully recorded and maintained from teacher to teacher and school to school.

What is education for the able?

For many people providing for the most able youngsters smacks of élitism. This is a philosophy far removed from the present volume. When we are talking about education for the able or gifted child we are putting the emphasis on three things:

... quality of provision,

... quality of teachers,

... quality of learning experiences.

Indeed, instead of discussing provision for gifted children, perhaps we should discuss gifted provision for all children.

In looking at our education system it would be appropriate to ask the same series of questions about the education of all our children, regardless of ability. These questions would include:

... What am I teaching?

    ... Why am I teaching it?

    ... How am I teaching it?

    ... Are the methods appropriate?

    ... What is the child learning?

    ... Why is this learning important?

    ... Are the learning methods appropriate?

    ... What does he need to cope with living in the 21st century (what Alvin Toffler has called Third Wave Civilization)?

    ... What does he need not just to <u>cope</u> but to function effectively - to accomplish - to live life with purpose and pleasure?

Consider the following list of aims in education, to which most educators would subscribe:

    ... to help a child to order his experiences so that he understands his world;

    ... to enable a child to recognize and develop his abilities and to strengthen his weaknesses;

    ... to promote a sense of independence of the individual together with a sense of inter-dependence of individuals within a society;

    ... to foster an appreciation of past culture, present culture, and to develop a sensitivity and a capacity to identify and evaluate problems, approaching the future with confidence and optimism.

These might well feature among the aims for educating our able pupils too. The scenario through which these aims are accomplished is based on personal experience; and in school those experiences are absorbed through the curriculum (both the overt and the covert curriculum) and through the interaction of pupil and pupil, and pupil and teacher. To use an analogy adapted from the Schools Council Working Paper 55, Chapter 1, the curriculum can be compared with a stage back-cloth which has the broad background and lighting for active learning but the child paints in the detail in co-operation with the teacher. There will be dialogue, monologue, ad-libbing, forgotten lines and scripted passages.
From the base of professional understanding and

expertise, the teacher identifies the child's previous experience, interests and skills and nudges the child forward into wider experiences developing cognitive skills and understanding, physical competence and mastery, social, emotional and moral awareness and effective functioning. Obviously it follows that improving teachers' skills and understanding through supportive guidance and regular in-service education, directly improves the quality of education for all children including gifted children, and this is a theme taken up explicitly in Chapter 4, and then throughout the rest of the book.

However, merely to state this as a broad philosophy, is to ignore the special characteristics manifested by exceptionally able children who present particular problems which can make excessive demands on a teacher. Also, if the special needs of exceptionally able children are to be set in the normal school, there are long term consequences which have to be considered. Clearly, though, a particular emphasis needs to be placed on the teacher's skill at devising individualized learning programmes to meet these special needs. It is to this topic that we now turn.

Individualized Learning Programmes

When we talk of individualized learning programmes we are not talking about providing access to high status knowledge for a few, and low status knowledge for the many. Nor are we talking about a superior curriculum versus an inferior one. The basic principle of designing individualized learning is to provide a background of materials and experience to which the pupil can respond at a level appropriate for him. The fundamental task of the teacher is to select appropriate learning experiences in consultation with the pupil - it is a process of negotiation - a synthesis of the teacher's breadth of professional understanding, knowledge of the subject and its divergent opportunities, and the child's interests, skills and level of understanding.

This idea of negotiation between teacher and pupil may be foreign to some teachers, and particularly for those who teach in the secondary sector. However, teachers need to come to regard this process not as a negation of professionalism, but as an integral part and manifestation of it. Too often teachers talk about able pupils doing 'more' work than the average, and about slow learners 'omitting' some tasks. This is probably an inadequate view of curriculum-building. The approach must always be positive: what does the pupil need to know by way of knowledge, skill or attitude and how can it best be taught?

To make appropriate curriculum decisions for the able, the teacher needs to know both the progressive stages of the educational objectives and also the sets of concepts

encompassed in the specific curriculum are،
extension programmes must be logical outgro،
random involvement in whatever happens to be
However, the spontaneous capitalizing on oppo.
present themselves is the art of a good teache.
also important to allow a child to find and tak،
paths to the same end. But it must always be re،
quantity of work is not as important as quality o،
and education must never degenerate into time-fill.

Any model of curriculum development serves two
firstly, it helps to clarify and detail aims and obj،
and secondly, it serves as a basis for action. The d،
lies in using such a model as a means of creating syst،
tidiness or perceiving it as an educational panacea. A
curriculum model, therefore, does not require undeviatin،
allegiance but serves as a broad guide by which the teach
analyses and refines the activities taking place in the
classroom. Moreover, the teacher must be primarily
concerned with the learning process as manifested in the
quality of the interaction and experience of the child.

It is also important to distinguish between
instructional goals, which give mastery of the tools and
techniques available, and expressive goals which make
creative responses possible. An expressive objective
describes an educational encounter and provides a pupil with
an invitation to explore - it is evocative rather than
prescriptive. An expressive objective provides a theme
through which skills and understanding learned earlier can
be brought to bear upon a problem while other skills and
understanding can be expanded and elaborated. An expressive
objective demands diversity of response, and the evaluative
task is not one of applying a common standard or blue-print
to what is produced but of reflecting upon the uniqueness
and significance of the response (Stenhouse, 1975, pp 70ff).

What makes an educational activity worthwhile ?

Perhaps this is the moment to pause and take stock. What
has been said so far encapsulates three clear messages.
First, that all children (including the able) should be
educated according to their individual capacities. Second,
that in order to do this the teacher needs to adopt an
individualized teaching approach. Third , that this
individualized approach implies a need to develop a
curriculum and curriculum materials in a planned and
systematic way. Much of the remainder of this chapter
looks at ways to approach curriculum building. Initially,
however, it is worth asking a value-laden question. What is
it that makes any educational activity worthwhile?

A possible response to this question is provided by
Rath (1971). He suggests that worthwhileness is found when

child

   ... makes informed choices and reflects on the
consequences of those choices;

   ... is active rather than passive;

   ... makes enquiry into ideas, applications of
intellectual processes or current problems;

   ... handles real objects and materials;

   ... can accomplish the task at a personally relevant
and appropriate level;

   ... takes intellectual risks;

   ... shares in the planning;

   ... is inspired to strive towards improvement.

In order to bring children to these ends the teacher
needs not just to reflect upon curriculum content but upon
his own rôle.

The rôle of the teacher

The teacher should be familiar with the procedures of
finding out: he should be able to teach study and library
skills, research methodology: he should aim at teaching the
child how to learn. Above all, the art of a successful
teacher is closely allied to the art of good questioning,
both the posing and the eliciting of questions. Attitude
is important, too. The rôle of the teacher should be that
of a co-learner, but a senior learner having greater
philosophical understanding and experience. This in itself
is important. As teachers, we can occasionally come across
youngsters who are, in terms of intellect and IQ, far
brighter than we are ourselves. But as educated and
professional adults we have much to contribute to the
fostering of minds young in emotions, choices and the
pathways to learning.

Bearing in mind what has been said we can now look in
more detail at ways to plan and execute a curriculum for the
able.

Preparing curriculum extension activities

It could be argued that the process of preparing curriculum
extension activities for exceptionally able pupils is no
different from the process of preparing curriculum activities

for all pupils. However, the special characteristics of
exceptionally able children mentioned earlier, plus the
extensive amount of time the teacher would need to spend in
preparation could cause considerable problems. It would seem
not only necessary but sensible to share the preparation and
pool expertise and ideas, and it is this goal towards which
this book is directed.

In the County of Essex, groups of teachers have undertaken to prepare curriculum extension schemes. Such schemes
are not meant to be prescriptive but are meant to offer
suggestions which a teacher can use flexibly, in negotiation
with the child. A broad curriculum plan is used for guidance
and is outlined in the three models which follow. The first
of these looks at factors which need to be considered in the
early stages of planning curriculum extension projects.

The second of our models looks at the sort of factors to
be considered in planning and evaluating a course of study.
Any course needs to be composed of appropriate knowledge,
skills and attitudes, and be mediated by apt teaching and
learning methods. Flexibility and variety are virtues
valued by teachers because they make teaching more rewarding
and provoke curiosity and enthusiasm in learners. Model 2
might profitably be used as a checklist in planning and
assessing the curriculum needs and achievements of able
pupils. Some of the headings of this second model are
discussed in more detail towards the end of this chapter.

Project plans are written out as a collection of ideas.
The teacher is encouraged to build a learning web with the
pupil before the project is begun, so that the pupil is
involved in making decisions about activities and can
discuss particular aspects of personal interest and concern.
Before this can be done, however, the teacher needs to be
aware of the aids and resources available to support
teaching and learning activities. To this end he can work
his way through the third model, checking each heading in
turn and listing what each can contribute to the study.

An Analysis of Cognitive Objectives

The three models given above can be built into a scheme for
curriculum building in the way described. However, reference
has been made already, both within the chapter and in the
headings of the models themselves, to cognitive skills. The
best available exposition of cognitive skills remains that
of Benjamin Bloom (1956). In the paragraphs which follow I
have attempted a summary of Bloom's classification of the
cognitive domain. Before turning to this, however, a word
or two of justification is in order.

This chapter takes the view that school is about
learning. A central message of the book is that able pupils
have both intellectual needs which require satisfying for

Model I: An Approach to the Preparation of Curriculum Extension Projects

Factors to be Considered

Teacher
Professional philosophy; knowledge and expertise in curriculum and method

Unusual content

Based on a group of subject disciplines

For a class project through differentiated activities

Teacher-learner interaction

Topic Project or Activity

Problems in past, present, future cultures

For a group activity

Child
Interests and background; level of understanding and development; level of skills and concepts

Conventional content

Based on one subject discipline

For an individual study

Model 2: Teachers Brainstorm Ideas/Activities

Planning and evaluation in the light of:

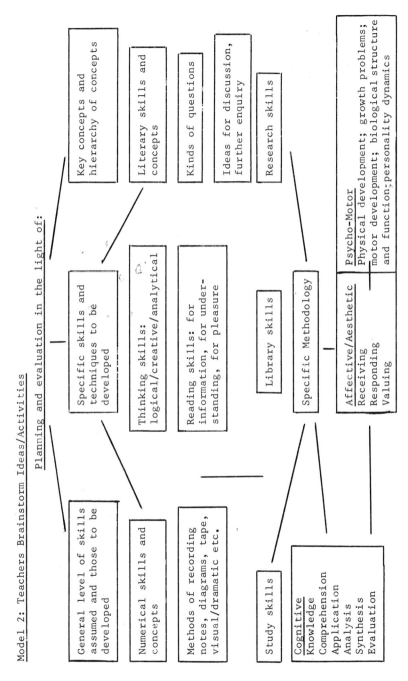

Key concepts and hierarchy of concepts

Literary skills and concepts

Kinds of questions

Ideas for discussion, further enquiry

Research skills

Specific skills and techniques to be developed

Thinking skills: logical/creative/analytical

Reading skills: for information, for under-standing, for pleasure

Library skills

Specific Methodology

Psycho-Motor
Physical development; growth problems; motor development; biological structure and function;personality dynamics

Affective/Aesthetic
Receiving
Responding
Valuing

General level of skills assumed and those to be developed

Numerical skills and concepts

Methods of recording notes, diagrams, tape, visual/dramatic etc.

Study skills

Cognitive
Knowledge
Comprehension
Application
Analysis
Synthesis
Evaluation

Model 3: Sources of Information - a network of possible resources

64

their own peace of mind, and also academic or creative skills which are of permanent benefit to themselves and, potentially, to society. For a teacher to achieve these ends it is necessary for him to have a grasp of the psychological steps in the process. What Bloom does so succinctly is provide another checklist against which curriculum content can be judged for its value, balance and intellectual demand. The checklist which follows illuminates the lowest left-hand box in Model 2, above.

A Summary of Cognitive Abilities based on Bloom's Taxonomy

1. Knowledge

The acquisition of various forms of knowledge is basic to all other forms of learning; it is analogous to a computer and requires the storage and retrieval of information when required. It involves memory and repetition and includes knowledge of appropriate materials, methods, processes, patterns and structures: eg,

- ... specific terminology and symbols;

- ... appropriate methodology and techniques;

- ... relevant facts and theories;

- ... ways of studying, organizing and judging;

- ... ways of presenting materials: styles and usual formats;

- ... accepted classifications, trends, sequences and categories.

2. Comprehension

The pupil is required to demonstrate some understanding of the knowledge acquired in the following ways:

- ... Translation: paraphrasing, explaining the meaning of words and selecting relevant information to answer a question.

- ... Interpretation: taking facts and re-ordering them, presenting a new view of the material, comparing and contrasting, and grouping or classifying according to specified criteria.

- ... Extrapolation: using given data to determine consequences and effects; ascertaining causes, consequences, implications, corollaries, results and effects.

3. Application

Although the acquisition of knowledge and the understanding
of that knowledge are important aspects of learning,
knowledge is static and passive unless it is applied to
solving problems. Application should involve:

... using knowledge in different areas of study and new
contents;

... applying acquired practices and theories to solving
problems;

... transferring methods or techniques to new situations;

... bringing general principles to bear upon new
questions.

4. Analysis

Analysis involves the process of breaking down the whole to
clarify the relationships between the constituent parts.
The activity involves:

... differentiating between fact and hypothesis;

... identifying hidden meanings;

... finding theses or patterns;

... understanding the system or the organization.

5. Synthesis

Synthesis is the process of creating or combining elements
to form a whole, rearranging, combining or reclassifying to
make a new pattern or structure. Activities include:

... organizing a set of ideas to make a new statement;

... developing plans to test a new hypothesis;

... creating a new form of classifying data or
phenomena;

... discovering new relationships;

... inventing and proposing alternatives;

... changing and improving.

6. Evaluation

Evaluation is the process of appraising, assessing or criticizing on the basis of specific standards and criteria. Evaluation demands:

... judging on the basis of logical accuracy and consistency in argument;

... verifying the worth of evidence or proof;

... evaluating materials according to specified criteria;

... comparing and discriminating between theories and generalizations;

... assessing work against recognized excellence;

... recognizing logical fallacies;

... arbitrating in controversial or opposing arguments.

It would appear from current research that teachers tend to concentrate on promoting learning activities within the levels of Knowledge and Comprehension, neglecting the levels of Application, Analysis, Synthesis and Evaluation. While it is desirable that all children should be given opportunities to experience activities which require all levels of thinking, able children function easily and effectively using the higher order thinking skills. Yet they are often denied the opportunity because teachers fail to build in appropriate activities. In the preparation of curriculum extension, therefore, it is essential to provide opportunities for pupils to function effectively at these higher cognitive levels. This is a case which has been extensively argued by the editor of the present volume (Kerry, 1980; Sands and Kerry, 1982); and the reader might also care to pursue the following references on a similar theme: Gallagher, 1975; HMI, 1977; HMI, 1978; Screen, 1981.

Learning and the affective domain

Having placed a good deal of emphasis throughout this chapter on the learning function of school it is perhaps time to redress the balance of emphasis: implicit, and often explicit, in what has been said has been the importance of the child growing and maturing as a social being in a climate of psychological security. Bloom is right to examine the learning which a child needs to cope with this

aspect of personal development. Again, a summary of Bloom's
ideas forms a useful checklist for the teacher, and these
headings serve to expand the lowest central box in Model 2
above.

Analysis of the affective domain based on Bloom's Taxonomy
1. Receiving

> ... developing personal awareness: building a
> consciousness of situations, phenomena, objects,
> stages of affairs, through the senses;

> ... perceptions of colour, arrangement, form, design;

> ... awareness of the symbolic representation of things,
> people, situations.

Receiving from others:

> ... listening to others;

> ... appreciating and tolerating religious, political
> and social national differences;

> ... developing sensitivity to human needs and social
> problems.

Selected/specific awareness

> ... listening and discriminating between moods and
> meanings, for example, in music;

> ... perceiving differences in human values and
> judgements through media such as literature.

2. Responding

> ... accepting basic rules for order and safety;

> ... participating voluntarily in activities;

> ... accepting personal responsibilities;

> ... seeking and deriving personal satisfaction through
> tasks pursued and accomplished;

> ... seeking, and responding with pleasure, to forms of

self-expression and personal enrichment.

3. <u>Valuing and appreciating worth</u>

... internalizing social values and developing personal values;

... ascribing worth to a phenomenon, behaviour, object;

... commitment to a value;

... discriminating between values;

... pursuing a faith, a loyalty, an ideal;

... assuming responsibility for social action;

... commitment to action motivated by personal convictions (fighting for democracy or human rights).

4. <u>Organization for living and personal philosophy</u>

... conceptualizing a value, identifying abstract qualities;

... relating abstract qualities to life (for example, anti-pollution or Welfare State);

... organizing and ordering complex and disparate values (for example, appreciating the interests of minority v. majority);

... synthesizing a new value;

... developing a consistent system of values;

... willingness to revise judgements in terms of issues, purposes, consequences.

<u>The psycho-motor domain</u>
Finally in this checklist of development comes the psycho-motor domain. In our Model 2 this area occupies the lowest right-hand box. Teachers of young children tend to be more aware of needs in this area than their secondary colleagues; but a glance at the list will show that these are areas of skill that are required, and developed, well into adult life.

Analysis of the psycho-motor domain

1. Physical development

... simple reflex movements, perceptual abilities, simple and complex movements.

2. Growth problems

... recognizing and accepting motor-development abilities;

... accepting divergence in physical development;

... recognizing and accepting sex role.

3. Motor development

... experimenting, manipulating and exploring to gratify intellectual curiosity.

4. Skilled movement

... writing, developing skilled techniques, using machinery, tools;

... involvement in sport, dance, music.

5. Structure and healthy functioning of the human body

... physical and chemical;

... mental and psychological.

6. Total movement as a person

... individual personality and group dynamics;

... using and responding to non-verbal communication.

Putting principles into practice

When teachers read education texts such as this one they often exhibit a healthy scepticism about the validity and practicality of the ideas presented. They tend to be suspicious of authors who are not practising as full-time classroom teachers. This is an understandable reaction.

However, in the present case, the ideas put forward have all been devised by teachers and have been tried out at the 'chalk face'.

The following details of curriculum extension projects show the principles outlined in the models above incorporated into practical schemes of work.

The flow charts show the initial planning although, obviously, the projects evolved further after consultation with the children. In the completed projects, the teachers' notes and suggestions for pupils' activities are written out fully with aims and objectives outlined in detail.

The teacher is encouraged to select and adapt according to the needs and interests of the pupil. Resources, such as films, exhibitions, reference books and fiction are also listed so that the basic preparation is done and precious time saved.

Project A

Project A was devised by Barbara Bexley, headmistress of an infant school in S.E. Essex. She and her staff worked as a team for a whole term on the theme of 'Working with Dinosaurs'. The work was planned for six-and seven-year-olds with above average ability. A conscious effort was made to reduce the recording to a minimum while providing opportunity for the higher order thinking skills.

Examples of activities 1 and 2
Collecting dinosaurs

Collect as many dinosaur names as you can.

Do you notice any similarities?
List your words, using these similarities.

Find a book that tells you the meanings of the dinosaurs' names, and add these onto your list.

Now can you decide which part of the word gives you information about your dinosaur?

Show your list to your friend or your teacher, and tell them what you have discovered about the long dinosaur words.

don	means	tooth
iguanadon		iguana tooth
dimitrodon		two sized tooth
dimorphodon		two types of tooth
hypsilophodon		high ridged tooth

PROJECT A

/This project includes a total of 26 activities; those given
here are examples only./

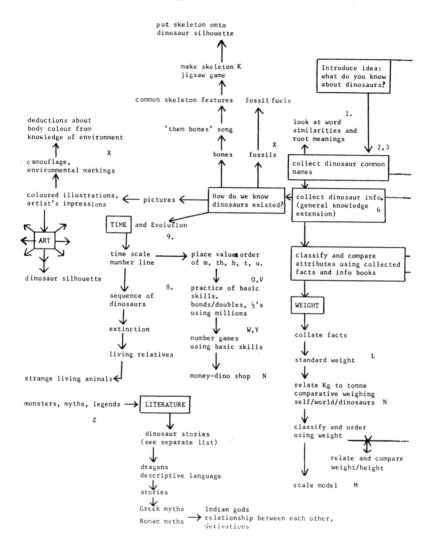

Curriculum building

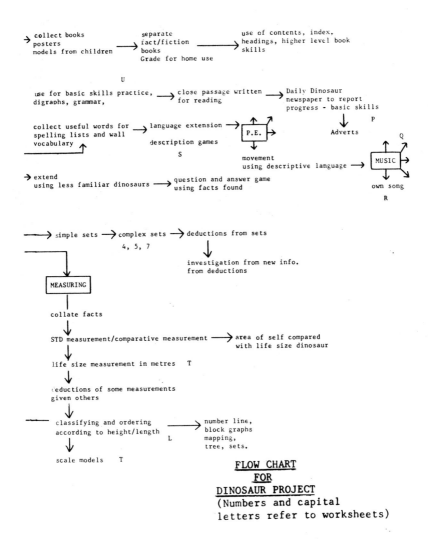

collect books
posters
models from children → separate
fact/fiction
books
Grade for home use → use of contents, index,
headings, higher level book
skills

U

use for basic skills practice, → close passage written → Daily Dinosaur
digraphs, grammar, for reading newspaper to report
progress - basic skills

P

collect useful words for → language extension →
spelling lists and wall
vocabulary description games P.E. Adverts

Q

S movement
using descriptive language → MUSIC

extend own song
using less familiar dinosaurs → question and answer game
using facts found R

simple sets → complex sets → deductions from sets
4, 5, 7

investigation from new info.
from deductions

MEASURING

collate facts

STD measurement/comparative measurement → area of self compared
with life size dinosaur

life size measurement in metres T

deductions of some measurements
given others

classifying and ordering → number line,
according to height/length block graphs
L mapping,
tree, sets.

scale models T

FLOW CHART
FOR
DINOSAUR PROJECT
(Numbers and capital
letters refer to worksheets)

pteradno<u>don</u>		winged and <u>toothless</u>
dicyno<u>don</u>		two dog <u>tooth</u>
megazostro<u>don</u>		big girdle <u>tooth</u>

<u>tops</u>	means	<u>face</u>
tricera<u>tops</u>		three horned <u>face</u>
protocera<u>tops</u>		first horned <u>face</u>
pentacera<u>tops</u>		five horned <u>face</u>
leptocera<u>tops</u>		slender horned <u>face</u>

<u>saurus</u>	means	<u>reptile</u>
bronto<u>saurus</u>		thunder <u>reptile</u>
tyranno<u>saurus</u>		tyrant <u>reptile</u>
psittaco<u>saurus</u>		parrot <u>reptile</u>
megalo<u>saurus</u>		big <u>reptile</u>
scelide<u>saurus</u>		limb <u>reptile</u>
corytho<u>saurus</u>		helmet <u>reptile</u>

A Dinosaur Name-Game

Most dinosaur names are long and have many syllables. Write a dinosaur name, leaving gaps between the syllables:

ty ran no sau rus
pter o dac tyl

Have you got the idea?

Write the name of a dinosaur on a long strip of paper, using a <u>different colour</u> for each syllable.

Now cut up the word, so that each syllable is on a separate piece of paper.

Mix the pieces up, and give them to a friend. Can he put them back together again to make your original dinosaur?

Now rearrange the syllables to make a new word: could rantyrusnosau ever have been King of the dinosaurs? Can a different friend guess the true identity of your beast?

To make the game more interesting, and more difficult, cut up three names, mix up all the syllables, and give them to a friend to sort out.

If you want to have a really difficult game, use lots of names. Find a way of marking the first (or last) syllable of each word so that your friend knows how many dinosaurs he has to find.

Keep your dinosaur name-game in a dinosaur envelope, so that you can find all the syllables when you want them.

Project B

Using the same planning method, project B was devised by a team of teachers from a number of schools and is suitable for middle junior children.

PROJECT B

9. Space history ...

- In fact and fiction ....

- Man's ideas of space throughout the ages

- His interpretation of the universe - superstitions and religious beliefs

- Some early stories of space travel

- Science fiction today - what makes for a good story?

8. Space in Mathematics

- Using space to make patterns and shapes of all kinds
- Strategies, planning, completion

7. The Laws in Space ....

- Man learns to colonise space -

(a) - how will he build a new society in space?

(b) - what laws will he have to make?

(c) - which earth laws could he take and adapt?

(d) - what interplanetary and intergalactic laws would be necessary for outer space?

TIME AND SPACE

6. 'Watch This Space' ....

- Communicating in a space age society ...

- The words we hear and write, the pictures we see ....

- Making our own space age advertisements

- Producing television programmes for the space age

- Using a video recorder and camera

5. Animals moving in, and using space ....

- How and what do we know of the way animals use space - individually and in groups ....

- Territorial patterns of chickens and other animals ....

- Migratory patterns - by land, sea and air

4. Survival in time and space...

(a) Earth's interior spaces ...

- Basic geology

- Volcanoes - Eruption of Mount St. Helens and other volcanoes

- Biological survival under extreme conditions

- The first colonisers - plants, insects, birds and animals - how they survive and adapt.

(b) Earth's inhospitable spaces...

- The Deserts ...

- Erosion and devastation

- Adaptation by plants, animals and men

Curriculum building

9. (cont'd)
- Favourite science fiction writers
- When has science fiction become science fact?
- The language and vocabulary used in space stories and poems
- What is 'the language of the spheres'?
- Geography of the moon

1. The Space around us ...
   Air -
   The amount of air
   - The effect of air
   - Its quantity and properties
   - Air in motion
   - The space surrounding our Earth
   - Getting things moving

2. Space and Time ...
   - The movement of earth in space
   - Time and the stars and planets
   - History of time measurement
   - Calendars
   - Time-tables - planning a space journey
   - Making 'clocks'

4. (cont'd)
- The drought escapers, the drought resisters
- Desert Nomads - The Bedouins and their culture
(c) The disappearing Australian Aborigines ....
- The Aborigines' life, language and culture
- Their physical adaptation of Australia's vast desert space
- history of white man's encroachment on this culture and the consequences thereof.

3. Using Space to live in ....
- Living 'space' and population growth
- Areas of high and low density population
- Living on an island
- Studies of growth of London and other settlements
- Making an ideal island

Project B: Detailed planning for 'space science fiction' section

Categorize elements
which constitute space
science fiction

Space	Technology	)In which are
Journeying into space	Robots	)they basic
Arrival/departure from	Machines	)to story or
point in space	Future	)mere padding?
Other planets	?	)comparing/
Aliens, primitive or	?	)contrasting
advanced?	?	)ordering/
	?	)selecting/
	?	)classifying/
	?	)analysing

Space science fiction
- from own reading
- short prescribed
  book list

Major themes in
space science
fiction

Man handling
new knowledge
- technology
- robots
- machines
- wealth/time

inferring, concept testing

Man examines himself
- microcosm against
  inter-galactic
  microcosm

evaluating, generalizing

DETAILED PLANNING FOR 'LAWS IN SPACE' SECTION

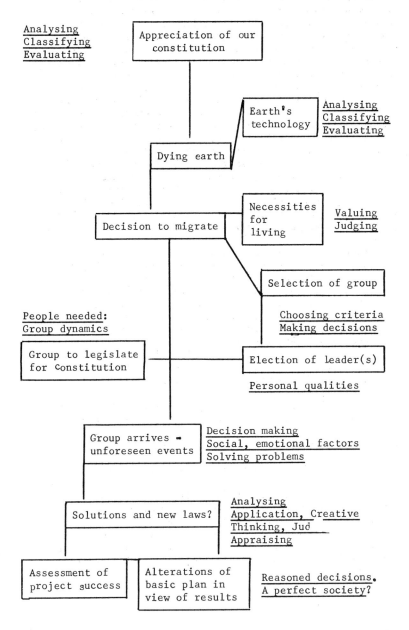

Analysing
Classifying
Evaluating

Appreciation of our
constitution

Earth's
technology

Analysing
Classifying
Evaluating

Dying earth

Decision to migrate

Necessities
for
living

Valuing
Judging

Selection of group

People needed:
Group dynamics

Choosing criteria
Making decisions

Group to legislate
for Constitution

Election of leader(s)

Personal qualities

Group arrives -
unforeseen events

Decision making
Social, emotional factors
Solving problems

Solutions and new laws?

Analysing
Application, Creative
Thinking, Jud
Appraising

Assessment of
project success

Alterations of
basic plan in
view of results

Reasoned decisions.
A perfect society?

At secondary level, examples of projects include a series
based on Mediaeval Studies devised by Stephen Baines. Pupils
are introduced to the intricacies of mediaeval estate
management and are required to run a mediaeval estate,
firstly as a Lord and then to switch roles and to survive as
a peasant. This involves a great deal of discussion of
social and moral issues, of justice and personal
responsibility. Another section deals with mediaeval castle
building in which pupils analyze the structures of castles,
plan their own and then work out the building programme in
time, man-power and money. Other aspects introduce pupils
to mediaeval literature, theology and science. The emphasis
throughout is on analyzing complex information and selecting
relevant facts, applying existing or creating new rules,
making decisions and justifying them, anticipating
consequences, posing and solving problems, debating
intellectual, aesthetic, moral and social issues.

In another secondary project, which is part of a history
series devised by Julian Whybra, pupils are given all
available evidence in relation to the Battle of Isandhlwana
(1879, South Africa). They are told:

> Your name is Colonel Hassard. The year is 1879 and you
> have been put in charge of a Court of Inquiry to look
> into a British military disaster at Isandhlwana on
> Wednesday 22nd January 1879 during the Zulu War, from
> which only a handful of Europeans escaped with their
> lives. The task before you is a difficult one and you
> are reminded that this is the only occasion in history
> when a British army has been defeated in battle by a
> native army. Six full companies of the 24th Regiment
> of Foot have been wiped out as have most of the leading
> families of the Colony of Natal.
>
> The public requires answers, clear-cut and decisive,
> and you are to give them. Your brief is twofold:
>
> 1. To discover how the disaster occurred.
>
> 2. To discover who was responsible for the disaster.

The evidence is fragmentary, gleaned from the few
survivors and the diaries or letters found on the dead
British soldiers. Pupils have to conduct an investigation
in the same manner as a Court of Inquiry. Choices have to
be made, men's motives and actions interpreted,
responsibility and blame apportioned and final decisions
justified.

In all the projects described the emphasis is not on acquiring factual knowledge and merely reproducing it, but on using knowledge for problem-solving and decision-making, as a springboard for action. These few examples illustrate the theme of the chapter in specific classroom examples. In the chapters which follow Christine Burke and Trevor Kerry take up more classroom themes.

(Note: It is planned that projects will be published and made available for all teachers and pupils on a commercial basis.)

Bibliography

Bloom, B S (1956). Taxonomy of Education Objectives, Methuen.

Crone, R & Malone, J (1979). Continuities in Education, NFER.

Devlin, T & Warnock, M (1977). What Must We Teach? Maurice Temple Smith Ltd.

Doll, R C (1978). Curriculum Improvement, Allyn & Bacon Inc.

Gallagher, J J (1975). Teaching the Gifted Child, Allyn & Bacon Inc.

Gallagher, J J (1979). Reaching Their Potential, Kollek & Son Ltd.

HMI (1977). Gifted Children in Middle and Comprehensive Schools, HMSO.

HMI (1978a). Primary education in England, HMSO.

HMI (1978b). Mixed ability work in comprehensive schools, HMSO.

HMI (1979). Aspects of secondary education in England, HMSO.

Holt, M (1980). Schools and curriculum change, McGraw-Hill Book Company (UK) Ltd.

Holt, M (1979). The Common Curriculum, Routledge & Kegan Paul Ltd.

Hooper, R (ed) (1973). The Curriculum, Oliver & Boyd.

Kelly, A V (1977). The Curriculum, Harper & Row.

Kerry, T (1980). 'The demands made by RE on pupils' thinking', Brit J Rel Ed.

Kindred, L W et al (1976). The Middle School Curriculum, Allyn & Bacon.

Kirk, S A & Gallagher, J J (1979). Educating Exceptional Children, Houghton Mifflin Co.

Kramer, A H (1981). Gifted Children, Trillium Press Inc.

Lawton, D et al (1978). Theory and Practice of Curriculum Studies, Routledge & Kegan Paul.

Povey, R (ed) (1980). Educating the Gifted Child, Harper & Row.

Rath, J N (1971). Teaching Without Specific Objectives, Educ Leadership, April, 714-720.

Sands, M K & Kerry, T (1982). Mixed Ability Teaching, Croom Helm.

Schools Council (1975). The curriculum in the middle years, Evans/Methuen.

Screen, P (1981). 'ESTEAM: a curriculum development for exceptionally able children in science', SSR, vol 63.

Stenhouse, L (1975). An Introduction to Curriculum Research and Development, Heinemann Educational Books.

Toffler, A (1981). The Third Wave, Penguin Ltd.

Vernon, P E et al (1977). The Psychology and Education of Gifted Children, Methuen & Co.

Weston, P B (1977). Framework for the Curriculum, NFER Publishing Co.

Weston, P B (1979). Negotiating the Curriculum, NFER Publishing Co.

Chapter 4

Trevor Kerry

Introduction

Few teachers deny that they feel inadequate to deal with the
brightest pupils in their classes. Why should this be?
There seem to be three main reasons.

First, there can be little doubt that training
institutions do not give much (in most cases, any) time or
expertise to this area at the initial training stage.
Pressures, both practical and academic, on BEd students are
for basic competence and confidence in coping with the
majority of pupils. Any additional emphasis is likely to be
upon slow learners, working on the assumption that 'the
bright will take care of themselves' (Kerry, 1978a) and that
they are unlikely to be behaviourally disruptive to the
point of being a discipline problem (Kerry, 1980). In a
PGCE course the eight months of training available simply
allow no time for anything beyond subject specific expertise
plus some very superficial skills training in areas such as
class management, which are applicable to a complete cross-
section of pupils.

Second, within the profession itself INSET has
for generations been too obsessed with subject specific
skills, at least within the secondary sector. Any course
advertised as concerned with 'Teaching subject X' will be
fully subscribed; any in-put labelled 'Teaching X children'
or 'Acquiring teaching skill X' is unlikely to gain enough
takers for a quorum (unless again the subject matter is slow
learners).

Thirdly, teacher attitudes are a direct reflection of
the norms of society. In the backlash which followed
comprehensive reorganization it became less than respectable
to admit the presence of, let alone give anything smacking
of special provision to, any already 'privileged' group of

children. This attitude affects not only our own society, but those of other developed countries (Kerry, 1978b) despite the fact that it is just the high technologies which demand highly able workers. (It is interesting to reflect that both the USA and the USSR are exceptions here.) As one teacher put it:

> the more able have had it too good too long; now we need to discriminate positively AGAINST them.

The same blinkered attitude can be seen at work in the history of Nottinghamshire's Curriculum Development Unit. Set up to experiment with innovative curriculum for bright pupils in a socially mixed division of the LEA, a change in local government control axed it as socially devisive. Now, no bright pupils of any social or ethnic background can benefit from its provisions. In some areas at least there can be little doubt that society has settled for, and is prepared to engineer, a levelling down in educational provision.

This chapter takes what to some will appear to be a partisan and unacceptable view. It maintains that, while equal opportunity should be a keystone of educational pro-vision, not all are academically, intellectually, musically or artistically equal. Mozart wrote a symphony at nine years old: few of us could do it at 90. But a genuinely democratic education system should be able to cater for Mozartian potential (as well as for, say, a slow reader). The argument goes on to accept that not so long ago about 20% of the population was regarded as sufficiently able intellectually to merit special educational provision. The reality is, these bright youngsters are still with us - often unrecognized, bored and unstimulated - often in mixed ability classes which fail to stretch them (Sands and Kerry, 1982) and being taught by teachers without specific skills to cope with their special needs.

Because the chapter takes this view it goes on to ask, and hopefully to answer, some specific questions:

... What kinds of teachers make successful teachers of bright pupils?

... What pupil needs should these teachers try to fulfil?

... What kind of training do these teachers require?

The answers, it is claimed, are neither partisan nor élitist, but are designed to secure only the fulfilment of the 1944 ideal: that every child be educated physically, mentally, morally and spiritually to the limit of his or her ability.

What kind of teacher?

We can take it as read that an effective teacher of bright pupils needs to have a good knowledge of his subject; but <u>any</u> teacher ought to aspire to this fairly limited horizon. More important, perhaps, is that he should have an enthusiasm, for learning as a process, and for the application of what is learned. In the days before teacher training became universal (only two decades ago) there were many who inspired generations of youngsters of all abilities to a real care for their subjects. They did it not so much by technical skills of communication (though they may have had some natural talent for these), as by their sincerity. Professionalism can provide polish, but only people exude emotion.

Teachers of bright pupils need to be sympathetic to adolescent development, with all its traumas. <u>All</u> teachers need this sympathy, <u>all</u> pupils pass through adolescence. But for bright pupils there may be the added problem of a mismatch between physical and emotional development on the one hand and intellectual development on the other. It is difficult to convey the full implication of this statement in the written word. It is relatively easy to communicate to someone of normal intelligence how it feels to be a slow learner. For example, the following brief instruction would be unintelligible to nine people in every ten without recourse to a dictionary:

make or find me a gouache.

Imagine yourself shut up in a room with all kinds of equipment from pots and pans to paint brushes, but with absolutely no idea of the meaning of the one key word. That's a bit like being a slow reader: so near and yet so far. On the other hand it is impossible to convey what it must be like to have a reading age of 17 inside a body of chronological age 7 years and with 7-year-old emotions.

As Belle Wallace has indicated in a previous chapter, the effective teacher of bright pupils must be skilled in producing varied and interesting curriculum materials, flexible in teaching method. These skills are always appropriate, of course. With the more able child, whose mind may be working ahead of the teacher's, the need to provoke, stimulate, interest and make curious is paramount. Games and puzzles stop being fun when you know you're going to come up with a correct solution every time. The child who comes home from school with ten sums right out of ten every day for a week is not doing well. He is simply under-stimulated: and this situation (which is so pleasing to many

parents) is an indictment of, not an accolade for, the
teacher.

Teachers of bright pupils need to practise and develop
their skills of questioning and explaining, especially the
former, and this is a theme to which we shall return in the
next two chapters. But English education is bedevilled by
the concept of bodies of knowledge: to be a scientist you
need to know x amount about science. Far from it. To be a
scientist one needs to ask good questions, develop
intelligent hypotheses and know how to test them. Teaching
through questions develops in pupils the ability to think in
a questioning manner. Some teachers find this threatening.
On the contrary, it is a measure of success.

Of course, a certain amount of memorized knowledge is
important in any sphere. To take a trivial example, the
child who responds instantly with the answer '49' when he is
asked 'seven sevens?' is going to save a lot of time on
simple computation (it beats the calculator by seconds!).
However, when I visit my GP and he takes a swab and consults
his manual of drugs I know he is more concerned to sift out
something specific to my personalized strain of bacteria
than when his opposite number elsewhere dashes off a
prescription and glances at his watch to check that the
appointment schedule is still on course for his coffee-
break. The latter has memorized some possibly appropriate
information but the enquiring concern of the former is more
reassuring. Sadly, the population at large often retains
its wish to think of the GP more as the wizard-like witch-
doctor than as the calculating scientist. In the same way
one should discourage youngsters from thinking in semi-
mystical terms of a space shuttle as 'a miracle of modern
man' (as one newspaper put it) and encourage the positive
approach that it is a brilliant technological achievement
by a skilled team of real people, more sweat than magic
wand. The time for attitude change is in school - for the
adult world there is little hope.

Another characteristic of the effective teacher which
is especially valuable in coping with bright pupils is the
willingness to guide rather than to dictate the progress of
learning. This is not to say that a child should be solely
responsible for evolving his own curriculum - he may be
potentially as bright or brighter than the teacher but lacks
experience or wisdom to make that kind of professional
decision. However, it is often more appropriate for a child
to pursue an interest actively than to be bound to the
straightjacket of a prescribed syllabus. Many teachers who
fight shy of this philosophy would complain about our
schools' tendency to make pupils specialize at too young an
age. But early specialization is exactly the trap of the
straightjacket against which one is arguing. On this issue,
one positive result of mixed ability organization in schools

has been to delay the start of the 'O' level syllabus with
its attendant specialization until the beginning of the
fourth year. (In passing it is worth remarking, perhaps,
that whatever one's view of the educational value of 'O' and
'A' level examinations, the fact is that teachers have an
obligation to help bright pupils obtain these passports into
the kinds of more relevant further education from which they
will benefit.)

An essential virtue of the teacher, and above all, of
the teacher of the bright, is that of humility. It is
strange that while anyone who has worked in higher education
is constantly aware that some of his students are potentially
or actually more able than he is (occasionally even, more
knowledgeable), in school teaching this phenomenon should be
swept out of sight. Yet it is a fact; and it is useful to
keep it in mind. If one's information, teaching methods or
points of view can be seen to be demonstrably wrong - admit
it. Mutual respect is a pre-condition for learning. In a
recent 'Peanuts' cartoon the little lad is pictured as
saying: 'I don't really wish to interrupt, I also don't wish
to be rude ... just as a matter of curiosity, Sir, has it
ever occurred to you that you might be wrong?'. Meantime,
the other pupils in the class have crept out. They know the
bomb is about to drop!

What are the pupils' needs?

The things which have been said about the kinds of teacher
needed for the bright pupil have already implied certain
latent needs in the pupils themselves. It is worth looking
at these needs a little more closely.

Clearly bright pupils need independence in learning,
encouragement to speculate, the security of psychological
climate to ask difficult questions of the teacher and the
stimulus of work at higher cognitive levels than average or
below average pupils. They need to solve problems and, more
significantly, to be encouraged to devise them.

Because of their high ability bright pupils may need
some specific social skills too. They need to compete, to
be failures and to learn to cope with failure. This should
help them to develop powers of discrimination and self-
criticism. The previous chapter made these points
effectively.

But it is a fallacy that bright pupils always <u>want</u> to
be best at everything: they often <u>want</u> to feel normal enough
to be mediocre at something. It's no fun playing chess if
you always win, or doing school work if it's always right.
The teacher must genuinely stretch the able child. In the
process the pupil will learn tolerance of others, a little
patience perhaps when <u>he</u> turns out to be slowest in a group,
or a little less perfectionism when he really struggles at a

task for a change.

Of course, co-operation is an important need for bright pupils as for others. Most bright youngsters are sensitive and need friendship. Sometimes their leadership skills or loquacity get in the way of these things. A sensitive teacher can be sufficiently interventionist to help the bright child learn to take more of a back seat, to enjoy the company of peers for its own sake as well as for the sake of a shared task.

Bright adults are often difficult to live with. Perhaps it will be ever thus. But the effective teacher can at least raise the youngster's level of consciousness so that he can become aware of, and begin to control, undesirable personality traits.

Some bright youngsters become obsessive about one field of knowledge or one interest. Here the need is for a more balanced approach, which the experience of the teacher can offer. This kind of broadening of educational or even leisure-time horizons may well prove fruitful, since many bright youngsters can cope with several different skills each at a high level. How often do we admire the high-jumper who can become an eminent barrister and still find time to be a proficient violinist? How much fuller his life must be than if he had developed just one skill, to whatever level!

What kind of training?

The in-service training of teachers in England is a well-intentioned hotch-potch of isolated gems engulfed in a stew of mediocrity. No one body takes ultimate responsibility, but everyone (the DES, universities, colleges of education and polytechnics, LEAs, teachers' centres and individual schools) cashes in on the act. The result is that keen young teachers turn up to do anything and everything in a fairly unsystematic way hoping for promotional rewards, but often in the current economic climate, not finding them. More senior staff who should be sharpening up on professional skills learned a decade or two ago often involve themselves not at all in further professional training, but by their seniority are seen to be rewarded. Above all, is the scandal that there is no need for <u>any</u> teacher to improve his skill (any skill - to manage a class, to question, explain, teach the able or less able) <u>at any time</u> during a professional lifetime. He can come out of college a mediocre student, be lucky or astute enough to find a job, and inflict even more mediocre teaching on forty annual intakes of pupils.

It would be difficult, then, to make suggestions about suitable training for teachers in the skills of teaching bright pupils without suggesting some overall review of the structure of in-service provision; though it would be unreasonable in this brief chapter to pursue the theme in depth. What can be said, however, is that training in teaching skills should operate at three levels in the profession:

... the initial training level,

... the probationer level, and

... progressively (and universally), throughout the teacher's service.

Participation and proficiency in this last phase should be as obligatory as that in phase one, and certainly more meaningful than the wine-and-cheese night and solitary advisory visit that often passes for phase two.

The emphasis at all levels of training needs to be on skills, and there are good precedents for this in England (eg the Teacher Education Project, 1976-1981), in Australia (the Sydney Microskills Unit, 1975 onwards), in the USA with the slightly more questionable Competency Based Teacher Education, and in Sweden where there is a good scheme for training special teachers of the less able.

In a general context one might suggest that, while many BEd and PGCE courses have been revised in the last decade, the probationer and in-service phases of training ought to contain at least four elements. These would include a study in depth of a teaching skill (class management, questioning skills, the skills of explaining, etc); a unit concerned with teaching the most and the least able; advanced skills in the teacher's curriculum area; plus perhaps an optional unit which might allow for career specialism in school or departmental management, counselling, research-based learning and so on. In all cases one would expect a teacher to be familiar with current developments in the field; and in each case there would be no artificial and unproductive divide between theory and practice. To be effective, thinking teachers need to be familiar with theoretical models, underlying philosophies and research techniques. To be effective, educational theoreticians and researchers need to be able teachers. Apart, each of two camps is like a wedding without the bride.

The specific knowledge and skills that might form the basis of a unit on teaching bright pupils would include not only the kind of information about identification contained in Dr Joan Freeman's paper in this book, but could involve more detailed studies of individual pupils (of the kind described by Belle Wallace in Chapter 2) so that the teacher would become more sensitive to individual needs and differences.

The evaluation and assessment of pupils' work would also

feature strongly. Too little work is marked according to its cognitive structure; far more often credit is given to the regurgitation of given facts, or even to incidentals such as neatness (however desirable this might be.).

Specific ways of working with bright pupils should be examined. In particular, emphasis needs to be placed on helping bright pupils develop effective study skills and study habits, and on ways of individualizing work so that bright pupils can make adequate progress at their own level in mixed ability or broad banded situations.

Ways of improving curriculum provision might be explored, and in particular teachers might do well to review the tasks they set to pupils. Here two things are important. One is to check that adequate cognitive demand is being made. The other is to look at ways to both broaden and deepen tasks for the more able. Examples of this approach are given in Kerry (1981).

Individual teaching skills appropriate to the education of bright pupils should be analyzed and practised. The skill of effective questioning is paramount here. A succession of authors have pointed to the failure of teachers to get to grips with this important aspect of teaching and suggested methods for improvement (Barnes, 1969; Kerry, 1982; Perrott, 1977; Turney, 1977).

Such a package-deal of skills pursued in some detail during the early years of a teacher's career, with the classroom readily to hand for real examples to scrutinize and experiences to draw upon, would be invaluable. Certainly, if consciously adopted, such a scheme would revolutionize the effectiveness of our educational provision.

Conclusion

This chapter has looked at the needs of bright pupils in relation to how teachers might be helped to meet them. The opinions it expresses have been formed following a sizeable study of what happens to bright pupils in both mixed ability and streamed classes (for the former see Sands and Kerry, 1982). Throughout, the stress has been on teacher effectiveness. This effectiveness has been shown to be of benefit not just to the bright pupils in schools: all pupils are likely to be taught better by teachers whose teaching skills are refined in the ways suggested. The theme of in-school and LEA-based in-service training is elaborated in Chapters 7, 8 and 9.

The chapter suggested that we do not need a new and different breed of men and women - a kind of alien super-teacher - to cope with these youngsters. Any teacher who is prepared to hone his skills and to think critically has something to offer, as the next two chapters suggest.

Rather what is needed is a change of attitude combined with the kind of mature professionalism that wears a human face.

FOR FURTHER STUDY

Barnes, D et al (1969). Language, the learner and the school Harmondsworth: Penguin.

Kerry, T (1978a). 'Teaching bright pupils in mixed ability classes', British Journal of Educational Research, 4.2.

Kerry, T (1978b). 'Some impressions of mixed ability teaching in Sweden' in Reports of Work in Progress, Teacher Education Project, Nottingham University.

Kerry, T (1980). 'Bright behaviour', Times Ed Supplement, November 1980.

Kerry, T (1981). Teaching bright pupils, London: Macmillan Education.

Kerry, T (1982). Effective questioning, London: Macmillan Education.

Perrott, E (1977). Microteaching in higher education, London, SRHE.

Sands, M K & Kerry, T (1981). Mixed ability teaching, London: Croom Helm (Chapter 7).

Turney, C (1977). Sydney Micro Skills, Units 1 and 2, Sydney: University of Sydney publication.

Chapter 5

THE ABLE CHILD IN THE PRIMARY SCHOOL

Christine Burke

We now turn our attention to classroom practice, in order to
examine how the individual teacher can extend the able child
in the context of the mixed ability primary class.

At Lowfields, in addition to work on basic skills,
integrated studies are well-developed; and my post is that of
consultant in this latter area.

This chapter looks first at some principles involved in
the teaching of thematic or integrated studies to primary
pupils. Here, examples are drawn mainly from environmental
studies but also from other topics explored recently in the
school. Basic subject teaching is considered next.
Throughout the text I have tried to give examples of pupils'
work to illustrate the points made.

LOWFIELDS SCHOOL

Lowfields School is a modern single-storey building set in
its own playing field on the edge of a new housing estate.
Currently a middle school taking pupils from the age of eight
until secondary transfer at twelve, at the time of writing it
is under threat of reverting to a primary school so that City
and County have a uniform age for secondary transfer.

Accommodation is fairly spacious, light and pleasant;
but the semi-open-plan classroom areas can appear quite
crowded. The school is too young to have benefitted from the
fat years of educational expenditure.

The Editor and author with to thank Mr George Berzins,
Helen Allen who contributed thoughts on maths teaching, and
pupils at Lowfields Middle School, Lincoln for their help
with this chapter.

In the paragraphs which follow I have described our environmental study on the theme 'The Normans'. This work is typical of the kind of integrated studies done in the school. Throughout the description reference is made to the skills required of the teacher in teaching such a topic and to the ways in which the abilities of all pupils, including the ablest, can be stretched.

ENVIRONMENTAL STUDIES

What is meant by environmental studies? The original stimulus of any study is limited to areas of interest inspired by the local environment. This can vary from a local industry, a piece of architecture, or a geographical feature, to a wide variety of subjects of interest to children. However, although the initial stimulus is taken from the local environment, the subsequent studies will explore far wider areas. It should also be understood that meaningful studies of the environment must include field studies outside the normal precincts of the classroom and library, and adequate provisions should be made for these in the pre-study plan. Variety in learning is important for all pupils; but for the able, any change from a routine they may find especially easy to cope with is to be welcomed.
For the purposes of this chapter, I have decided to set out the aims and objectives, method of execution and subsequent assessment of a study on 'The Normans'. This theme is based appropriately in Lincoln, using the facilities available and aimed for children in the 10-11 age group. But each teacher would, in practice, need to become familiar with the potential of his or her own area as a source of material for study.

Formulating the aims of the study
Before embarking on an environmental study the teacher should set out quite clearly the aims and objectives underlying the theme. The main point of environmental studies is not the accumulation of knowledge but the acquisition and understanding of the skills required to obtain that knowledge. This is particularly important for the more able child, who should be encouraged at all times to extend fully the use of new skills by applying knowledge and by formulating questions in new fields of study.
It is of vital importance when planning a study for the teacher to formulate his or her aims, as early clarification of these will make their achievement more likely. The teacher will have a clearer picture of the direction in which he wishes the study to go. Furthermore, with aims clearly written down, the teacher will be able to

ensure that the activities on which the child embarks will be both purposeful and valuable. To some it may seem like a chore, but I would strongly recommend the discipline of committing aims to paper. Aims are relatively long-term and global, as opposed to objectives (which will be discussed later).

Some aims underlying a study of the Normans with children in the 10-11 year band would, I suggest, be as follows:

... to learn about previous culture which has influenced our landscape and institutions eg dimensions of land, establishment of law and order, and the characteristics of the people

... to understand and appreciate some of the strengths and limitations of the Normans and their culture

... to encourage and develop research skills. (These are not to be construed simply as fact-grubbing; what is important is to learn where to acquire useful information and how to extract and abstract it.)

... to use outside visits in order to encourage the child to think critically

... to help children ask questions of their own and form hypotheses

... to clarify and present knowledge assimilated in the course of the study

... to encourage the social skills, eg those requisite to working in multi-ability groups or to interviewing specialist adults whom they may meet in their study.

It may be that not all pupils will be able to achieve all these aims. Some of the skills are quite sophisticated. However, the above list includes provisions for allowing and encouraging the more able child to extend fully his potential in the developing and the subsequent testing of hypotheses. The potential for stretching the able pupil is thus built into the first stage of planning.

From long-term aims we turn to shorter-term objectives.

Objectives
Formulation of detailed objectives prior to embarking on a

new study will help prevent children being plunged into investigation lacking the basic concepts needed to solve problems. If the class teacher is fully aware of the children's individual needs he can gear the objectives towards filling in the missing areas. The objectives appropriate for children depend on their ability level, and not upon age. Objectives can be achieved in a variety of ways. It is not necessary for all children to share the same experience in order to achieve the same objectives. In the same way, it is possible for several objectives to be achieved from one activity.

The objectives behind a study of the Normans could be as follows:

... ability to collect information from a variety of sources

... to evaluate information

... to make judgements and hypotheses

... to test them and arrive at generalizations

... to plan an enquiry

... to present a report in an appropriate and creative way to other pupils

... to become aware of man's group behaviour, involving the basic concepts of communication, power, values and beliefs, conflict and consensus, similarity and difference, continuity and change, causes and consequences

... to be aware of man's individual behaviour and an empathic understanding of other people's attitudes and values

... to develop individual research skills such as the competent use of a table of contents, an index, an encyclopaedia and a library

... to interpret data, eg photography and maps

... to take notes, plan, organize material and present written findings.

Pathways to planning
In making longer and shorter term plans it is useful to have some scheme in mind. Many teachers use a flow diagram to

this end. One which I find especially useful comes from
Rance (1968) and appears as figure 5.1 in this chapter.

Preparing Resources

When planning a new project such as 'The Normans' it is, of
course, vitally important to gather together as many
resources as are available; the wider the variety of
resources, the more challenging and ultimately rewarding the
project, especially for the more able child (who should be
able to evaluate evidence and to reconcile apparently
opposite or contradictory evidence, but is all too frequently
left to 'find out' for himself from a pile of school library
books).
    For a project on the Normans, I would envisage using the
following visits as resources:

       ... outside visits to the local Norman churches

       ... a visit to the Norman west front of the cathedral

       ... visits to local Norman domestic buildings

       ... a visit to the village of Laxton to examine the
           strip field still in existence

    It would also be necessary for the teacher to make
the effort to visit Blackfriars Museum in London, if
possible, the Archives Office and the Cathedral Library to
view the Magna Carta. If possible these visits should also
be available to the pupils. The able child more than any
other will gain benefit from the experience of carefully and
critically examining genuine records; and appropriate open-
ended questions should be posed in order to direct the
child's thinking in the most beneficial and challenging
directions.
    In addition to possible visits the library service
would provide a project collection and information leaflets
and, if informed prior to the project, ensure that adequate
books are available for children to borrow. The local
Teacher Training College or Teachers' Resource Centre would
provide appropriate film strips, slides, video-tapes and
wall charts. Local archaeology groups could be consulted
and their literature made available. A glance at the Central
Film Library catalogue should provide a film dealing
generally with the period. The teacher should also check
the fiction shelves for any suitable historical fiction.
The wider the variety of resources the more challenging the
project, and the more scope there is for the able child to
develop fully his potential in research skills.

Figure 5.1. A Planning Guide

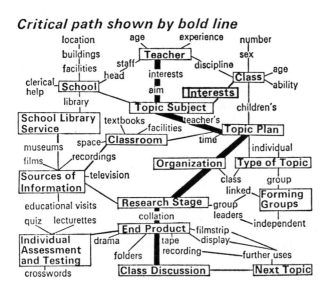

Critical path shown by bold line

Source: Teaching by Topics by Peter Rance,
         Ward Lock 1968

Teaching activities

In environmental studies, where a child is frequently
involved in pursuing his study outside the restrictions of
the classroom, he is doing far more than adding to his
factual knowledge, rather he is developing attitudes, skills
and concepts appropriate to all his future education. The
teacher should be aware of this, particularly when dealing
with an able child. This may mean skilful questioning on the
part of the teacher, or providing further more demanding lines
of enquiry. These important means of guiding a child could
easily be overlooked unless prompted by specific activities
both written down in a pre-study plan and firmly lodged in
the teacher's mind. A good example of a web of classroom
activities to aid planning can be found in 'With Objectives
in Mind', Guide to Science 5-13, on which Figure 5.2 is
based.

Figure 5.2 A planning web

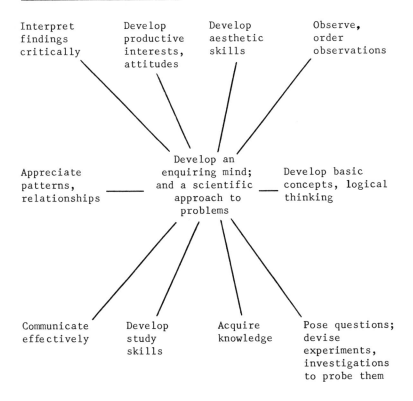

99

Getting down to work

It is at the point where classroom work begins that all the
planning and pre-project organization come to fruition. At
this stage the teacher must select the method of working most
suitable for the children in his care. One school of thought
considers the best way for the more able children to work is
for the teacher to give instructions such as 'find out as much
as you can about the Normans', and to provide a pile of
resources. The child is then left to get on. However, I
feel it would be more valuable for the child to be
incorporated into a group situation, but given questions to
answer that are both challenging and open-ended, allowing
him to examine fully the issues whilst remaining under the
guidance and supervision of the teacher.

In my own classroom I would work through the following
sequence.

First there would be a lead lesson - this to include a
film strip (showing selected frames), an introductory talk,
and an overview of the period just sketching the main
features. At the end of the session the children would be
provided with a typed worksheet. Parts of this would make
specific provision for the more able. This could either
take the form of a separate sheet, or of carefully worded
questions so the less able would give the more obvious
answer, but the more able would feel obliged to delve
deeper.

Following the lead lesson, the class could be prompted,
by means of a time-line, to give an idea of life expectancy
and how it has been expanded over the centuries. Questions
such as the following could be put to the class in order
that they may begin to think more carefully about the
period, and as a prelude to the division of the class into
research groups:

... who were the Normans? Where did they come from?

... why did they come here? Which invaders did they
    replace?

... what did they do when they got here?

This work could be completed with the help of a film
strip on the Bayeaux tapestry. A BBC Radiovision filmstrip
provides excellent pictures; and the Schools' Council
stimulus materials on 'The Normans', published by Macmillan,
are excellent and specially designed for the more able.
These reinforce the aims of analytical work and the
evaluation of evidence. For example, there are several
accounts of the Battle of Hastings by various observers, and
pupils are asked to identify the bias of these and to
suggest the nationality of the writers.

The children could then be divided up into mixed ability groups to research subjects such as the following:

... village life

... castles and defence

... town life

... buildings and technology

... transport, travel and navigation

Each child might be expected to cover at least two areas of study, for individual research. Shared groupwork would be of a practical nature eg model making, sketches, illustrations, plans, board games, crosswords,with the emphasis on social skills. Each individual would contribute information gathered, relating to the practical tasks. The groups would be given a question sheet and suggestions for practical tasks, and it is here that special provision can be made for the able child, bearing in mind that an able child need not necessarily be academically gifted in all curriculum areas or skills. There exist children who are academically quite average but who achieve remarkable results on the practical or aesthetic side of a study. Examples of some possible questions are included. Examination of these will show a high proportion of open-ended questions suitable for further research, together with practical tasks for the more practically gifted child.

Examples of possible questions

(a) Individual tasks

1. Look at the poster and slides showing the Bayeaux Tapestry. Find the section in which Harold is killed. In what way did this single incident affect the people of Lincoln?

2. In what way did local leaders and clergy help William I secure his position in England?

3. Why did William I need to build so many castles? Find out where these castles were. Mark, on an outline map of England, the position of some of these castles. Why were these sites chosen?

4. The Normans possessed advanced building technology to help build stone castles and cathedrals. What type of mechanical devices did they possess? Make working models

of some of the machinery, using the Meccano, woodworking tools and strips.

5. Find out the function of a keystone in an arch. Using clay, produce building stones to form a Norman archway. When is the arch secure?

(b) Group Projects

6. Why was the Church so important to both the leaders and common people?

7. What was the original purpose of the Domesday Book? How important was it to William I? How important is it to us? Do you think it is an accurate document? Why, or why not?

8. Build a model of a Motte and Bailey castle. Label clearly the name and function of each part.

9. After visiting the Norman buildings in Lincoln, read p 10-13 of Lincoln, the growth of a medieval town by Dulcie Duke. Discuss the quality of life in Norman Lincoln.

10. Using the Bayeaux tapestry as a source, design and complete a small tapestry or piece of appliqué, depicting either one aspect of life or one character from Norman Lincoln.

Monitoring progress

Throughout the working of the project there should be continuous assessment of the situation and feedback from the child to both group and teacher. This can be done on the basis of informal discussion and observation. The teacher should ask himself if the child needs redirection or requires additional information to stimulate a new line of enquiry. Discussions with the child whilst he is working, and at the end of each session, should take place as a matter of course so as to draw in all loose ends and help either answer questions or redirect the child to find the answer for himself.

The culmination of the study

Presentation of a project is an important skill that is frequently overlooked or considered of little importance. However, it is important for all children, and in particular for the more able, to have the opportunity to both criticize and receive criticism from his peers. I suggest that, as the culmination of a project, the children join together in subject groups and select from the individually prepared books pieces of work for display and aural presentation to the rest of the class. This will involve a high degree of social interaction. The group is thus responsible for selection of the work to be presented, and the best way in which this can be achieved. After each group has presented its work the rest of the class is free to question and comment: a valuable exercise in social and oral skills.

Evaluating the work done

Having completed an environmental study it is necessary for both child and teacher to assess value and progress. It is of vital importance for the more able child to have the opportunity of assessing his own work in isolation and in comparison to other children, both of lower and equal ability. The teacher must formulate his own criteria for assessment of success in environmental studies as no standardized test exists to help him. I suggest he will need to look at his pre-plan aims and objectives in relation to the finished studies. The assessment or evaluation will emerge from the objectives of the study, and in it provision will be made for assessing the progress of the more able children. Looking back to our aims and objectives we can begin to formulate some evaluation criteria. For example, have the pupils acquired a more critical approach to use of evidence in support of their conclusions?

As previously stated there are no standardized tests available for this kind of work. However, there are a variety of ways open for the class teacher to ascertain how many of the original aims and objectives have been achieved. These methods of assessment are also of benefit to the children as they will show up any glaring omissions and misunderstandings. Commonly teachers use:

... quiz tests

... cloze procedures - to be discussed in small groups, not individually

... group discussions

... class discussions; or

... children may make up board games

... children make up or complete crosswords.

At Lowfields we have devised a Class Record to begin to track the progress of work in the environmental study area.

This record looks at four main areas of pupil learning. The first of these is concerned with progress in study skills, eg

... coping with library skills (using a catalogue/ finding a book)

... using a table of contents

... using or making an index

... finding information from an encyclopaedia

... following up cross references

... reading Ordnance Survey maps

... interpreting graphic data

... taking notes

... planning written work for the study

... organizing the material logically

... presenting material attractively

Some attempt is made, too, to monitor whether the individual teachers have made children aware of key concepts. Some specific examples are:

... communication

... power

... beliefs and values

... conflict and consensus

... similarity and difference

... continuity and change

... causes and consequences

The class record also asks teachers to check that they have given pupils scope to develop certain qualities:

... as toolmaker

... in communicating knowledge to other pupils

... in social areas

Finally the record keeps track of the content of work
covered so that it can be seen in context. Here the crucial
questions are about the ways in which the study relates to
basic subjects on the one hand and to past and future
curriculum content on the other. This record is a good way
of ensuring that pupils are not bored, that the most able are
not simply 'time-filling' or going over areas of knowledge or
skills already covered while neglecting other important
areas.

Setting the tone
So far in this chapter I have attempted to show how the
practising teacher can, with forethought and planning,
prepare an environmental study project such as The Normans,
suitable for a mixed ability class but with special provision
for the more able members. It is a rare practising teacher
who has time to prepare individual pieces of work for every
member of his class, yet every child has individual needs.
The problem is how to cope with every child's individual
needs without detrimentally affecting other members of the
class. It has been my experience that all too often the
more able child is left to fend for himself whilst the least
able receive the bulk of the teacher's time and patience - a
practice which is not educationally sound, as the more able
also need direction and guidance, but for far different
reasons. Within the framework of environmental studies it
is possible to cater for all needs; especially through the
medium of the open-ended question, which allows the less able
to give an obvious answer whilst encouraging the more able
to look beyond. Environmental studies also caters for
children who are gifted in other, less academic ways, eg
needlecraft, model making, drawing and painting.
    Whenever a teacher has two or more children to work
with he is dealing with a mix of ability, and it is his job
to plan his schemes of work to cater for the varying needs
and not expect the able child to work in isolation. To this
end, the remainder of this section looks at some pre-
requisites and pitfalls of work of the kind described above.
    Planning is critical to successful classroom work; and
in mixed ability classes it is at the planning stage that
special work can be built into the study (for the able, the
least able, for poor readers). We try to plan in outline a
whole year ahead, and in detail about one term ahead. At all
stages, staff in each year group have informal as well as
formal meetings to put things into shape.
    The actual content of work covered is variable; though
under the environmental studies umbrella we attempt to keep
a balance between arts, humanities and the sciences. Some

recent work has included the following themes:

... autumn

... hibernation

... growth

... the growth of crystals

... a local history study

... the work of the police force

... France: language, customs and people

Enough has been said to demonstrate that factual content is less important than the skills required from pupils. This work, which may take up about a quarter of the pupils' time, is characterized by enjoyment. It is essential for the teacher to feel enthusiastic and to convey that message. The children must want to talk to each other informally about the work, and show enough keenness to bring cuttings or objects of interest from home. This work uses the skills learned in basic subject lessons and helps the pupils to apply them and see their practical value.

One distinctive feature of this work in relation to the more able pupil is the independence it requires of the pupil in finding and using information and developing the skills reviewed above. This independence is of great importance; and in teacher-pupil relations should lead to genuine dialogue or conversation. The sensitive teacher will have an eye to quality of work, drawing out each child's potential and refusing to accept second-rate offerings. Pupils must, though, be made to feel that they are contributors - to groupwork, to ideas, to planning, to classroom display. Perhaps the best way to sum up the atmosphere of the classroom would be in these four words: independence, enthusiasm, commitment, contribution.

SOME PUPILS AND THEIR WORK IN ENVIRONMENTAL STUDIES

I have chosen to illustrate this environmental work by glancing at three able pupils. Each is described briefly, and an example of work is included in the boxed sections. These will serve to illustrate some of the points made above.

Ian: aged 11 years
A popular well-balanced child with supportive parents who are

very interested in his progress and well-being at school. He
is a very conscientious and diligent worker, tackling
everything in a very thorough manner; a methodical worker who
does not skimp on detail to save time.

A good average in maths, above average for environmental
studies, English and related areas of curriculum. Not very
creative, but thorough and accurate; he likes a challenge. A
keen sportsman who enjoys football and plays for school teams.
From his record card he appears to have developed
academically in the last two years and was not previously
considered above average, though the reasons for this are
unclear.

This pupil's work on unidentified flying objects (of
which small sections only are included) shows ability to
choose an interesting topic, to research effectively, to
sustain a narrative and to make judgements. The English is
uncorrected.

Sophy: aged 11 years
A quiet, methodical child, very hard working and diligent
with a definite musical bias. Supportive parents who are
very interested in her progress. She is always keen to do
well and does not skimp on detail to save time; a studious
child. Good average in maths, above average for integrated
studies and English but untidy in presentation. Creative
writing is good, but not outstanding. She has one or two
close friends and is never frightened of speaking her mind to
adults, being quite relaxed in their company. A quietly
determined child who likes a challenge. Her record card
supports these comments, she appears to have been above
average from the beginning of her school career.

Karen: aged 11 years
A quiet but determined character who will speak her mind if
necessary. Very fastidious in presentation and keen for
accuracy but with very small handwriting. She has a real
talent for creative writing and writes long sustained stories
and pieces of descriptive prose that reflect a more mature
attitude than one might expect from an 11-year-old. Above
average for integrated/environmental studies and creative
writing, good average for maths but frequently experiences
difficulties. However, she always perseveres and does not like
to fail. Popular with a small group of friends and has a mature
attitude towards adults. Enjoys a challenge. A good gymnast.

From her record card she appears to have always been
considered able but inclined to chatter and make careless
mistakes. However, her attitude is now far more mature and
she is usually diligent and conscientious.

Ian's work on
Unidentified Flying Objects
I chose to write about this subject because I have
always been interested in them ever since I saw one.

Earth's UFOs
Not all UFOs come from outer space but aircraft
engineers designed lots of odd looking machines that
could have easily been mistaken for UFOs.
Unfortunatly for UFO enthusiasts, the disc-shape does
not fly very well, in fact the one which I am about
to tell you about did not fly very well because it
wobbled so much it had to be tied down by steel
cables.
It's safest height was only 1.22 metres off the
ground.
Other designers changed their ideas from round to
oval and they found better results.
But people think that a winged object such as the
aeroplane flies best of all.

The Avro-Avrocar
Once there was a flying saucer called the Avro-
Avrocar which first flew in Canada in 1959.
It was designed to take off upwards, stop in mid-air
and hover at any height. It could reach a maximum
of 480kph but it wasn't a success and the project
was abandoned.
This saucer had three J69 jet engines which were
arranged in a triangle around the central fan.
The exhausts from the jet spun the fan around to help
it lift into the air.
It had a central fan which was driven by the three
jets to provide the lifting power for the saucer.
It had a two man crew which sat under bubble shaped
canopies either side of the machine and the pilot
sat on the left and the observer on the right.
The saucer was 5.48 metres wide, weighed 1,815
kilogrammes and could carry a 907 kilogramme load.
The outer rim of the saucer had a split running
around and under it and the exhaust gas roared out
of split so the saucer could cruise just above the
ground like a hovercraft.
There were eight circular vents which covered the
air-intakes for the jet engines.
It had a compartment which carried different types
of test instruments.

Fliegender Pfannkuchen
This tiny plane called the 'Fliegender Pfannkuchen'
was build during the Second World War in Germany.
Few details of this flying pancake are known but it
was only a research machine equipped with wooden
propellor but unfortunatly never went into active
service.

Flying Flapjack
This twin engined plane was called the Chance Vought
XFSU-1 and was designed to fly from America air-craft
carriers.
It could take off in very short distances - less than
60 metres - yet it could still fly at over 600kph.
It's engines were buried in it's saucer shaped wing,
single seater cockpit and a turbine propellor unit.

Westland Wisp
This odd looking machine is almost the cause of some
aero-space reports in years to come.
It was a remotely piloted helicopter which had a
television-eye equipped and designed for armies for
spying on enemy troops.
It has twin rotors which are used to lift it into
the sky.
It can be carried on an ordinary jeep and can take
off from any small flat space.
It can take off vertically, cruise at nearly 130kph
and then return to its pilot sitting in his jeep.

In what way can further study of UFOs increase our understanding of space
It may be difficult to increase our understanding of
UFOs in space when most UFO sightings have been
proved to be false, but in the unlikely event they
exist:-
Are they what they seem?
Are they hostile or friendly?
Why have they come? Is their planet over populated?
Are they going through the same crisis that earth is
going through?
They might be time travellers visiting other planets
as well as earth and can inform us of what is going on
on other planets.
Is it likely that earth beings could ever live on
them? It would save a lot of time and money if a
friendly UNFOnaut time traveller could let us know
whether it is worth while to venture into space -

the uncertain future holds the answer.

Sophy's   work
People I would like to meet

1.   Kenny Dalglish

If I was given the choice between three people to
choose just one of them I would like to meet Kenny
Dalglish. If Liverpool or Scotland are playing on
television my dog has to wait for his game because
I have to watch him.
My dad is alway teasing me and calling him the Wee
canny Scotsman and I'd tell him that I've wanted to
meet him because he isn't a thick footballer or one
that boasts alot about nothing. I think I would
probably take my friend along and make her do all
the talking because I'm shy. I would like to ask
him what is it like to be on the football field .

2.   Peter Davison

I would like to meet Peter Davison because I adore
the way he can change his character from programme
to programme and yet he can still be an extremely
good actor. I think I would ask him what his real
name is. What it is like to be on television and
also on stage. I would probably be very nervous
because I'm nervous even talking to other people
dads. I wouldn't want to meet him as much a
Kenny Dalglish because I don't think he would be
quite what I expected but Kenny Dalglish's
character is easy because I have read books. But
I don't know what he is really like.

3.   Mrs. Thatcher

I would like to met Mrs. Thather for many reasons
but mainly because I admire the job. She's made it
to the top in a male chauvanistic world and I wonder
if they could do the job as well. I would ask her
how it feels to be Prime Minister. I would also ask
how it feels to talk to some of the worlds highest
officials and also wheter she thinks that extra
housing should be provided for the unemployed that
can't pay for the house they were living in. I
would tell her that I think this would be a bit
silly because if you saved you would be able to but
it would mean no going to pubs or having expensive
treats.

Karen's work

The Sea and the Storm

The sea lay peaceful feebly lapping the restful
village sighing and purring like a sleepy kitten.
Suddenly the wind began to play tricks and a spiteful
face appeared on the clouds. The wind began prowling
around the sky and then it flew into a furious tempest,
and began howling and screaming as it had never done
before, it raged and raged ear-splitting the villagers
with its loathing scream. The sea began to toss and
turn reluctantly to become part of the storm, but the
wind tormented and forced the poor sea until it had to
chase the wind in its furious, destructive torrent.
The sea began bucking and kicking like the fiercest
bucking bronco ever, it tossed its mane no longer was
it a playful kitten softly sighing. It began tearing
and scrambling at the poor village huddled together
cowering from the terrible storm. Then the sea
seemed to have a mind of its own as well as an overpowering will. The wind raged on screaming howling
and whistling in delight. The sea began grashing
and gnawing at the village, giving no known mercy.
Thundering and crashing the sea lost total control
of itself. And the wind tossed and leaped in pure
joy. The sea reared fearfully in fingers reaching
like flames over the land. Then the wind began
dying tiring with weariness, never the less its
terrible task was done. It began to grow restful
and slowly but surely disintegrated back into the
sky. Now the wind was over the sea came back to its
senses sighing until it was just a silent murmer
hardly a breath of sound. Then it rolled over and
fell into a silent slumber purring in contentment.
It had grown silent at last.

THE BASIC SKILLS: LANGUAGE

As well as a full and rounded curriculum related to daily
living and future needs - the kind of curriculum which is
provided in environmental studies - it is important that the
primary teacher maintains a good standard for all pupils in
the basic skills of language and numeracy. This section and
the next look briefly at the basic skills areas and suggest a
handful of ways in which the teacher can stimulate the
performance of the able pupil in these contexts.

Language work is usually divided into reading, talking
and listening, and writing; and we shall consider them in
this order.

1) Reading

A recent HMI Report (1982) on first schools concluded that
pupils of eight and nine were often not making adequate
progress. Competent readers were, it suggested, kept on
basic reading schemes too long when they should have been
tackling more demanding and interesting books. Sometimes a
school's book provision was inadequate. But even when this
was not the case, pupils were not encouraged to do more than
browse; they were insufficiently guided in reading choice by
teachers and they were not enthused with personal enjoyment
in reading. It has to be remembered that our brightest
youngsters of this age are often extremely able readers; and
the success of the teacher is a two-fold phenomenon: he must
help the pupils to read in an applied and purposeful way, and
also to enjoy the experience.

A lot of classroom reading time is devoted to listening
to individual pupils. For able pupils the emphasis must
change to discovering advanced reading skills. It is an
unfortunate fact of educational life that the more able
readers tend to be neglected whilst the teacher devotes most
energy and resources in the direction of the remedial
readers. LEAs should make far more classroom help available
for the slow reader so that they do not consume a disproportionate amount of the class teacher's time. At primary
level, children are at their most responsive; the majority
want to learn and make progress. However, reading is
frequently viewed as a means to an end rather than a
pleasure in its own right. In order to develop advanced
reading skills time must be provided in which children 'just
read', ideally amongst an abundant and varied supply of
books. Time is also needed for the child to define and
examine his own response to a book through exploratory
writing and discussion.

The Bullock Report (1975) clearly states that the
extension of reading skills in and through normal learning
activities is likely to be more effective than separately

time-tabled specialist reading periods. This can be seen in
an environmental study, where the more able child will be
capable of more sophisticated research which depends upon
reading fluency, comprehension and analysis of what is read.
The more able child should be taught how to 'skim', for
example, thus acquiring a skill which frees him from
dependence upon single-speed reading. Some of the skills
requisite to reading with understanding may be acquired
incidentally in the course of work in the non-formal
curriculum, particularly if the teacher has made appropriate
provision for them in his aims and objectives. Some would
merit more specific teaching. The following are some ideas
that a small group could follow.

> ... skim a given passage to gain an impression of the
> content or to find the answer to a specific
> question

> ... learn when to skim and when to read carefully

> ... list the key words in a sentence, paragraph or story

> ... list the key ideas in a passage

> ... read to deduce answers to questions about things
> not explicitly stated

> ... follow written instructions precisely

> ... use cloze procedure to encourage careful
> observation of punctuation, grammar and precise use
> of words.

The more able reader will benefit far more from discussion
of his work and the books he has read than if the teacher
merely hears him read a page of his book out of context.
Far too much importance has been attached to the hearing of
children read. The more able need in-depth discussion and
analysis of books, writing techniques and authors' styles
and intentions. An excellent review of advanced reading
skills can be found in Drummond and Wignall (1979).

2) Talking and listening
Most primary pupils are fairly willing to talk; able pupils
often have a great deal to say. Obviously, before any real
education can begin all the pupils need to learn the
groundrules, eg simple politeness about when to talk and
when to listen; they also need to know the difference
between productive talk and mere attention-seeking.
Encouraging pupil talk depends upon establishing these

groundrules and then signalling that, in the right context, talk is productive and welcome to the teacher.

Able pupils should be given many opportunities to express their ideas in talk. They can be shown that there are different kinds of spoken language. English (in Sutton, 1981) divides talk into:

... describing events or feelings

... recalling or reminiscing

... summarizing

... giving instructions

... persuading

... extracting information from someone, questioning

... evaluating

Each kind of language is appropriate in given circumstances; and each can be practised. He lists ten ideas or tasks for small group classroom talk:

... comparing and contrasting two similar objects

... deciding how to set about a task

... finding the thread of an argument

... predicting events or consequences

... identifying an unfamiliar object

... devising questions for others to answer

... designing something

... drafting a document or a set of rules

... guessing the identity of an unseen object from a description

... imagining other people's points of view

Obviously, too, there are countless other ways of encouraging pupils to talk: informal conversation with the teacher, rôle playing, giving a talk to others, dramatic production - all these have a part to play. All pupils benefit from them; but able youngsters are going to benefit particularly by discovering how to communicate more effectively what they know.

Often, however, able pupils are less good at listening. Obviously the teacher needs to encourage these youngsters to obey the groundrules of discussion and to be polite. But listening is a more active skill than simply sitting still, silent and inactive. Various listening games and activities can enhance the skill of productive listening. Pupils can be asked to follow complicated instructions, to discover what is missing from an explanation, to follow and reproduce a line of argument, to undertake aural cloze exercises, to take efficient notes from a period of teacher talk, or to analyze the soundtrack of the piece of film or videotape.

Listening or talking, the skills advocated here are those which are going to help able youngsters to analyze, think effectively and communicate with others. They may also enhance pleasure, and perhaps this is best illustrated at story-time.

3) Writing

A large proportion of a teacher's time is spent in teaching the routine skills of writing, punctuation, sentence construction, spelling etc. However, this has become such an important part of the curriculum that it is easy to lose sight of its original purpose. We should ask ourselves, particularly in relation to the more able, how often we ask children to use these skills in the production of something individual and lasting. The development of a child's ability to write clearly and imaginatively is closely connected with the quality and depth of their experiences and it is the task of the teacher to provide a wide range of stimulii. This can be anything from listening to a record, to touching an old bottle or looking at an intriguing photograph. The following is a list of stimulii that I have found useful:

... pupils' own interests and hobbies

... stuffed birds and animals

... old bottles and keys

... fungus and lichen

... a coat with 'objects' of interest in the pocket

... a parcel 'abandoned' in a public place

... unusual shaped pieces of wood

... melted plastic

... skulls and bones

... music, including sound effect records

... photographs, pictures and posters

... poems and extracts from books and other children's work.

It is important to remember that before children write, we must provide situations which create the need for them to formulate and express their ideas. For example, if an old key were used as a stimulus, children would need to guess, think and touch, formulating ideas as to its origin, purpose and any story that might have been attached to it.

Language is something that every child must be taught how to use in a variety of ways according to his individual requirements and as an instrument of communication. The majority of the writing we do as adults fulfils a purely factual and utilitarian role. The writing a child does in school serves several functions, one of which must be to prepare him for the writing he will require in the adult world. Therefore, when a child puts something into words it should be one way of clarifying his thought process. If we want children to develop a variety of thinking strategies, we must make demands which will help them. Children also need to develop skills in using words, clearly and economically, without becoming ambiguous. Teachers can help by encouraging children to give verbal/written instructions for simple tasks: eg boiling an egg, making a journey from school to home, cleaning one's teeth. Our aim should be to make children aware that there are different ways of using language to serve a variety of purposes: a time for emotive language and a time for factual statements, the transactional mode. Children need time to think, plan and execute. A set hour once a week will not be adequate help for children with ability; time should be 'made to measure'. It has always been the role of the school to help the child develop to the limit of his ability, into an autonomous person. Language is an integral part of this development and is the basis of all school work. Language is in use throughout the day, so the teacher must be <u>constantly</u> aware of the quality of language used by both himself and the children at any time and not merely in a portion of the time-table designated 'language development'.

Two pieces of written work will serve to illustrate some of the points made about language. The first is quite a good example of a pupil making out a case and then pursuing a line of argument, in this instance for the establishment of a wildlife park. The second combines reading and writing into the production of a book review about <u>The Wind in the Willows</u>, and is characterized by some excellent turns of phrase.

A Wildlife Park

If I was a member of the Lincoln Council and if I had lots of money then I would make a wildlife park in Lincoln because at the moment we haven't very many facilities in which a whole family can go somewhere together. I would build my village park on the north common because this is a wide space of field which is only used by golfers and horses, but I would still leave some of the field for horses and golfers. If the people around the north common didn't like the idear for a reason like the noise of the animals and the chance of them escaping, then I would say that I would have a sepret pen for each animal or group of animals, and at no time will the animals be allowed to roam the common without its keeper. I think this park will be of great value to children who go to schools all over Lincolnshire, because it will help them to identify and understand animals more. Also, it will benefit to the unemployed because it will take alot of workers to run the park. And in its turn this will help most of the people who live in Lincoln, because there will not be quite so much vandalism. To make my park a more exciting and interesting place, I would have a mini fair with lots of rides, I would also have a crazy golf course for the golfers, then there would also be souvenier shops and refreshments. There would also be a picnic area with a park in it, and I would have a quiz for school children which would ask them all sorts of questions about different animals. If for some reason I couldn't have my park on the south common, then I would have it on the west common, because it will have as much space, and because so far it is not quite so crowded around with houses and office blocks.

The Wind in the Willows

This wonderful book will definately appeal to animal lovers. The magical antics of mole, rat and toad are so well described in this story that you can put yourself in their character entirely.

The story begins when the mole meets rat near rat's house in the bank of the river. Mole is a rather quiet character who likes to please everyone, while rat is a cheerful animal with a strong sense of humour. Then there is the impossible toad, he is very rich and lives in a big mansion called Toad Hall, but although toad is rich he is not wise as it so often is, he squanders his money on new cravings which he has every day. But one day something tragic happens to Toad, he is taken to prison for stealing. But in prison toad made friends with a little girl who pities toad, and helps him to escape by disguising him. The next part of the story dedicates itself totally towards toads flight to freedom. In which he sneaks on a train, buys a horse and meets up with a rather unfriendly barge woman, as well as some other intriguing and exciting adventures. But it was all for no avail because toad's welcoming gesture was a tragic one, his hall had been over-run. And if you read this book you will find out exactly what happens when toad, rat, mole and Badger, a solitary grumpy fellow at times, try to overthrow Toad Hall's intruders.

Altogether a magical, lovely book out to capture any interest.

THE BASIC SKILLS: NUMERACY

HMI (1982) found that only a quarter of the first schools they surveyed covered a wide range of mathematical work, most concentrating rather on computation. For able children, as for others, this is an important skill to develop; but as in other curriculum areas, so in mathematics, able pupils need a more problem solving approach. One class of eight-year-olds was given the template of a tetrahedron. This measured ten centimetres at the base, was eight centimetres high and measured six centimetres across the top. They were asked, from what they knew about finding the areas of square and oblong figures, to find one or more ways of calculating the area of the tetrahedron. After about half an hour of discussion amongst themselves they came up with two solutions. First, to lay an acetate sheet marked with centimetre squares over the cut-out and to count squares and part squares. Alternatively, they made a scale drawing on squared paper, cut out the 6 x 8cm rectangular centre portion, slotted the remaining two triangles together to form a rectangle 2 x 8cm, and calculated the answer as 64 square centimetres. This was slightly different from their first attempt, because of the difficulty of estimating the size of part squares in the earlier solution.

Not everyone would agree with Bertrand Russell that mathematics is 'exact, rigorous, exciting, beautiful'. Nevertheless, there is quite a lot which can be done to show pupils that maths can be challenging, interesting and even practical. Mathematics is concerned with the discovery of pattern (and, sometimes, its absence) and with the communication, in a variety of ways, of the pattern found. Patterns of all kinds have a mathematical basis, in number, algebra and geometry, in natural and man-made forms.

A mathematically able child often possesses an intuitive tendency to arrange numbers and look for pattern. He can describe that pattern in words, use it elsewhere and extend it. Mathematics is an abstract subject; an activity of the mind. It is, therefore, important that all children, including the most able, are provided with concrete materials to stimulate their imaginations. Many able children need to see the appropriate objects in order to solve a problem and perhaps extend that problem.

How best can we create a mathematical climate in which the mathematical potential of the able child can flourish and ripen? If, as in many schools, the teacher employs a style of teaching which uses the same material for the whole class, pitching it at the level of the average child, then the more able children are likely to be unstretched. Whatever the style of teaching, whatever the classroom organization involved, the talents of the more able child can only be matched if there is some measure of individuality in

the work they are expected to do. The more able child needs
to be set problems which require sustained effort and which
can be pursued in depth. Open-ended assignments, with an
opportunity for a child to explore a problem or a concept
and perhaps end with half-formed ideas or even additional
questions,are required even if they are difficult to evaluate.
Questions should be investigational in nature, with perhaps
many solutions, and more than one approach to those
solutions. They should be designed to encourage divergent
thinking and creativity.

To enable children to spend time in exploration and
questioning we must encourage discussion. It is in
discussion that children attempt to verbalize their
thoughts, they use each other as learning catalysts. The
atmosphere needs to be co-operative rather than competitive.
The emphasis should be on learning rather than teaching. The
teacher organises situations in which conversation and
discussion play a major part. He must know when to add
comment or withdraw, he must judge when to stop a
discussion. Most of us learn faster when we are able to
verbalize our thoughts and concepts. Through talking with
other children and adults,children interact their ideas with
those of others and gradually modify their own thinking.
More able children can communicate their excitement in
solving a particular investigation and so enlist the
support of others in class, so all the class benefits.

To help children learn that mathematics is useful and
relevant in many situations we must ensure that mathematical
techniques and operations are embedded in a wider framework
of mathematical thinking. The Open University, in their
Mathematics across the Curriculum Course, suggest that this
can be done by allowing children to encounter real problems.
In solving these problems, children can see a reason for
using mathematical skills and so acquire the incentive to
gain new skills. They suggest that any problem chosen
should:

... have an immediate effect on children's lives

... offer solutions which lead to some improvement of
the situation

... have neither known 'right' solutions nor clear
boundaries

... require children to use their own ideas in solving
it

... be 'big' enough to require many phases of class
activity for any effective solution.

Recently I co-ordinated the efforts of a class of mixed ability 8-9 year olds to solve the problem of making the playground a happier place to spend time in during playtimes and lunchtimes. They felt very disgruntled with their treatment from the older children, 'bullying' they seemed to think. Diplomacy was necessary not only when dealing with the older children but also with the lunchtime supervisers. With the help of the acronym PROBLEMS the children were able to find some solutions to their unhappiness. PROBLEMS stands for:

   ... Pose the problem

   ... Refine into areas of investigation

   ... Outline the questions to ask

   ... Bring the right data home

   ... Look for solutions

   ... Establish recommendations

   ... Make them happen

   ... So what next?

During their investigation they learned such skills as reading and using plans of the school, sampling, questionnaire design, data organization and statistical interpretation. Interaction between small groups and the whole class was vital. As well as the exchanging of ideas and information class discussion helped each small group to consider how their work contributed to solving the problem and to decide what further investigations were necessary. These discussions kept me in touch with whatever was going on and where any help was needed. I was thus able to keep the work organized and use all the teaching opportunities that arose. It was easier to introduce a mathematical skill when the children were aware of the need for it than attempt to teach it in a 'maths lesson'. Real problem-solving uses skills which are not developed by teaching mathematics in isolation, it emphasises the relevance of mathematics. I found it a very useful idea with much scope for the more able children, not only opportunities for mathematical learning but also observation skills, decision-making and communication skills.

When considering the able child it can be a problem for a teacher to decide whether to push on more rapidly with the main core of the mathematics course within the school or whether to explore the topics being studied in greater breadth. This problem is more acute in the primary or middle school than at a later stage because pupils subsequently transfer elsewhere. I suggest that where there is doubt it is preferable to choose greater breadth because of the risk of boredom if work is repeated later.

It has to be admitted that many primary teachers are not mathematically inclined, and some will feel unable to cope with the problem-solving and abstract approach advocated. In schools where this happens the whole situation should be raised at a staff meeting as a management issue. Most schools have one or more members of staff who would be prepared to specialize as maths teachers for part of a timetable or who are already holding posts as subject consultants. Amicable arrangements should be made as a matter of policy to use the talents of such people to further the skills of the most able mathematicians.

Above all, the individual teacher must become aware of the opportunities for mathematical work. These can arise in various ways: one can find interesting problems in books, or in magazines such as Junior Education; there are a number of well-known mathematical games; mathematical problems arise spontaneously from studies in other curriculum areas. Some good examples are given in the following paragraphs.

Networks that can be drawn without taking the pencil off the paper or going over the same line twice are called UNICURSAL, which means ONE LINE. Which of these is a unicursal network? Pupils should answer the question and then try the problem at the bottom of the page.

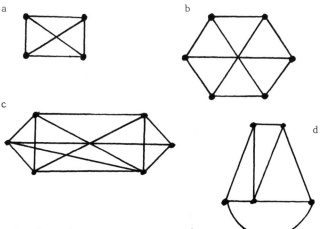

a   b   c   d

(c. is the only unicursal network)
By drawing networks of your own attempt to discover any rules applying to a unicursal network.

Concepts learned from the network activity can be extended to solve the Königsberg problem. The town of Könisberg has two islands in the middle of the river Pregel that runs through the town. There are seven bridges linking the islands to the banks thus:

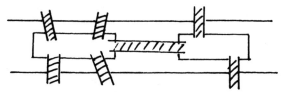

Can the citizens of Könisberg walk around the town crossing every bridge once only? Use the knowledge you have of unicursal networks to see if the walk is possible.

Activities with dice interest children and the concept of probability is a useful one to explore. Throw two dice and add the scores. Repeat this 36 times, recording each result. Draw a frequency graph to show how often each total appears. Which total occurred most often? Least often? Repeat with another 36 throws. Are your results what you expected? Make an addition table for numbers one to six. Which number(s) occurs most often in the table? Least often? Draw a frequency graph of your addition table. Compare the two frequency graphs. Discuss the chances of throwing a double six in Monopoly. The activity can be extended by using three dice instead of two.

Suggestions for games for two or more players would be BRIDG-IT and SPROUTS.

Game devised by David Gale in 1958 for two players. Isometric dot paper needs alternate rows to be coloured in, say, black (represented here by thick lines) and blue (thin lines). Each player uses a different colour. The object of the game is to join any pair of adjacent dots, horizontally or vertically, trying to form a connected path from one side of the board to the other. No lines can cross.

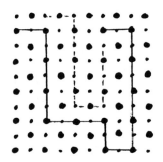

SPROUTS was invented by two Cambridge University mathematicians. It is a game for two people involving drawing a network. Two points are marked on a sheet of paper. The players move alternately, by drawing an arc from one point to another or from a point back to itself. When an arc is drawn, a new point is drawn somewhere on it. No arc may cross itself, another arc, or pass through a point. A point has only three 'lives', that is, no more than three lines can start or finish at it.

The object is to leave your opponent without a move to make.

| original points | 1st play | 2nd play | 3rd play | 4th play |

This shows an unfinished game starting with two points. Is there a limit to the number of moves that a sprout game can last? What conclusions can you make? <u>Brussel Sprouts</u> is a variation that uses three or more points to start.

Finally, an example of mathematics arising from environmental studies would be as follows. A group of pupils was studying a farm which was crossed by a disused railway line. As well as the history of the line and a study of its wildlife the pupils raised questions about the cutting through which the line travelled. They learned it was hewn by navvies; and were led on to measure its length and depth and to calculate the volume of soil moved. By working out how much soil a man could move in a day and by checking old records to find the number of men employed the youngsters were able to work out how long the operation might have taken and were able to appreciate some of the labour involved.

Mathematics should tax the most able conceptually, compel them to think abstractly, and encourage them to solve and devize problems. Tackled in this way it is by no means as much of a wilderness area as many people believe. By keeping abreast of the professional magazines every class teacher should be able to find enough stimulating ideas to make the subject fun as well as to raise the level of intellectual demand.

This chapter has set out to review an approach to the able child in the primary school class which is both practical and effective. It is perhaps most appropriate to end with a word about record-keeping. The progress of each individual pupil must be carefully monitored in basic

subjects in the same ways as were suggested for the
environmental studies discussed early in the chapter. But
the teacher, too, needs a checklist against which to measure
lesson performance. Figure 5.3 sets out just such a checklist as a quick but reliable way of monitoring the teacher's
own professional activity.

FOR FURTHER STUDY

BULLOCK, Alan (1975). A Language for Life, HMSO.

DRUMMOND, D & WIGNALL, E (1979). Reading: a Sourcebook,
        Heinemann.

HMI (1982). Mathematical development no. 3, HMSO.

SUTTON, C R (1981). Communicating in the Classroom, Hodder
        & Stoughton.

Figure 5.3

Checklist of provision for able pupils in primary
classes

Have you given your able pupils opportunities to ...

1.   tackle more demanding workcards or tasks?

2.   work independently?

3.   develop their own areas of interest?

4.   work at their own pace?

5.   tackle open-ended problems?

6.   be innovative or creative in response to set
     tasks?

7.   be imaginative?

8.   pursue areas of interest at home or beyond the
     classroom?

9.   work with other able youngsters as stimulus?

10.   form hypotheses and test them?

11.   respond to high-order questions?

12.   ask questions of you?

13.   read widely around the topic?

14.   make judgements and draw conclusions?

15.   argue effectively, both orally and in writing?

16.   explore more demanding resource materials?

17.   produce detailed and well-presented work?

18.   think laterally?

19.   learn how their written work might be improved?

20.   consult you about their strengths and
      weaknesses?

                              TK/CB 1982

Chapter 6

Trevor Kerry

I want to begin this chapter with two descriptions of classrooms I have visited. There's more than an even chance that
you will recognize them, too.

Our first classroom visit is to Knotwaving Comprehensive.
The day is half over, and the residue of several crisp
packets proclaims that lunch has been taken. A gym-shoe,
hidden under a landslide of banda sheets on the floor causes a
minor skirmish as we enter and inadvertently trip over it.
The room is deserted, but a little after the bell some pupils
arrive in noisy, giggling groups. Soon the teacher,
breathless, follows, apologizing for lateness and announcing
her intention to move the desks so that we can all see the
filmstrip better.
    While the pupils slide chairs and desks into unfamiliar
places we have time to take stock of the walls. The paint is
ageing, but is slightly newer than the peeling Fire
Regulations. A newspaper cutting held up by three drawing
pins yellows on a pock-marked but otherwise deserted notice-
board. Meanwhile, Miss Slipshod is setting up the projector,
without major mishap, and delegates the loading of the
filmstrip to a pupil who is more fluent with its operation
than she is.
    'Thanks, Charlie,' she says.
    'Any time, Miss,' he flirts. 'Do you know your jeans are
fraying?'
    'Yeah. Still, no use wearing decent clothes here ...'
    Charlie turns the filmstrip from frame to frame while
Miss Slipshod reads from the printed commentary. The room is
stuffy in the blackout and whispers break out. There's the

subtle aroma of chewing-gum. At frame 57 the bell goes.
'Damn. I'll do the other five next lesson if I remember
to book the projector. Now come back here. I've got some
notices for you lot. Here, you in the blue jersey, sit
down ...'

The classroom at Goodhope Comprehensive is clean, safe, tidy
and well aired. Furniture is not in the first flush of youth,
but the teacher arrives back early from lunch to slide it
quickly into appropriate patterns for the coming lesson.
There is a small class library, a reference collection,
cupboards for sets of texts and to store in neat piles those
exercise books awaiting marking and return. Classroom walls
are full of stimulus materials and pupils' work. Exhibits
are held up with map-tacks or blu -tac; and eye-catching
posters on a board near the door attract the pupils'
attention as they enter. They converse spontaneously about
them; the teacher picks up the conversation and uses it later
as a lead into the lesson. Administration is kept to a
minimum; more notice-boards fulfil some of this role, while
verbal notices are kept for lesson ends.
Over the years Miss Slick has gathered a sizeable
resource collection of pictures, charts, tapes, slides and
magazines. Each item is selected for quality and relevance
to the curriculum. Most are available for children's use: a
simple but efficient card-index locates items which are
housed in an improvised filing system. The simpler hardware
is available in the classroom and pupils have been instructed
in how to operate it. Each subject in the card index is
served by several stimulus items, covering a range of reading
and cognitive abilities. Today, Miss Slick is to use part of
a filmstrip to illustrate her theme. Equipment has been
booked in advance, and she has set up the projector, checked
that it functions, and wound on to the appropriate section of
the resource.
When the final bell goes Miss Slick can look back on
this lesson as a success. She was there to greet the pupils
at the classroom door, she chatted to many informally,
calling them by name, as they moved quietly into their
places. They conversed in whispers until all were gathered
and appeared to be ready. A spontaneous silence fell.
'So you liked my new poster, Marian? What do you think
it added to what we discovered yesterday ...?'
The lesson was under way. She checked with her eyes,
constantly, that all were involved, interested. At the
change from question to answer to filmstrip, from filmstrip
to pupil task in groups, she was there - apparently
everywhere - and she drew things to a conclusion just before
the bell; giving out her notices and watching the departing

pupils as she moved them unhurriedly out of the room ready
for her next group ...

These two incidents spell out not the difference between a
good teacher and a bad, not between a favoured school and an
underprivileged one (for they often occur under the same
roof). They show what we are prepared to tolerate, and the
minimal acceptable standard of professionalism. Miss Slick
is not a paragon, her classes not made up of angels, Goodhope
not in a middle class ghetto. To believe that is self-
deception. But Miss Slipshod is with us in every large
school and many small ones and, tragically, Knotwaving is
'knot waving but drowning' as Stevie Smith might have put it.
     So let us be clear before we begin this chapter. The
strategies offered are set against the background of
Goodhope. Until the Knotwavings are eliminated there will be
little or no true education for anyone: able, average or
remedial. Some not too incompetent childminding, perhaps;
but no education.
     Accept, if you will, my thesis; at least for the present.
What epitomizes the goodness of Goodhope centres around quite
separate, though related, strands of skills. The first is
that of management and organization. A second is to do with
planning for learning and teaching. Finally, there are
specific teaching skills and strategies. This chapter now
examines those three strands in more detail, relating them
particularly to the education of the able in the normal
classroom.

MANAGEMENT AND ORGANIZATION

Class control and discipline

Class management is the largest single drain on the mental
and physical resources of the teacher. Contrary to the
popular mythology teachers are not normally subject to
physical threats from pupils. In an extensive study carried
out by the Teacher Education Project (1) it was found that
less than 1% of all disciplinary incidents in comprehensive
schools involved any physical aggression; and when it did
occur it was always between pupils and was of a very minor
nature. There are schools and localities where such events
do take place, but the point is rather that they have rarity
value. What the teacher is more likely to be up against on a
daily basis are these:

          ... pupils who talk noisily so that others can't get on

          ... behaviour which is inappropriate to the task in hand

... pupils who talk about things which are not part of
the task

... the inappropriate use of equipment (tapping with
rulers instead of drawing with them)

... eating and drinking in lessons

... movement by pupils around the classroom at the wrong
time, at the wrong speed or to the wrong place.

In just a page or two of text it is impossible to give a
complete breakdown of the skills and sub-sets of skills
involved in class control. However, some attempt will be
made to outline the main elements which are pre-requisite for
pupils' learning. This, then, is the underlying assumption:
no effective teaching or learning can take place until proper
class control has been established.

Let us examine briefly what is NOT implied by this
statement. I am not advocating the rigid sitting in silent,
motionless, unresponsive rows which typifies (in the popular
imagination) the 'good old days' of English education.

No. Rather, we must accept that the first priorities
are to do with safety, comfort, and politeness. The teacher
must, from the very beginning, establish his own working
relationships and standards with pupils. From the first day
in the classroom he must spell these out and stick to them.
There will be a few attempts to put him to the test; when
these fail the novelty will wear off. Advice about a
teacher's general approach might go like this:

> The first priority is to exude confidence. Even when
> you are nervous you must learn not to show it in look,
> voice or gesture. You must always give instructions as
> though you expect them to be carried out. A calm
> approach is preferable. Collect everyone's eyes - once
> they are looking at you keep them interested (good
> lesson preparation will help here) and occupied (bored
> pupils seek diversions). At first, minimize pupil
> movement; when you want the class to file out or move
> into groups allow them to do so a few at a time. Be
> mobile yourself. Move around, but develop routes for
> walking round the class so that you keep everyone in
> view. Vigilance is paramount. The normal arc of vision
> is quite restricted, so don't stay at the desk.
> Remember, too, that early in a lesson or as soon as a
> task is set, you should get round quickly to everyone:
> this encourages pupils to start working. You can go
> round again later to deal with specific queries or
> problems. Give instructions clearly; then do not
> allow silly and unnecessary questions: pupils must get

into the habit of listening. If you are using stimulus
material at the front of the room, a wallchart, OHP
transparency or slide picture, teach from the back for a
while. With the pupils' attention pointing forward they
are then unaware of where you are looking, so cannot so
easily commit minor acts of deviance.

Above all, try to persuade pupils to take the
sensible attitude towards school. They're going to
spend seven hours a day there for a long period. The
classroom must be both a home and a workshop. Here they
must make good social relationships, chat to each other,
be able to be relaxed and informal when the time is ripe.
In between it must be used as a place to carry out tasks
safely and sensibly because the learning really is
valuable (good curriculum planning will ensure that it
is!).

The top ten class management tips given to students by
experienced teachers in the Teacher Education Project's
research were these:

... start firmly, you can always relax later

... get silence before you try to teach or talk

... control the pupils' entry to the classroom

... know pupils' names, and use them

... prepare and structure your lessons

... arrive before the pupils

... prepare furniture, apparatus and equipment in
advance

... be sure you know how to use apparatus and equipment

... be mobile

... get lessons started with a bang, and then sustain
the curiosity.

This is sound enough advice, even if one might wish to
add to it, modify it or change the order of importance.

Sound class control is an <u>enabling</u> feature of the
teacher's repertoire of skills: it allows learning to take
place in a variety of ways (for example, in groups or through
individual independent study). It permits the build-up of
good teacher-pupil relationships. It fosters the kind of
atmosphere in which teachers can ask, and encourage pupils to

ask, important questions and to seek the answers to them. All these points are taken up again as this chapter progresses, and first we go on to look in more detail at the question of social relations.

Social relations in the classroom

Teaching, like any other interpersonal relationship, is at its best when the parties enjoy each other's company and get spontaneous pleasure from being together. The best teacher-pupil relations are characterized by firmness and friendliness. In other words, the pupils should feel free to speak openly about work, to ask questions, to discuss, to express opinions, to disagree, and also to talk about personal problems or simply (most importantly, perhaps) to hold conversations with each other and with the teacher. Humour is an ingredient. But there should be recognized boundaries. School rules should be obeyed; politeness should be prevalent; few teachers prefer to be addressed by christian names; there should be no swearing, slang or rudeness. Trust has something to do with it, too. In a well-run classroom youngsters will accept trust and can therefore be trusted. This in no way relieves the teacher of the duty to be present with the class or to exercise vigilance. What this package adds up to is a relative informality with a set of guidelines that ensure security.

A word which is often used to describe this security is climate. A climate in which effective learning can take place must leave room for the individuality, skills and personalities of all the participants. These guidelines are valid for all pupils, but it will be recalled from the Introduction that creative thinkers and under-achievers are particularly at risk in repressive classrooms.

Some common mistakes here are to err on one side or the other of the firm/friendly dividing line. An authoritarian teacher may give out sound information; he will not persuade a timid pupil to voice an opinion or offer an enquiry. In the same way even able, creative pupils will rarely volunteer to answer a question unless they are certain of the answer. One piece of research which examined wrong answers given by pupils concluded that they were given in one of two sets of circumstances. A teacher who pressurized individuals to answer, calling on them by name, might extract incorrect responses or guesses. The only other circumstances in which these occurred commonly were where pupils trusted a particular teacher not to ridicule or censure an incorrect but genuine attempt. These pupils were prepared to speculate, an essential ingredient in the successful education of the bright pupil.

Some teachers try to keep control by currying the favour of the pupils. They may ape pupils in casualness of speech,

dress or manners. But pupils see through these ploys, and
the strategy is doomed to failure.

Sound advice is to become involved in some form of
extra-curricular activity with pupils: a school team, a
lunch-time club, a dramatic or musical production, a school
trip. Here teachers and pupils can learn to accept each
other as human beings away from the pressures of the
classroom. Similarly, try to discover the interests and
hobbies of pupils in your classes, especially of the more
timid. In this way you can open up a channel of
communication which depends rather less on the conventional
teacher-pupil roles. Able pupils often have well-defined
areas of interest in which they are quite expert, so be
prepared to do a little homework!

Learn by experience when to say 'Yes' and when to say
'No'; and avoid idle threats or, worse still, unfulfilled
promises. What pupils respect most are the twin virtues of
consistency and fairness.

The corollary of this approach is that pupils are
thinking, self-motivating learners, for bright pupils in
particular must never be spoon-fed. Indeed, this should be
the aim of all education: so it is opportune to shift the
emphasis from managing and organizing to learning and
teaching.

PLANNING FOR TEACHING AND LEARNING

Curriculum planning

The preceding section has raised important curriculum issues.
Some of these will now be explored in a little more depth.

A month or two ago I visited a small suburban school.
In conversation, after the pupils had gone home, I asked a
small group of staff when they had begun to plan aspects of
their work for the autumn term. One teacher acted as spokes-
man for the group:

> After the first television programme of the term. We
> usually follow the series, but advance information is
> too sketchy to permit us to prepare much before we've
> got the flavour of the programmes.

Let it be said immediately that teaching involves the
ability to think on one's feet; to adapt, change or modify
one's prepared schemes; to be flexible in approach.

But this reply was unsatisfactory.

Longer-term planning needs to take place at intervals:
a year, a term, a month, a week ahead of the lesson.
Planning at these various intervals may be more or less
detailed, more or less concerned with educational issues,
more or less bound up with organization or administrative

detail. But each stage is vital in the chain of events. Let us take an example.

Several staff get together and decide that they want to re-model part of the work of the second year pupils. Up to a year in advance they will meet and plan, together, with the department head, with the deputy head (curriculum) and even the head. Sometimes advisers or other outside consultants may be asked to join these early discussions. At this point the outline of the new curriculum will begin to emerge. Over the next few months a philosophy, agreed aims and a syllabus or course content will emerge.

Once agreement is reached, some administrative arrangements will need to be made well ahead of the new academic year: visits have to be planned, coaches hired, the time-tabler approached for co-operation.

A term in advance detailed plans for individual lessons may emerge, and decisions will have to be made about employment of man-power and teaching methods, and about the use of plant and resources. Orders for equipment or resource materials will be placed.

A few weeks in advance individual teachers will be preparing lessons for at least the first half-term or term: they will meet, chat informally, swap ideas and exchange materials.

Finally, a week in advance, audio-visual equipment will be booked from technicians, and the final touches will be put to individuals' lessons.

Even where other colleagues are involved, each teacher will need to go through these motions, his thoughts crystallizing over a long period so that he is _au fait_ with his proposed methods and materials.

So what does course-planning of this kind imply? Certainly, a consideration of the issues set out in Figure 6.1. And at each stage of this model the needs of pupils with special learning needs must be taken into account: those of the slow reader, the poor writer, the less numerate; but also those of the quick worker, the individual specially talented in this area, the creative thinker or the pupil of general all-round ability.

When the curriculum planning is over, the teacher will need to translate the emergent syllabus into individual lessons.

Figure 6.1 Questions pertinent to curriculum planning in the secondary school

QUESTION	GENERAL PROVISION	PROVISION FOR THOSE WITH SPECIAL LEARNING NEEDS
How are curriculum decisions reached and communicated?	By head? deputies? heads of department? individual teachers? other means?	Teacher/Department with special responsibilities? Staff awareness of these pupils raised by curriculum planners?
How effective is course and lesson planning?	Is it done well in advance? Its results communicated to all interested parties?	Teaching methods suitable? Flexible enough to allow a range of pupil activities at once?
What machinery is there for innovation?	Visiting speakers? Courses? Department meetings? Informal discussion by staff? Research initiative?	Latest curriculum and research findings monitored? Curriculum content monitored for suitability to whole range of pupils?
What resources/ facilities are available?	At school/ classroom/extra-curricular levels?	Resource banks contain material for pupils with special needs? Equipment available to allow pupils to study independently? Quality of home-made resource items monitored? By whom?

Lesson preparation

Anyone who becomes a tutor in a college or university department of education will soon gather that his students are regularly given advice by old hands in the profession. One common piece goes as follows: 'Don't waste your time with all those lesson notes; once you've left college you won't bother again - they're just there to keep the tutors happy'.

Like most propaganda, this kind of advice is dangerous because of the grain or two of truth it contains. Lesson notes are tangible evidence of preparation: to compile them is of value for one's tutor, for in this way the writer reveals the amount and appropriateness of his thinking about the job in hand. Full-time teachers are free not to commit these thoughts to writing.

In reality, however, the notes serve to build up useful habits both of planning method and of subsequent behaviour. At the training level, they are of value; and to denigrate them is evidence of both ignorance and irresponsibility. This kind of conversation undermines the trainee's confidence. In practice, too, many teachers do go on writing truncated versions of lesson notes; and the better teachers are certainly influenced by the kinds of considerations which are typically covered by such notes. Let us review the typical headings to be found in a set of lesson notes.

Aims, intentions or objectives. Once you have decided upon the scope of a lesson it is necessary to have some quite clear ideas about what you hope to achieve by the end of it. Various terms can be used, but the three listed here cover most purposes. I use them to mean rather different things.

Aims are longer-term. For example, a continuing aim in a cookery course or a science scheme may be to inculcate safety in working. This aim may be included in every lesson throughout a course, with particular points made at fitting moments. These aims can be about things to be learned (ie content), about skills to be acquired, or about social factors (eg learning to work co-operatively).

Objectives are essentially short-term and are probably easily measured. The objective of a domestic science lesson may be to make an edible shepherd's pie - and the proof will be in the eating. An objective in a history lesson may be to make a tape of someone describing his or her experiences in World War I. The tape is evidence of achievement.

Intentions cover those areas which are less easily 'measured'. The teacher's intention may be that pupils will become more sensitive to the feelings of others after studying the Joseph story in the Old Testament. It is partly possible to discover whether this is so, at the theoretical level. At a personal and practical level any achievement (for example, in improved ethical or social activity) by the pupil will be outside the teacher's domain.

Between them, the three words aims, intentions and objectives cover what the teacher hopes will be the longer and shorter-term outcomes of the lessons. They are crucial concepts in lesson planning, for without them we cannot go on to assess whether the lesson has had any success in practice.

Content. This section describes the scope of the lesson in relation to information, skills and concepts and it need be in outline only. In training students it is as well to encourage a brief description here lest they become dependent upon it and begin to teach by reading from their notes. For the experienced practitioner preparation under this heading serves also to highlight those areas in which he might need to learn at his own level.

Teaching methods and organization. Both the aims of the lesson and the things which the teacher wishes to communicate have implications for teaching methods and classroom organization. For example, if the lesson is aimed at teaching sensitivity through mime then this section spells out the need for pupils to plan and execute tasks in groups; it will raise issues about how the teacher plans to introduce the theme (perhaps through stimulus materials viewed by the whole class); and it will show how the room space is to be utilized to accommodate eight groups of four youngsters. Both administrative and educational considerations need to be taken into account for the lesson to run smoothly and be effective.

This section of the lesson note should include planning for the needs of individual pupils: poor readers, slow learners, the able pupil. Any special activities or tasks, such as extension work for bright youngsters, should be recorded here.

Resources. This section of the lesson note serves as a memory bank. It should consist not only of what resources are available and how they will be used, but also of where they can be located and of details of whether necessary hardware and software bookings have been made.

Special attention should be paid to the needs of able youngsters. Resources make varying demands on reading skills, abstract or conceptual level thinking or on evaluating their content for bias. Resources for able pupils should not simply be of the kind which imply rote learning of supplied facts.

Evaluation. No lesson is complete until the teacher has measured what, if anything, the pupils have gained. The commonest assessment of pupil achievement is the attainment test but this usually measures little more than data recall. It is unlikely to be an effective barometer of whether the aims and intentions of a lesson have been achieved. When considering evaluation of pupil learning the teacher needs to look back to those original aims, intentions and objectives, tailoring ways of making evaluative judgements to each kind of aspiration. For example, if the intention of a lesson is to teach sensitivity, then the test of sensitivity is not ten multiple-choice questions but to put the pupil (at least in a second-hand way through film or literature) into a position of having to respond to people and situations, to make judgements or show empathy. Sometimes evaluative procedures can be very simple (how many pupils remember to tie back long hair while cooking); sometimes they demand a more sophisticated approach (did bright but tactless Johnny actually manage to work with a slower inarticulate colleague to produce a genuinely co-operative end-product).

The findings from these evaluative efforts need to be recorded. Later in this chapter we shall take a clear look at evaluation and record-keeping techniques, especially as they affect the progress of able youngsters.

Self-assessment. Finally in this section we turn our attention to the teacher's self-assessment. No lesson should be allowed to pass without some thought being given by the teacher to his own performance. This may be comparatively brief and involve answering the simple question: what was most and least satisfactory about this lesson?

The purpose of this self-assessment process is always the same: to decide what changes need to be made (if any), to one's teaching skills or in one's approaches to lessons or to individuals. It is part of that flexibility and sensitivity to their role which able teachers recognize and admire in others.

To sum up, lesson planning is a vital skill in gaining pupils' attention, stimulating their curiosity and giving the teacher himself confidence.

Teaching and learning are two sides of a coin, but the teacher cannot and should not teach by exposition all the time. Many tasks are tackled more effectively using group-work or with pupils working alone (this theme is expanded later in the chapter). To cope with these alternative teaching modes, however, the pupils must learn how to learn.

This is particularly crucial for able youngsters. Too often they finish work quickly and are simply given more examples to work or an essentially similar task to repeat. By making the able pupil independent, that is by teaching study skills, he or she is less likely to seek attention, become bored, or simply consume a disproportionate amount of teacher time. Nevertheless, he will remain occupied purposefully rather than just be kept busy.

A minority of comprehensive schools do provide courses of study skills for first year pupils. I have come across many primary teachers who do the same. Yet even among college and university students many of the most basic skills are lacking. What are these skills which make youngsters independent in learning?

Two important sets of these skills are what are often described as advanced reading skills and research skills. The latter title is often a misnomer. Research is concerned with identifying problems, suggesting and testing hypotheses and drawing conclusions. What teachers more commonly mean by research is simply finding out, ie looking up information in books and writing some form of précis of it. Therefore, we can look at this cluster of reading and finding out skills together. They consist of the following abilities on the part of pupils:

... to hunt, skip or scan when consulting books

... to skim or conduct an organized search

... to discriminate about what is important information

... to reject irrelevant information

... to précis, summarize or take notes

... to describe types of literature (novel, biography)

... to copy or apply the style of various types of literature

... to find one's way about an index, contents page, catalogue, etc.

... to use timetables, directories, etc.

... to extract information from a variety of sources (eg maps, plans, graphs, slides, tables)

... to distinguish shades of meaning

... to recognize and be able to use synonyms, antonyms, metaphor, simile

... to cope with various kinds of dictionary skills.

These skills imply also the acquisition of various comprehension skills. Sadly, as has been already indicated in this chapter, much so-called comprehension in schools takes place at the lowest possible level and demands no more ability than to regurgitate accurately. Bell and Kerry (2) demonstrated that one can score good marks at comprehension even when the stimulus passage is nonsense, provided it has internal consistency. Comprehension in its higher sense involves the following abilities:

... to recognize key ideas

... to follow directions

... to put events into sequence

... to analyze types of material (fiction, documentary)

... to interpret facts

... to classify and group data

... to evaluate ideas

... to perceive an author's intentions and motives

... to be aware of the motives of characters in the passage

... to recognize bias

... to anticipate possible turns of events

All of these skills are appropriate to printed stimulus materials; many have equal relevance to graphic or audio resources. Effective watching and listening may still need to be taught in the first instance. To get the maximum benefit from a film or television programme pupils may need to be taught such skills as these:

... to observe composition

... to take account of picture shape (verticals tend to be more menacing, for example)

... to notice background and foreground detail

... to be aware of lighting - its spread, direction, colour, intensity and quality

... to learn from close-up sequences about things otherwise invisible

... to recognize the distortions of wide-angle and telephoto shots

... to appreciate the editorial effect of camera angle

... to notice tricks, for example, the use of filters to emphasize clouds, distort colour or produce particular lighting effects.

In the same way aural skills have to be practised and
learned, so that a discriminating use can be made of stimulus
or resource material. Sounds can have various qualities
which convey meaning. They can be hard or soft, raucous or
soothing. They may give away emotion in a human voice,
convey messages even in animals (the snarl of a leopard).
In speech, the same word used with varying tone or inflection
can convey quite opposite meanings! The duration of a sound
and its context are important clues to meaning. Pauses, or
even silence, are powerful 'sounds'.

Once the pupils have acquired these abilities to deal
with the raw materials of learning (and there will be others,
too - for example, manual skills in technology or biology,
observation skills in all the sciences and so on), he can
begin to work alone. This is important. The teacher has to
divide himself by about thirty pupils during every lesson.
An equal share of the teacher's attention in a typical day
might be a total of about nine minutes in seven or eight
short bursts. Though bright children do demand a lot of
teacher-time they are also (as teachers themselves report)
left to get on. That 'getting on' may in reality be marking
time unless practical steps are taken to ensure a proper and
purposeful independence. Even when the skills have been
acquired these bright youngsters need to be clear about what
next steps are available: the teacher must approve of some
self-marking and self-pacing, and must make clear where the
directions of travel are to be.

A final word in the section must go to written work.
The apparently simple task of essay-writing is a closed book
to many students in higher education in spite of their having
written thousands of prose passages in order to obtain their
college or university place. In humanities, teachers should
inculcate the disciplines of planning an essay in sections,
with an introduction and conclusion. They should show how
each section can, at the planning stage, be individually
ghosted by the listing of relevant points. Above all, the
simple skills of logical sequence and sustained argument
should be acquired by pupils at the first opportunity. In
the same way, scientists should teach the conventions of
transactional language and of technical reporting. Bright
pupils need to be encouraged to combine originality of
thought with appropriate conventions for recording in the
various subject areas, for it is through these conventions
that we communicate with one another. A brilliant idea
gains credence by means of its being passed on to, and com-
prehended by, others.

Deciding on teaching mode

With curriculum strategies established, lessons prepared and
pupils trained to work independently through the acquisition

of study skills, we are now free to end this section on
preparation for teaching and learning with a closer look at
the appropriateness of the three main teaching modes.

1.   Whole class teaching
Whole class teaching is one of three common teaching modes,
the other two being groupwork and individualized learning.
In a study of five first year mixed ability classes in comprehensive schools it was found that about three quarters of
all lessons consisted of whole class teaching. Popular
belief suggests that whole class teaching is used to
introduce lessons, to give general instructions and to
draw the threads together at the end of lessons. But in
between these activities it is typical to see pupils working
alone but all on wholly identical tasks, or in groups but
simply to share equipment or so that they can sit with
friends. This kind of activity also counts as whole class,
since the activities themselves are not graded, selected or
tailored in any way to the needs of individual pupils. (3)
     How appropriate is whole class teaching for the
education of able youngsters? What problems are inherent in
it? What are the alternatives?
     In mixed ability classes the philosophy is that each
child's needs are catered for. The research already
referred to failed to support that view of reality. In a
further unpublished survey of some 640 tasks set to pupils
in these classes by 36 different teachers, the vast majority
were set to all pupils without differentiation (this is
discussed in more detail later in the chapter). Given that
this research reflects a picture which is widespread, the
able pupils are being asked to do work which is no more
demanding than that set to both average pupils and those of
below average ability!
     Perhaps even more worrying is that the whole tone and
tenor of whole class lessons must be aimed at the average
and slightly below average pupils in the class. The language
the teacher uses, the work he sets, the concepts he puts
forward - everything must be determined by the need to hold
onto some interest, understanding and commitment from the
less able. It takes very little imagination to deduce that
able pupils are understimulated in these lessons (4).
     In banded classes the problem is lessened, and it may be
progressively so in setted and streamed situations. Where
there is some comparability of ability, and pace of learning,
by pupils in a class, more whole class work can go on because
the teacher's language and ideas can be uniformly at a higher
cognitive level. This does not mean, however, that whole
class teaching is a mode appropriate to seventy-five per cent
of work done, even in homogeneous classes.
     One major problem teachers face in whole class lessons

is to keep pupils anywhere near to one another in terms of ground covered. In studies carried out by the Teacher Education Project, I and my colleagues came to adopt the term 'zeroing'. Zeroing described one frequent approach to mixed ability work. The teacher would start all pupils on a new topic or subject, for example the life-cycle of the butterfly. The most able would soon cover the ten question worksheet and be looking for extension tasks; the fastest might complete several of these. Meanwhile the average pupils would have worked honestly through the ten basic questions. Some slow learners would have covered seven out of ten questions. One or two may have had trouble with even reading the worksheet, so have had to wait for teacher help. Perhaps they had reached question two. By now the gap between able and slow would have widened so much that the teacher would feel the need to call a halt. Rather than enlarge and extend the topic he would take a new theme, where everyone could start from scratch again. He had 'zeroed'. For able pupils this meant that just as they were getting to the things that were likely to stretch their abilities they were called back to basics on another topic. Since the early stages of most topics represent the informational aspects, these pupils were constantly bombarded with data but rarely asked to apply, analyze or evaluate it.

The upshot of these comments is not necessarily to dismiss mixed ability organization nor to suggest whole class teaching is a waste of energy. It is rather to pose the question: when is whole class teaching appropriate, especially in a mixed ability setting? Let us take a concrete example.

Pupils in 4X are studying personal relationships. They are being encouraged to think about issues such as children's attitudes to parents, race relations, relations between the sexes, and relations between groups of people holding diametrically opposed views. To get things off the ground on this last issue the teacher decides to show a film. The film is a documentary of how the bye-laws in an American park forbid singing. Someone is arrested for this apparently trivial offence. The following Sunday thousands of outraged, ordinary people turn up for a peaceful protest. They walk, singing, through the park. But the local police chief decides to enforce the regulations. He builds up his forces, on motor-cycles, in cars and vans, with batons and shields. The quiet middle-class singers become involved in a violent and sometimes bloody battle. But who was to blame?

Obviously it is wholly fitting that the stimulus material should be shared - all pupils view it simultaneously. Some follow-up discussion is also likely to be relevant to all pupils. But the scope and variety of tasks which emerge from the film suggest that at this point pupils should have more carefully structured assignments according to need.

To be effective, then, whole class teaching should satisfy these requirements:

... it must involve material which is capable of being shared by all pupils

... it must be pitched linguistically and cognitively at a level which is acceptable to all

... it must involve tasks that everyone has an equal opportunity to complete efficiently.

As soon as whole class teaching has to depart from these criteria it must, for the sake of the individual pupils of whatever ability, give way to groupwork or individualized learning.

2. Groupwork

Genuine groupwork must satisfy one or more of the following criteria:

... the pupils work co-operatively

... the task is shared (ie not the identical task for each pupil)

... each person's work contributes to a collective end-product

... there are opportunities for leadership within, and self-direction by, the group.

Of course, classroom groups will not always be chosen by the pupils themselves; nor will the able pupils always be grouped together. A purpose of groupwork for able pupils would be to give them experience of different ways of working. Sometimes one able child might be a leader of a group of average or less able youngsters. Sometimes he would be just one contributor to a co-operative task co-ordinated by another pupil. Sometimes he would be assigned to work with others as bright as, or brighter than, himself. Groupwork is not just about learning but about social relations and the teacher should bear this in mind.

The use of groups allows teachers to tailor tasks to pupils' needs while retaining a social context within which activities take place. Since pupils are occupied on the tasks set, the teacher is free to circulate. Given the proviso that the teacher's time is shared equally between all the pupils, how can this time be most productively used to help pupils - the bright, the average and the least able?

In the Teacher Education Project's study of mixed ability classes it was discovered that, while teachers quite properly circulated around the class when pupils were working in groups, their input to the learning was minimal. Typical of these blocks of time were fleeting exchanges between pupil and teacher. Imagine a science lesson in a laboratory with children working in fours. These were the kinds of things which teachers said:

... Everything OK, John?

... Tighten that joint or it'll collapse.

... Where are you up to?

... Which metal are you using now?

... Get a cloth and wipe that up, Ann.

Pupils' responses were monosyllabic, or simply wordless compliance. We called these exchanges 'contacts', but concluded that cognitively they were of little value.

A whole world of teaching and learning opportunities is being lost here for bright pupils and others. The sensitive teacher may need to say some of these managerial/administrative things; but he will also be pitching in provocative questions designed to test what has been learned, to see how much deduction has taken place, and to provoke speculation about the results of the experiments in progress. It is absolutely essential for the effective education of all pupils, but especially the more able, that teachers learn to capitalize on these opportunities.

It may be that at first this skill does not come easily - it's hard to break old habits. Perhaps part of the lesson preparation may be to think out possible questions to ask during these periods when work is being monitored. But it is essentially a 'thinking on the feet' job, since it requires knowledge of individual abilities and relates directly to the stage a given group has reached (5).

3. Individualized learning

Individualized learning or independent study is one of the most practical solutions to the teaching of able pupils in mixed ability classes, or even in banded or streamed ones; though it ought not to be used exclusively lest it lead to intellectual and social isolationism.

Individualized learning is where the pupil is provided with a programme of work selected or designed to meet his or her specific needs and stage of development. Since the pupil is working independently he will need the study skills

already outlined in this chapter. Motivation must be provided
in two main ways, through contact with the teacher and because
of the intrinsic stimulus of the work set. Pupils will also
need to self-mark, self-pace and to make decisions about at
least some of the directions in which their work will progress.
As in groupwork, the teacher is freed to monitor progress; and
it is partly in the quality of this monitoring that the
success of this teaching mode lies.

The most common forms of so-called individualized learning
in secondary schools take place in maths lessons. Pupils tend
to follow a specific maths scheme, usually the School
Mathematics Project materials, and each is allowed to go at
his own pace. After a while the pupils are working on widely
differing topics. In other subject areas self-pacing of this
kind is comparatively rare; although the increase of various
forms of project work, as in the CSE examinations, sometimes
gives pupils scope for initiative. Project work of this
kind, however, is also open to abuse with pupils merely
copying or at best summarizing, from textbooks. More is said
about this subject in the section below which deals with
classroom tasks.

Individualized learning implies that teachers should
review and modify their role in the classroom. In whole
class teaching, the teacher is essentially expert, expositor
and director. By contrast, when children are learning to work
individually the teacher becomes planner, co-ordinator,
helper, facilitator, provider of resources, academic
counsellor and adviser. Part of the skill of the teacher is
to be able to change rôles quickly and sensitively according
to teaching mode and the needs of the pupils.

Much of the success of individualized learning comes
down to the effectiveness of the tasks pupils are given to do,
and the reader is referred to the appropriate section below.
Another key teaching skill in this context is the ability to
ask penetrating questions. It is to these and other teaching
skills and strategies that we now turn our attention.

TEACHING SKILLS AND TEACHING STRATEGIES

Effective questioning

A systematic study of classroom questions reveals that
questions are commonly used by teachers to check pupils'
recall of information recently conveyed, or to make sure that,
at a simple level, a written passage or piece of work has been
understood. In a sizeable piece of research into teacher-
pupil interaction all the questions asked by 36 teachers in
147 lessons across eight academic subjects were recorded and
analyzed. Analysis was designed to estimate the cognitive
demand of the questions - to what extent they required of
pupils thinking skills rather than regurgitation (10). Based

147

on the famous taxonomy of thinking by Benjamin Bloom (6), the
categories of analysis were as follows:

    Q0   management
    Q1   recall
    Q2   simple comprehension
    Q3   application
    Q4   analysis
    Q5   synthesis
    Q6   evaluation

Results from the analysis showed that the vast majority
of teachers' questions required only a simple regurgitative
ability from pupils. The following table shows a breakdown
of the 6,928 questions asked into the three broad categories,
managing, informing and stimulating questions:

Managing questions (Q0)	21%
Informing and checking information (Q1, Q2)	75.5%
Stimulating thought and exploring higher cognitive levels (Q3, Q4, Q5, Q6)	3.5%

These findings were made in first year mixed ability
classes in comprehensive schools. Clearly, in this mixed
ability setting, bright pupils were not being greatly
stimulated by the questions teachers asked. Such a diet of
simple fare for the able and active mind must inevitably lead
to untold boredom. So what can be done about it?
To answer the question we might look briefly at three
separate classroom contexts.
This first is where whole class teaching is involved.
In a mixed ability class it is often difficult for the
teacher to conduct the whole class mode of teaching in a way
which will both stimulate the able, and be fully
comprehensible and slow enough in pace for the least able.
Take a typical situation: the demonstration of an experiment
in a science lesson. The teacher works at the bench,
explaining apparatus, methodology and principles as he goes
along. To keep the ablest interested, however, he needs to
throw out constant challenges.

'Suppose we changed the apparatus thus ...?'

'What would happen if we used copper not zinc?'

'Can you think of a practical application?'

'Do any appliances in the home work like this?'

In practice, we found these questions and challenges which demanded the application of knowledge, its use in new situations, and a critical or experimental approach to be very rare indeed.

Groupwork frees the teacher to circulate and cater more sensitively for particular needs. In this situation the questioning skills come into their own once more. In a history lesson, groups may be looking at life in the 1850s. For the teacher, the task is to challenge them; not simply to grub together a few impersonal facts but to use imagination, empathy, evidence and judgement. He might ask:

'Are there any trends in local rural populations discernible between 1850 and 1950?'

'How do you account for the different attitudes to poaching and wildlife between then and now?'

'What evidence can you find in our village of the incidence of childhood disease and early death?'

'Were the Victorians really as humourless and straight-laced as they seemed?'

Individualized learning allows the teacher to be even more specific in pushing individual pupils to explore topics in detail and to make 'thinking capital' out of them. Here, even more than in groupwork, a sequence of progressively more difficult tasks can be built up. For example, for a pupil studying poetry a possible sequence might go somewhat as follows:

Read George Macbeth's 'Owl' and Laurie Lee's 'Town Owl'.

What factual information do the poems contain about owls?

Is this information accurate in all particulars?

Each poem has a 'message' about the nature of owls - to what extent do they agree?

Do they convey this message in similar ways?

What is distinctive about the style of each writer?

From evidence in the poems can you reconstruct the circumstances which led each writer to put pen to paper about his chosen bird?

Which phrases from each poet are the most evocative?
Why?

Using the style of each poet in turn can you write a
couple of poems about another bird, for example a
buzzard, a starling or a crow?

Questioning is a kind of ferreting about in the mind of
another person to explore his or her depth and range of
response. It is crucial to the process of learning -
responses to questions are the externalization of knowledge or
feeling previously only half-realized by the respondent.
Verbalized knowledge or feeling becomes more truly one's own
and can be put to more practical advantage. This sort of
challenge is essential to the most able who, as Torrance put
it, like to 'take on tasks which are too difficult for them'
and to prove that they aren't.

From the research into questioning reported in this
section it was possible to calculate that an average career
teacher might ask a million and a half questions before
reaching retiring age! Refinement of question technique is an
imperative, therefore. But if teachers ask a lot of questions
they spend even more time talking to classes.

Examining teacher talk

Research in five first year mixed ability classes (already
described) examined the nature of classroom talk by teachers.
Using a simple coding system, all periods of classroom talk
by teachers in the sample were coded for the cognitive
demand which they made on pupils. The coding system was as
follows:

TO - talk concerned with class management, giving
demonstrations or instructions

T1 - information giving

T2 - talk which involves the giving of explanations or
reasons, or the use of concepts

T3 - talk which is about rules, laws, generalizations or
abstract ideas.

If one accepts the premise that the kind of talk a
teacher uses forms a signal to the pupil about the kind of
thinking he requires, it quickly becomes clear that the T2
and T3 levels of teacher talk are essential in coping with
and stimulating able pupils. In what proportions did these
two categories occur in the sum total of teacher talk? The
following brief table gives the answer:

TO 58%
T1 37%
T2 4%
T3 less than 1%

Clearly, the messages teachers convey by their own classroom talk is that learning is about knowledge or the acquisition of information within a context of orderly behaviour. For able and creative pupils this message is, to put it bluntly, a dull one.

Of course, class management is vital. This point was laboured early in the chapter. But it consumes too much of the average teacher's energies. For individual teachers within our sample it took up 80-90% of their classroom talk. The minutiae of class management MUST be settled once and for all early on in the relationship between a teacher and a class. This done, the teacher should find as many ways as possible to streamline administrative tasks. A trivial example might be the giving out of exercise books. For the teacher to hand them out, in lesson time, to one pupil at a time, is a waste of learning time. Two quiet and efficient monitors could be primed to arrive quickly and complete this chore as other pupils filtered in to the classroom.

Given a stream-lined, orderly context it still remains true that teachers need to think more seriously about the nature of education. While one sympathizes with the objection that GCE courses demand a major element of factual recall it is also true that few schools put pupils on that examination treadmill until the third (sometimes the fourth) year. But, even with first year classes, the simple absorption of data was a major classroom task in the schools observed. Yet for able pupils gaining information is done with characteristic facility. Rarely can the pace of the lesson match their speed in assimilating the information supplied. Once more, we are face-to-face with a recipe for boredom. So the case must be made for an alternative approach.

The most logical alternative approach is to view learning as the acquisition of skills; the information (be it in history, science or music) is the raw material on which the skills are practised, and the characteristic disciplines of the subject area become the methodologies by which these skills are applied and the criteria upon which judgements are made.

To illustrate this point it might be appropriate to close this section with two examples of teachers talking, using similar material as a starting point, to see how this would work in practice. Which method do you think an able child would find more interesting?

Teacher A: The poem we're going to read today is by a modern
poet called Ted Hughes.   It was published in about 1960 in a
book called <u>Lupercal.</u>   It's a violent poem, and it's called
'Hawk Roosting'.   Before we begin there are one or two
things you ought to know.   First, hawks are woodland birds
with strong beaks and claws.   They live by catching smaller
birds or things like mice or voles.   Part of the hawk's
special equipment for feeding is his eye-sight; this helps
him to spot the prey before it spots him!   They sometimes sit
in the tree tops and wait for small movements below, which
are a sort of give-away that a possible meal is on the move.
The poem is quite short, just six verses of four lines each.
Right, listen and I'll read it ...

(144 words)

Teacher B: Shortly we're going to look at a poem called
'Hawk Roosting' by a modern poet called Ted Hughes.   I want
you to look out for some interesting things.   Jot a note or
two about each one when we read it together.   Hughes tells us
a lot about the life-style of hawks.   What does he tell us?
Then again, he gives the bird some human characteristics.
Watch out for them.   And he mentions Creation a lot.   Why?
Lastly, try to work out the rhyming scheme.   Is it regular?
If not, why not?   What does it add to the poem?   I'll read
it over once while you follow the text; that'll help you to
get the feel of it.   Then I'll read it over again while you
think and scribble notes.

(124 words)

Explaining effectively

One specific skill in teacher talk is the giving of clear and
lucid explanations.   Since this skill enables teachers to
convey material which goes beyond the purely informational it
is worth pursuing in a little more detail.   The advice on
effective explaining given here is amplified by Brown and
Hatton (7).

   Explaining is defined as the giving of understanding to
another person and it functions through a series of linked
statements which form 'keys to unlock that understanding'.
Explanations may be classified as interpretive, descriptive
or reason-giving.   Interpretive explanations clarify terms,
statements or issues; they answer what ? questions - what is
chlorophyll?   Descriptive explanations describe processes,
procedures or structures; and they answer how ? questions -
how is chlorophyll produced?   Reason-giving explanations
answer why ? questions, and they involve reasons,
motivations, justifications or causes - why is chlorophyll
important to plants?

   Explanations, like lessons, should be planned.   The

topic to be explained should be analyzed and broken down into main parts or keys. The relationship between each part should be established and the logical links forged in the teacher's mind. Any rules, laws or generalizations should be spelled out at this stage. Then the teacher should decide which kind(s) of explanations are required: interpretive, descriptive or reason-giving. Finally, the explanation should be adapted to suit the needs of the learners. In doing so, there are a number of factors which should be taken into account.

Above all, the teacher should have an eye to clarity and fluency. This means he should:

   ... define new technical terms

   ... use explicit language and avoid vagueness

   ... give emphasis and interest

   ... use appropriate visual aids or resource material

   ... make use of pauses and silences for 'thinking time'

   ... use phrases or ploys to signal important steps (eg repetitions or such expressions as 'Now this is an important point (pause) ...')

In presenting explanations concrete examples of what is, and what is not, meant are extremely useful. The sequence of the explanation is crucial: it must be correct and logical, and link-words and phrases (therefore, next, so) are useful to cue in the listener to the sequence. Once the explanation is over, or at appropriate intermediate moments, the teacher should test the understanding of the pupils by question or task.

Some common errors in the presentation of explanations are these:

   ... not understanding the topic yourself

   ... missing out a 'link' or 'key'

   ... going too quickly

   ... using language which is not shared by the listeners

   ... forgetting to give any instructions in an equally clear fashion

   ... leaving out the feedback stage.

The ability to give clear explanations is one particular way in which the cognitive level of classroom work may be enhanced. To that extent it is beneficial to all pupils, and it is yet another manifestation of the phenomenon that sharpened teaching skills for all pupils are of special benefit to the able child.

Considerable emphasis has now been placed on teacher talk so it is opportune to redress the balance and to look at pupils' verbal contributions to lessons.

Encouraging and enriching pupils' talk

A sizeable majority of classroom misbehaviour consists of excessively noisy or irrelevant chat; a major teaching need is to keep pupil talk on-task. There are three main kinds of pupil contributions which facilitate learning. The pupils

... may respond to teachers' questions

... may initiate conversation or questions

... may take part in more formal classroom discussion.

We shall look in turn at each of these kinds of pupil talk.

Earlier in this chapter research was quoted to suggest that, if teachers signalled by their talk that they wanted a low level of cognitive involvement, then pupils would respond appropriately. During the 140 or so lessons observed in that research project (1) pupil responses to teachers' questions and the incidents of pupil-initiated talk with teachers were logged. Some 18,963 transactions took place in this way and they were analyzed on a scale which went as follows:

RO responses or initiatives concerned with management or administration

R1 responses or initiatives concerned with information or data

R2 responses or initiatives concerned with concepts, reasons or explanations

R3 responses or initiatives concerned with abstract ideas, laws and generalizations

Of these pupil-teacher contacts only about $4\frac{1}{2}\%$ fell to categories R2 and R3, the higher cognitive levels. This clearly has a detrimental effect on the involvement and motivation of able pupils. How can this situation be improved?

Two solutions have been suggested already: that teachers should encourage by example classroom talk which deals in concepts, laws, abstract ideas, and the use of empathy and imagination. Pupils would then improve their use of language and the register of their ideas by imitation. Secondly, the skilled use of question technique would provoke more insightful and extended answers from pupils. To this we need to add the points already made about the importance of pupil-teacher conversation, the encouragement of hypothesizing and problem solving as methods of working, and the necessity of conveying to pupils that they should regard it as normal behaviour to ask questions and to take a critical stance about the work which is put before them.

A more formal approach is the contrived debate or discussion. Debates have their own groundrules. A class discussion requires special skills of the teacher as leader, and a redefinition of his rôle. The rôle of chairman of a discussion group might require the leader to:

... be a good listener

... protect the opinions and feelings of minorities

... avoid stating his own position

... provide a suitable climate for a frank exchange

... ask only questions which are open

... request evidence for unsupported statements

... summarize the state of play at the end of the discussion.

Some of these rôles are not readily accepted by teachers; so, in order to function effectively as a discussion leader, the teacher may need to do some self-training and practice(8).

Effective learning is a participant activity, and the skill of the teacher lies to a great extent in his ability to muster the potential participants into action. Having looked at oral activity we now turn our attention to other kinds of classroom tasks in which pupils participate.

Setting classroom tasks

What kinds of classroom tasks do teachers set to pupils?

To find the answer to this question all the tasks set to pupils in the five first year mixed ability classes referred to above were recorded. The 36 teachers set, between them, 640 tasks during the 147 lessons observed; an average of 4.3 tasks per lesson (this included work set in advance for homework). Once the tasks were logged they were scanned for patterns, and the various categories were labelled 'higher level' or 'lower level' according to cognitive demand. Tasks at the lower levels of cognitive demand were as follows:

L1 Work set for disciplinary or management purposes

L2 Administrative tasks

L3 Draw or colour

L4 Put a heading; copy from board or text

L5 Read aloud around the class

L6 Read silently while slower pupils catch up; watch; listen

L7 Rote learning and memorization

L8 Complete a revision activity

L9 Carry out a demonstrated experiment; make simple factual observations

L10 Simple cloze or simple comprehension

L11 Reinforce by practice, examples, repeating words etc

L12 Look up, find out from a resource text

At the highest cognitive level six kinds of task could be identified:

H1 Task demanding imagination or empathy

H2 Task asking for deduction, reasoning, collecting evidence

H3 Task asking for application skills

H4 Task asking for analysis skills

H5 Task asking for synthesis skills

H6 Task asking for evaluation skills

Fuller discussion of the findings from this research will be published elsewhere in due course. For the moment, the crucial issue is the discovery that 85% of all tasks were classified at the lower level of demand. Only a handful of tasks were directed at individual pupils, or even at groups. So the corollary is that bright pupils are given undifferentiated tasks of which only 15% make a higher cognitive demand. When it is realized that for any given task to be classified as higher order only a small part (say one question out of ten) needed to be at the higher level the picture is even more depressing.

In teaching able pupils, the message to the teacher is loud and clear. He must learn to treat pupils as individuals, and to grade the work which he sets in the classroom to stretch the abilities of this group of youngsters.

Evaluating and record-keeping

What has been said in the preceding sections has put a great deal of emphasis on effective learning; and it is important for the teacher to monitor this learning process. In fact, if the reader cares to glance back to the section of this chapter which deals with lesson planning he will see that we have now come full circle, to the problem of evaluation.

Evaluation is the assessment of what learning, and what degree of learning, has taken place. It has to be done in the light of the original aims and intentions of the lesson and by the use of appropriate, often tailor-made, activities. Let us take a brief example.

In English a series of lessons has been planned to improve the pupils' ability to write imaginative prose. The teacher hoped to go some way to achieving each of these ends:

... to improve pupils' sentence construction and use of appropriate particles

... to show the importance of proper paragraphing

... to encourage pupils to plan an essay or story in broad outline

... to teach them to apply the same principles to planning individual sections of the writing (chapters or episodes)

... to write sustained passages of prose

... to keep up an argument or story-line

... to be creative in devizing plots

... to use a series of climaxes to sustain the reader's interest.

157

It would be possible to give the pupils the task of writing a story on a set theme eg 'Lost in the Dark'. But the marking scheme would have to reflect the individual skills of the lesson intentions. A simple nine out of ten rating would mean nothing to the pupil - except a general level of approval. Since the teacher would be assessing each of the skills indicated in the list above, by means of a few moments work with a Banda master it would be possible to produce a marking grid for each pupil of the kind shown in Figure 6.2. This scheme would be issued to the pupils in advance so that they were aware of what was required of them (there is no virtue in being tested on your skills at x when no-one has told you what exactly you are being tested on). The instructions for the task to evaluate this short course might be as follows:

Over the last few weeks we have been looking at the skills listed on this Banda sheet. Now I am going to see how well you can do each of these things. Bearing these skills in mind I want you to write me a story with the title: 'Lost in the Dark'. You have to supply me with three things by next Monday. First, a fair copy of the completed story, length about 7,000 words. Second, your outline plan of the story into chapters - rough work will do. Third, your detailed planning of episodes and paragraphs - again, rough work will do so long as I can read these last two items. Marks will be given according to the scheme on the Banda sheet, and I hope to return your work on Monday 20th.

When the teacher begins marking he has a guide in front of him already; the pupils' work will be more effective because they know exactly what is required of them; the assessment will have meaning because it will look at specific skills; and the marking scheme will be of use to the pupil in guiding his attention to strengths and weaknesses. Teachers might well contemplate setting fewer classroom tasks, but making them a greater aid to learning in the way suggested. This would benefit all the pupils, and the more able would be challenged a great deal more than by more conventional attainment tests.

Part of the skill of the professional teacher is to make judgements about pupils' abilities, progress and potential. These judgements have to be communicated in school (to colleagues such as heads of year), and outside school (to parents and potential employers). Some of this liaison is in the form of written reports; sometimes there is face-to-face contact.

There is nothing more frustrating for the recipient of a verbal or written report than to be faced with bland generalizations. Parents, indeed, find it particularly

Figure 6.2: Possible marking scheme for an essay: Lost in the Dark

Name:

Story: 'Lost in the Dark'   5.9.82

Class: 3B

Skill	Comment if required	Possible mark	Score
Sentence construction		7	
Use of paragraphs		7	
Planning outline		5	
Planning in detail		5	
Ability to sustain story-line		10	
Quality of the plot		8	
Use of climax		8	
GENERAL COMMENT			
TOTAL MARKS		50	

insulting if teachers cannot make insightful and detailed
comments about their children.

Let us reconsider the evaluation proforma in Figure 6.2.
By the judicious use of a piece of carbon paper the teacher is
able both to give the pupil a copy of the evaluation and to
keep one himself. Over a period these evaluation proformas
would build up, pointing the teacher to individuals' strengths
and weaknesses by the study of recurrent patterns. This helps
the teacher to plan remedial programmes for the individual
(and here let it be said that even able pupils have relative
weaknesses, and it is the teacher's professional
responsibility to identify and improve on these areas). But
the collection of proformas also provides an important and
detailed bank of specific information for use in reporting on
the pupils' progress to interested parties (10).

By contrast, a string of marks in a ledger is of so
little value it is questionable whether their compilation was
even worth the effort.

Specific strategies for helping the able

The bulk of this chapter has set out, quite deliberately, to
concentrate on those activities which a teacher can employ
for all pupils, and by using them effectively can stimulate
the able youngsters in the class. Before leaving the work of
the secondary teacher, however, it is fitting to cast a brief
glance towards special strategies which might be used to
capture the interest of the more able.

Some specific strategies mentioned by teachers include
the following:

... holiday projects such as compiling a tape, writing a
novel

... use of Young Scientist and other public competitions

... occasionally using the pupil as a teacher

... asking extra stimulus questions in odd moments such
as breaktime

... setting voluntary homework tasks

... giving the able pupil a class or school
responsibility

... setting up out-of-school clubs and societies

... giving able youngsters the chance to learn an extra
language

... building appropriately difficult units into school
or class resource collections

... enlisting the help of interested outsiders to foster
special talents eg in nursing, photography,
conservation, archaeology

... asking parents, advisers or university staff to
visit the school to give talks

... making the able pupil mark his own work objectively

... setting an able pupil the task of devizing the
class's next workcard

... providing the able youngster with a chance to talk
to a group of peers about a topic of special
interest

... providing opportunities for able youngsters to work
co-operatively with other pupils as ordinary team
members.

Wherever possible any special strategy of the kind
indicated should be dovetailed into normal classwork; and
able youngsters should not be made to feel 'different'.
Such a situation may sometimes lead to them becoming the
target of unpleasant attentions from other pupils. Bullying
and social pressure to conform is a major cause of underachievement.

Self-appraisal by the teacher

Finally in this chapter we turn out attention back to the
teacher to ask how he can assess his own performance in
handling the able pupils in his classes.
    For too long teachers have made their classrooms into
private bolt-holes in which any outsider is regarded as an
intruder. But a teacher who genuinely cares about his own
professional development cannot do this. As yet we don't
have any compulsory element of further professional
development of the kind described in Chapter 4. So the
responsibility rests with the individual to promote the
blossoming of his own skills. Three simple ploys would aid
this process while making very little demand on teachers'
already heavy commitments of time and energy.
    First, it is not too difficult to tape a lesson in
progress and to do so unobtrusively. If a teacher is
interested to know how well he explains, whether he asks
higher order questions, or which pupils offer responses and
at what cognitive level, then he can easily take home the

tape and play it over in the privacy of his own home. Here it can be transcribed and analyzed. Conclusions can be drawn, and alternative teaching strategies planned. Further tapes will reveal whether there are changes in behaviour patterns by teacher or pupils.

A more sophisticated technique of the same kind is microteaching. Usually, contrived lessons are taught to small groups and the results recorded on videotape. Gesture, facial expression and movement round the group can be monitored in this way. However, even where the equipment is available, this process is more demanding than the use of sound tape. It is always a good idea to start with the simplest method.

The second way to make teaching a more open and self-critical activity is to organize some departmental time for team-teaching. Team-teaching often involves a lead lesson by one team member given to the year group or part of it, followed by class-based follow-up. The discipline of giving lead lessons and receiving informal comment on them is a useful one.

Thirdly, self-appraisal may take the form of observational pairing. By this is meant the deliberate request by the teacher to a colleague to watch him at work. The observer may make general comments or use specific observation instruments such as those in the Focus series of workbooks which are referenced in the Further Reading section of this chapter. This is a sizeable step for some teachers to take; but the lessons to be learned from it are worth the effort in overcoming initial reluctance. None of us is a perfect classroom practitioner, and no group of human beings is wholly predictable - so in every lesson something of value will emerge. Usually the observer will concentrate on just one small aspect of teaching skill, such as vigilance or mobility around the class. In this way real change can be monitored. Next lesson, the observer and teacher change rôles: so it is important to build up a fair degree of trust and comradeship in this activity. The key-notes are honesty and the willingness to learn.

Conclusion

This chapter has been detailed and wide-ranging. Some will see it as not sufficiently revolutionary; perhaps they would prefer tight streaming methods or the very open and self-motivating approach of a Summerhill. Others will regard it as wholly unrealistic with too much demand on the teacher. For myself, I would offer it as a minimum professional standard at which all teachers should aim. But in the real world of restricted release for in-service education and heavy timetables it should, of course, be tackled a little at a time. If the headings of this chapter are seen as topics

in a programme of self-training or of staff development, then
many teachers will be adequate or better on a proportion of
them already. The priority is to discover the weak points
and work on those in isolation, one at a time.
    Systematic improvement of staff skills in finding and
helping the able child are not pie-in-the-sky. In the
chapter which follows Roderick Thompson, a deputy head, tells
how he set about the task in his school. This is followed by
an account by an Advisory Teacher of initiatives at a county
level. Finally, Carolle Kerry surveys the variety of
approaches to be found nationwide.
    Somewhere in these accounts the reader will find
strategies to suit his own situation.

Notes and references to Chapter 6

(1)   This study is to be published as one of a number in a
      volume to be edited by Professor E C Wragg and
      available from Croom Helm in 1983.

(2)   The principles outlined here can be found in Bell and
      Kerry (1982) in the Further Study section below. They
      apply as much to the able as to the slow learner!

(3)   Sands M K and Kerry T, 1982, Mixed Ability Teaching,
      Croom Helm.

(4)   This point is made throughout the DES Survey:
      HM Inspectorate 1978 Matters for discussion no 6:
      Mixed Ability Work in Comprehensive Schools, HMSO.

(5)   See the reference to Handling Classroom Groups in the
      Further Study section below.

(6)   Bloom B S, 1956, Taxonomy of Educational Objectives,
      Methuen.

(7)   See Brown and Hatton in the Further Study section
      below.

(8)   Further information about pupils' classroom talk can be
      found in Sutton C R (ed) 1981 Communicating in the
      Classroom, Hodder and Stoughton, Chapters 3 and 4.

(9)   See Sutton C R (op. cit.) Chapters 1 and 2 on setting
      and responding to written work.

(10) An interesting summary of approaches to measuring pupil
      attainment is to be found in Brown F G, 1981, Measuring
      Classroom Achievement, Holt, Rinehart & Winston.

FOR FURTHER STUDY

The Teacher Education Project's Focus Series published by
Macmillan. The individual titles and dates are as follows:

Teaching Bright Pupils	Trevor Kerry	1981
Class Management	Professor E C Wragg	1981
Teaching Slow Learners	Peter Bell and Trevor Kerry	1982
Mixed Ability Teaching	Trevor Kerry and Margaret Sands	1982
Effective Questioning	Trevor Kerry	1982
Giving Effective Explanations	George Brown and Neville Hatton	1982
Handling Classroom Groups	Trevor Kerry and Margaret Sands	1982
The New Teacher	Trevor Kerry	1982

Chapter 7

Roderick Thompson

Background
This paper is concerned with the initiatives a school can
take, through its own in-service programme, to make provision
for the teaching of bright children. It is an account of the
process and methods of an in-service undertaking, and indeed
of the delicate public relations that are part of any
innovation in school, rather than a detailed description of
the course content of each department. We set out here to
show what can be done - the problems, pitfalls, short cuts to
take - and we leave the 'subject by subject' matter for
others to devise their own schemes. It is the method that is
important rather than the content.

The school concerned is a fully developed 11-16 comprehensive school which has about 850 pupils on roll. It is
situated in the industrial conurbation of the Midlands Black
Country. Its catchment area tends not to produce a 'balanced'
intake but one in which the lower socio-economic groups pre-
dominate. Nevertheless it has its fair share of bright
youngsters, and all its pupils are encouraged and directed
towards the ideal of 'personal fulfilment and personal best'.

(A) Identifying the Need
Early in 1980, as part of the school's reappraisal of
curricular organization and teaching methods, we were
concerned that the brightest of our pupils may not have been
performing up to expectation; that they were not doing as
well, perhaps, as they would have done in the selective
system and that their individual talents were not being
fostered effectively. The evidence for this was subjective
and derived from 3 sources:

165

   ... our view of the organization of teaching groups as
it applied at that time

   ... our external exam results, which indicated that quite
a number of individuals <u>ought</u> to have done better as
judged by their potential on entry to the secondary
school

   ... the supposition that, willing though they were, the
parents of some of our bright youngsters were not
always able to provide the intellectual or academic
impetus needed to promote a more effective learning
situation.

Our hopes for them were not those of an élitist school
of thought; that such children should be separated from the
mainstream; but that they should not simply have to 'look
after themselves'. We felt that the precept of extending
the ability of each individual pupil to its limit (whatever
it is!) should apply certainly to those youngsters who had
talents in a number of directions.

In short, we asked the question of ourselves: regardless
of the form of curricular organization in operation (setting,
streaming, banding) <u>are</u> we doing the best for our brightest
scientists or artists or musicians and so on? Our answer was
not securely affirmative. Thus we decided to embark upon a
project which we hoped would identify our ablest youngsters
and improve our professional ability to cater for their
special needs.

It was decided at that time that this project would be a
major innovation for the academic year 80/81 and that it
should be organized under the aegis of the in-service
training programme. In this way all our staff would be
committed in some degree to participate!

Definitions

At this point it is necessary for the reader to understand
what is meant by 'brightness'. There are always problems of
definition, since 'bright' is a comparative term. However,
early on, we evolved a working definition which, in retro-
spect, served our needs well enough.

Here are some possible characteristics of a bright child:

   ... those whose performance standards should enable them
to pass four or more 'O' levels (or CSE Grade One)
in their fifth year.

   ... those who absorb instruction and information and
make rapid progress.

... those who are capable of better work than is normally expected of them in lessons, and who would be held back by teaching at the 'middle' of the class

... the top 20% of the ability range

... any child with an IQ in the region of 130

... one who shows an outstanding talent in any ONE field of schoolwork which sets him/her notably above other pupils in the class or age group.

Thus in the present context we are talking about a small number of pupils who, whilst not being outstandingly gifted, were identifiable to us, if we applied the above criteria. For some bright pupils the means of identification was not always apparent.

Planning

Having decided that this project was to be a major in-service initiative various plans had to be made, and questions posed, in the months that led up to the Autumn Term 1980.

... Sources of information. No 'handy pack' of ideas seemed to exist and no book with all the solutions in, although we became aware through our Advisory Service of other schools who had shown similar initiatives and of various academic institutions or agencies which had also worked on the general theme of bright or gifted children. HM Inspectorate had also previously published its Gifted children in Middle and Secondary Schools, and this became a useful work of reference.

... Launching the project. As with any major innovation there was a need to be auspicious in the manner in which we embarked upon it! Impact upon the staff was important from the start.

... The longer term plans. What form should these plans take? Should the whole project be unfolded at once, or should we adopt a pragmatic approach and plan a bit at a time?

... Aims and Objectives. To what extent did we need, in advance, not just clearly understood aims, but the means by which to implement them?

The Director of Studies (the Deputy Head appointed to promote in-service work) was, at this stage, able to identify

a major source of information that was of inestimable value.
The Teacher Education Project, based at the University of
Nottingham, had developed and tested ideas and materials
concerning the able child, for use in the classroom. The
emphasis of the Project was on classroom practice and the
materials that the Director of Studies obtained when he
visited Nottingham to see the project co-ordinator, proved
subsequently invaluable, and indeed formed the basis of other
more 'home-spun material' that was devised from within the
school. Shortly after this the DOS (1) visited a school in
Coventry which had also linked with the Teacher Education
Project and through its annual staff conference had
stimulated work on the bright child. These two visits
provided the basis for the detailed planning that was
essential initially if a project was to be successful. The
DOS was thus able to avoid some of the pitfalls that might be
inherent in a 'go it alone' in-service venture.

Preparation

The staff were kept aware of these developments since they
were referred to in the staff briefings, and dates were set
for commencement of the work early in the Autumn Term. We
were fortunate in acquiring the services of HMI Margaret
Caistor for the first of the two full staff sessions. She
had been the secretary to the Working Party which produced,
in its series 'Matters for Discussion', Gifted children in
Middle and Comprehensive Secondary Schools. She was to
provide a lively and learned introduction to the whole
in-service course. A third prerequisite was to set out some
aims, some goals, that would give credence to what it was we
were endeavouring to do. Those aims which had begun the
Coventry school's work seemed appropriate to our situation
too and thus we adopted them. They were as follows:

... to raise our level of awareness of able pupils
throughout the school

... to explore ways of identifying able pupils in the
classroom

... to increase and improve our professional ability to
cater for the needs of these pupils

... to evolve guidelines for further action.

These aims were incorporated into a paper which was
circulated to the staff at the first in-service session and
which set out the rationale for the early part of the scheme.

1. Director of Studies

We did not suggest any methods by which these aims might be implemented at this stage and this we later felt was a mistake. Having aims is one thing. How to attempt to put them into practice is another matter! Without clearly stated procedures we subsequently realised that the project took off in various well-meaning directions which were not always productive.

In-service session 1

Miss Caistor's contribution on this occasion was apposite, pithy and formed an admirable backcloth to the ensuing debate. She itemised the contributions that various agencies should make to successful work with bright youngsters, ranging from the LEA contribution to the nature of the school organization, the role of the Head of Department and of the individual teacher within each department. Other aspects mentioned were the ethos of the school, its library facilities, pastoral links with other academic institutions and use of local expertise. In short, she produced a check-list which a school could use to judge its own success in helping bright children. She also gave an important pointer to success in such work by underlining the prominent role of the HOD (1). We were to discover subsequently that no amount of careful planning or bureaucratic overbearance could match the enthusiasm of the HOD in guiding the work of his own department. The remainder of that first session was given over to the problem of identifying bright children and the staff talking together in working groups. Staff were given a questionnaire (devised by the Teacher Education Project at Nottingham) which could be used for such a purpose, together with a list of bright child 'characteristics' suggested by colleagues and supported by other source material. The term 'enrichment' was introduced ... a change in quality of work rather than a change in quantity. The term enrichment was to be a key word in the more detailed departmental planning later.

Two points need to be made at this stage:

> ... it should be clearly understood by staff that providing bright children with extra (ie 'quantity') is not the answer - once bright children have grasped a point they do not necessarily need too much practice, but rather work 'in depth' which takes them into the 'uncharted waters to where most youngsters would not plot a course'

> ... some schools of thought advocate a change in curricular content for bright children, but this is often difficult from an organizational point of view

1.   Head of Department

and stretched limited resources. It can also be too
'separative' and as such ideologically unacceptable.

And so, from the start, our working groups argued the
case for enrichment material and a 'common' curriculum.
Finally, at this first session we adopted as an educational
slogan the phrase 'achieving atmosphere' and conjectured as
to how we could create such a corporate feeling. /It is
important to mention in passing here the value of organizing
group work and establishing (and briefing beforehand) group
leaders to keep the work moving along/.

In-service session 2

The second full session was held 10 days later, and in the
intervening time staff were busy with their questionnaires
identifying bright children and thinking out ways of
creating and enhancing an achieving atmosphere.

The working groups which had been organized for the
discussion work in session one were re-established and this
aided continuity. A second paper was distributed forming the
basis of the work planned. There were 3 elements to this
session:

  ... identification of the bright child - a comparison of
      pupils' profiles

  ... teachers' questioning skills (together with some
      practice material)

  ... general strategies.

Colleagues had worked well between sessions and a
sizeable number of pupils had been profiled. Data was
compared (the DOS having asked that each child was studied by
at least 2 teachers). Lively group debates ensued, the chief
discussion centering around what actually we meant by
brightness and whether there were some common features
amongst bright children. This was an important debate
because we were learning something new about our bright
pupils and thinking more deeply about their problems and
aspirations.

We turned our attention next to the skills needed for,
and problems associated with, teaching bright pupils. A
sample worksheet had been prepared with 'enrichment' material
- what we later termed extension material. Staff were
invited to comment on Kerry's analysis of questions. Kerry
(1982) had categorized question types which ranged from data
recall, through observation (closed types) to speculative,
discriminatory and problem solving - higher order questions.
The vital importance of questioning skills was clearly seen

if bright children were to be 'stretched'. Sources other
than Kerry's put questions into similar categories of
information, comprehension, analysis, synthesis, application
and evaluation (eg Bloom, 1956).

Finally in this second session, groups discussed
teaching strategies for bright pupils and began to evolve
guidelines for further action on the longer term. Group
leaders, of course, had prepared beforehand 'prompt'
suggestions so that discussion could go ahead with some
ideas in mind. As this second full staff session ended
colleagues were invited to produce their own 'trial' worksheet. This material was to embody the skills acquired
during this session and could be tested and evaluated in the
classroom.

Thus ended two hard-working but fruitful in-service
sessions, which at the near start of the academic year were
to provide the momentum for much of the work at departmental
and individual levels for the rest of the year. One cannot
stress enough the value of gathering together all staff in
such a way and organizing the work on a part lecture, part
workshop, part discussion basis. A differing pattern of
organization maintains and stimulates interest.

Evaluation: a first phase
With two important sessions behind us, and thoughts for
future action in mind, evaluation was now essential. An
evaluation questionnaire had three components, the first of
which was to ascertain how far the AIMS of the project were
met. The second asked simply what aspects of the in-service
sessions were rated as successful or influential in
improving our knowledge of the needs of the bright child.
Thirdly, staff were asked to complete a grid (a-e) concerning their enthusiasm or otherwise for a large number of
'achieving atmosphere' items which they themselves had
previously suggested as being worthwhile goals.

Insofar as this was the first formalized feedback the
evaluation exercise provided a good deal of information,
accounted for a variety of views, and indicated strongly
what the school should be doing with its bright children.

Space prevents anything more than a cursory appraisal
of the evaluation exercise, save for the following general
points:

>   ... aims 1 and 2 (level of awareness of able pupils and
>   exploring ways of identifying them) had been well
>   met in the first session. Miss Caistor's
>   stimulating talk had revealed for many colleagues
>   the need to think again about our teaching relation-
>   ships with able pupils. To be able to identify
>   brightness was essential.

... Aims 3 and 4 (improving professional ability to help
bright pupils and to evolve plans for the future)
were not so clearly met and this was largely due to
the over-abundance of materials provided for
colleagues to work with, and lack of time to
assimilate ideas and consolidate them.

... As regards the 'Achieving Atmosphere' staff
responded strongly for:

increased provision for departmental resources

encouraging positive attitudes towards
excellence

improvements in the school library and in
display or exhibition work generally

the teaching of study skills

... They responded strongly against:

allowing bright pupils to sit 'O' levels in
Year 4

making one member of each department responsible
for bright child work (ie feelings were for a
departmental drive!)

streaming or separation

and, oddly enough,

increasing extra-curricular provision or
promoting ideas of leadership.

Other ideas that came through quite strongly included
comments on the value of group discussions - a 'cross
pollination of ideas'; the need to reappraise questioning
skills; to look again at our worksheet provision for bright
pupils; and to build into lesson plans provision for
extension material.

The evaluation exercise had indeed been a successful
exercise and pointed the way forward more clearly than
before, although it was important that this collected
information should be passed back to staff. This was done
via the Heads of Department. In hindsight, perhaps another
in-service period for the whole staff would have been of
value.

Continuing initiatives

In the months that followed (November-February) work proceeded at departmental level. This took the form of a series
of meetings involving each department in turn with the
Director of Studies. Much of what had been part of the full
staff sessions and the evaluation process was now taken up and
looked at in more detail.

Each department was set some tasks or set to answer some
questions:

... What provision has been made for bright pupils
    hitherto and what more can be done? What actually
    happens to bright pupils in your department?

... List the bright youngsters you encounter and specify
    the nature of their talents.

... What changes in departmental aims and objectives are
    needed to take account of the bright child?

... What is the nature of progression of difficulty in
    your subject (ie what makes it more difficult and
    how can this be used to provide extension material)?

... Work out a strategy for your department's teaching of
    bright pupils and be prepared to discuss this at a
    later stage.

... Work out a strategy for monitoring and evaluating
    the work of your department.

... What do you see as the benefits of such work?

... How can your department aid a school philosophy of
    an achieving atmosphere?

In order to give further force to departmental work some
optional pilot schemes were suggested. Although some of these
were not taken up they are recommended as a basis for 'warm
up' work, before establishing a longer term departmental
philosophy (Kerry, 1981):

... improving a task. (Aims and objectives, teaching
    method, resources, content of lesson, assessment of
    lesson.)

... testing pupils' study skills

... task analysis (of lessons set to bright pupils)

... checking teachers' questioning skills: a self-

173

assessment

... providing extension work (ie planning a series of
lessons in which a subject is made more demanding in
so far as it is deepened or broadened).

Response to these exercises was varied, some departments
taking them up as pilot schemes while others began soon to
plan longer-term work. The exercises were not monitored by
the DOS and although there was a good deal of communication
between departments and the DOS, the latter could perhaps
have pursued a policy of checking pilot schemes somewhat more
assiduously! However, formal meetings were held and
'In-Service - the bright child' appeared as an item on the
HOD Meeting agenda with regularity.

It is appropriate to mention at this point that the
bright child project should be viewed as only <u>part</u> of a busy
school's week-by-week business. However much those who
initiate schemes are keen to make such work their <u>raison
d'être</u>, the reality is that only so much time is available for
planning and adopting new teaching methods. Departmental
heads will rightly argue the case that they have to establish
various other priorities. This is perhaps why, from time to
time, in-service work gets shunted up a side track! However,
some benefit was derived from this initial work and early in
1981 we were able to proceed with longer perspectives in
mind.

Longer term plans

Early in 1981 departments were asked to look at some part of
the syllabus that they were about to teach. From this they
were asked to plan work with bright pupils in mind, having
regard to (a) any pilot schemes they had undertaken, (b) the
work previously done in the in-service meetings. Heads of
Departments were required to name a topic currently being
planned for teaching and to indicate what class or classes
were to be involved, what materials and resources were to be
used (worksheets, booklets, oral, other source material).
Further, they were advised to monitor the work, provide some
means of evaluation, and to be prepared to report back later
in the term.

I shall give here only the briefest of reports concerning
departmental responses. Each school and each subject area
will have its own ideas regarding materials, method, assessment and evaluation and perhaps the only common ground will
be the desire to improve teaching, to cater for the needs of
the bright child. Suffice it to say that the responses
given were thoughtful, generally well-planned and carried
out with good-will and vigour! The variety of work
undertaken is shown in what follows and demonstrates the

Subject	Topic chosen	Year Group	Duration	Intended outcomes for the bright pupil
Technical Studies	Design a sporting figure or insect form	½ year group Year one	½ a term	(1) To extend the creative potential of the bright child. (2) To provide opportunities for solving design problems.
Mathematics	Directed Numbers	Year one 2 classes, one of which was a 'control'	4 weeks, including time for assessment	(1) To provide extension work at regular intervals and to pursue the sub-topics in depth. (2) To devise open, interpretive, inventive and investigative types of questions.
English	A thematic approach 'The American West'	Year one 2 classes, one of which was a 'top' band	½ term	To design and implement a comparative exercise which will evaluate the differing approaches to content and method employed in teaching the two classes.
Geography	Farming	Year two Whole year group	1 term	To provide extension work built in as an addendum to the normal classwork.
Commerce	Transport	Year four 2 exam groups	½ term	To give credence to the topic by solving some real problems connected with transport.
Religious Education	The Life of Jesus	1 class top band	½ term	To demonstrate pupils' understanding and interpretation of the topic.

Subject	Topic chosen	Year Group	Duration	Intended outcomes for the bright pupil
History	Second World War	Year three 1 group	1 term	Questions of a higher order planned. (1) To be able to synthesise material from various sources to evaluate it and recognize bias. (2) To be able to comprehend more difficult historical concepts such as dictatorship, justice, persecution, etc.
Art	Pattern → Tessellate → Environmental trail → Composition and production of tiles	½ year group Year one	½ term	(Pupils taken through stages shown in topic column. Pupils convert sketches into a composition which is interpreted in clay and applied to the tiles.) To show an awareness of problems of perspective and to appreciate simple answers such as overlapping shapes.

Subject	Topic chosen	Year Group	Duration	Intended outcomes for the bright pupil
Home Economics	Looking at foods (in particular eggs)	Year one	1 month	(1) To enable pupils to develop an interest in the foods they eat. (2) To teach pupils to observe and learn about varieties of appearance, textures, aromas and flavours of various foods. (3) To encourage observation of chemical changes in food (eg appreciation of heat, freezing.

The Science Department had already begun by this time to redesign its worksheets in year one and, like the History Department, was building in extension work in the form of higher order questions. This new material was being tested in year one as the project proceeded.

range and nature of the work.

Evaluation phase 2

By the end of the Easter Term we were ready to look back over
the term and to evaluate, albeit subjectively and without too
many precise analytical procedures.

In anticipation of this across-the-board evaluation by
departments the DOS had circulated a series of papers which
gave the outlines of what each department's contribution to
the project had been. As part of his own monitoring procedure
he had spent some time in each department talking to
individual teachers and noting progress. Of course, the
informal staff room banter was an invaluable means of keeping
colleagues informed!

Just prior to Easter each department was asked to submit
a brief report of its in-service contribution during the preceding term or so. The verbal reports were to be supplemented
by materials used to extend the bright child and examples of
pupils' work in response to these materials. The report was
required to be in the same form as the guidelines set down by
the DOS in January so that continuity could be maintained.

Our Heads of Department meetings have for some time been
noted for an open, honest and forthright approach to matters
educational - indeed 'openness' is encouraged - and this
meeting was no exception. It proved to be a lively,
intelligent and extremely interesting public examination of
what we'd been trying to do - a public accountability, as it
were - and as such was one of the most successful highlights
of the in-service work. Successful from a number of points
of view: colleagues were honest enough to admit any mis-
givings they had about the work of their department whilst
modestly highlighting those features of their schemes which
they rated highly. Reports were delivered thoughtfully, each
department going through the various stages of its work
leading up to production of materials, pupils' responses and
other outcomes, intended or otherwise. The presentation of
pupils' work provided a focus of keen interest and much time
was spent in examining folders, exercise books, models
designed in technical studies, pottery and art departments.
Examples were given of research projects undertaken by some
pupils, where they obtained source materials from,what skills
they had acquired in completing the work. More than one
department spoke of the pitfalls inherent in any work without
adequate resources. (It pays to plan!)

The two interlinked issues that were emerging from this
public forum gave rise subsequently to more profound
thinking about 'where we were going' with regard to our
teaching methods. Firstly, it became apparent that some
departments had used the project to take off in other
directions - there were other matters they wished to pursue,
other areas of their curriculum they now had the opportunity
to explore using the methodology of the bright child project.
Secondly, and this was true for all departments, as the work

178

of each department proceeded it began to re-examine its teaching strategies for all pupils and it began to think seriously about improvements it could make in the teaching performance of individual colleagues. The question was posed 'How can we become better teachers?'. So, at least the bright child project had had two interesting consequences - research techniques refined and teaching methods improved.

Perhaps our evaluation of what we'd accomplished was not as refined and methodical as it might have been (a few departments had attempted to measure improvement and had methodically kept a log of events); but we were able, at least, to say that we'd improved our professional ability to cater for bright children and that guidelines for further action were already being laid down.

The Spring Term gave way to a busy Summer Term and departments were given a free hand to develop any features of their own work which they had rated as promising or proven. Thoughts now focussed on the longer term: the lessons we had learned could now be taken as part of our day-to-day planning and be institutionalized. The phrase 'on a permanent basis' encouraged departments to think out strategies that would, for the future, have relevance for the brighter child.

The more distant future

Towards the end of the Summer Term departments were asked for a statement of intent - how each department saw its bright child work proceeding and to what extent it could incorporate this into a statement of aims. The outcome was a series of productive plans which are already becoming reality. A selection of departmental statements indicates the range and type of work envisaged from the Autumn Term onwards:

Home Economics

A reconstruction of worksheets with more emphasis on pupils 'finding out for themselves' and, for some children, a more theoretical approach to back up the skills learned practically.

Technical Studies

An extension of the problem solving approach in design, and provision for bright children to 'extend' or 'design' their own problems.

Art

The development of an art appreciation course with the compilation of 30 packs of work called 'Looking at pictures'.

One school's initiative

This is a building up of additional resources in 'figure', 'colour' and 'portraits'.

History

A reappraisal and 'rebuilding' of the worksheets to include bibliographies and original source material. (Here, there has been a sound financial investment to stock up on resources.) Emphasis is again on the types of questions being asked in the worksheets, which require the deeper skills of the more advanced historian and the calling for the controlled use of imagination and empathy.

Geography

This department will continue to provide extension and enrichment material in its topic approach.

Sciences

The worksheets here have been redesigned in year one (and shortly in year two) and the scientists plan an evaluation exercise of their worksheets later in the Autumn Term.

Mathematics

The department has approached the work from an organizational point of view and is keen to improve the efficiency of coping with the bright child in teaching groups by restricting the ability spectrum. As far as the curriculum is concerned they are augmenting their store of resources so that staff have a library of materials and can select work appropriate to individual needs.

English

This department is establishing its own in-service work that will include demonstration lessons and workshop sessions.

Other departments not mentioned previously in this account are the Physical Education department, and here in Educational Gymnastics the department encourages an open-ended approach for bright youngsters who, whilst not gifted in PE nonetheless can demonstrate creativity in solving problems in the gymnasium.

The Modern Language department is planning to produce a pack of articles, magazine extracts and other materials which will aid dictionary work for bright linguists. They also have in mind a 'bright linguist' competition.

Music, of course, provides much in the way of stimulation for its bright musicians and its various instrumental clubs typify the 'extension' work it provides.

Thus, such creditable work is becoming institutionalized and part of the fabric of the whole school - a recognition that bright youngsters need looking after as much as those less well endowed (who have, by the very nature of curricular organization been cared for over many years).

What has been achieved?

Briefly, we turn to the whole-school policies and plans. Departments tend to work out their own salvation and it is (rightly) left to senior management to formulate a corporate philosophy. It is a management job to place values on academic and other forms of success, to establish priorities in timetabling, to make arrangements for INSET opportunities and to inculcate the kind of school ethos or atmosphere that will engender worthwhile endeavour.

Our achieving atmosphere has begun to become apparent:

... display work, exhibition of pupils' work and reward for endeavour are all features in the daily life of the school.

... Regular half-termly review and progress meetings report on the work of individual children.

... Some monitoring of the individual bright child is done at DOS level and particularly at form tutor level and Head of Year level.

... A working party was set up early in 1981 and has now produced an informative working document concerning study skills which we hope will be a blueprint for good teaching practice this coming year.

... All staff are encouraged to appraise their questioning skills and bear in mind questions of higher order.

... Reorganization of mixed ability groupings in years one and two to allow for a 'top ability' band working in depth, has taken place.

... Emphasis, through our school aims, on improved teaching performance is apparent.

... There is the beginning of a scheme of evaluation: how can we 'measure' the worth of what we are attempting to do?

Other plans yet to materialize include:

... identification of new entrant bright children in more effective ways

... an extension of extra-curricular work and use specifically of teacher 'talents'

... full staff conference to assess materials, resources and to evaluate our work thus far

... linking with other agencies to further our own knowledge and using more of the materials prepared by the Teacher Education Project at Nottingham.

Summary

The author has tried, in a linear fashion, to outline the stages in planning, implementation, evaluation and policy-making that are part of one school's attempt to meet the needs of a small number of pupils (whilst recognizing the beneficial effect of such work upon all). In doing so he has alluded to the problems and pitfalls that beset any major innovation. A retrospective view is inevitably the wiser. A reiteration of the major points would seem to make a meaningful conclusion to this chapter.

* Planning beforehand, and at each subsequent stage, is essential; and crucial in this planning is the need for clearly stated aims.

* The commencement of the project should be an auspicious occasion so that a corporateness can be engendered. Such a corporate view of what it is we are doing should be maintained throughout.

* A senior member of staff should co-ordinate and promote the work, with preferably a small working party, so that a teamwork approach is possible. This aids good communication which is essential for effective promotion of work.

* It should be seen as INSET and given adequate publicity throughout the year in departmental, Heads of Departments and full staff meetings.

* Monitoring and evaluating procedures should be sophisticated and well thought out. Each department should have assessment and recording techniques.

* Remember that we are concerned with the individual child. There is no substitute for regular communication with individual teachers, too.

* Adequate resources, financial, material, human, must
  be found.

These are some of the ways in which a school can help
itself to get the best out of its youngsters. Above all,
there needs to be a measure of humility as a prerequisite.
Mistakes are made, things take off in different directions
and the best plans don't always work. However, if the course
is charted and colleagues begin to think sensitively about
the important matter of academic (and other forms of)
excellence - the training and nurturing of the bright
intuitive mind - then that is a good starting point upon
which to build a sound educational institution.

FOR FURTHER STUDY

Bloom, B S, 1956, Taxonomy of Educational Objectives,
        Macmillan.

HMI, 1977, Gifted children in middle and comprehensive
        schools, HMSO.

Kerry, T, 1981, Teaching bright pupils, Macmillan.

Kerry, T, 1982, Effective questioning, Macmillan.
        (The school was allowed to experiment with trial
        versions of materials from the Teacher Education
        Project.)

Chapter 8

Belle Wallace

In the previous chapter Rod Thompson described an approach to
professional improvement in provision for the able based upon
in-service training. Now the spotlight turns to what an LEA
can do to identify and help some very able youngsters to make
the most of their abilities against a background of
psychological security.

Background
For the last fifteen years, the County of Essex has shown
concern for the needs of gifted children. 'The Brentwood
Experiment' (1969) is an account of Dr Sydney Bridges' work
at the Brentwood College of Education, Essex. Bridges felt
that it was necessary to give student teachers experience of
working with the brightest children so that they would be
sensitive to the intellectual needs of these pupils and,
therefore, more aware of the need to provide extension of the
normal classroom activities.
   Twenty pupils from local primary schools, who had verbal
reasoning scores of 130+, were brought to the college for one
afternoon a week over a two year period. Students taught a
variety of subjects: nature study, physics, chemistry, maths,
art and craft. One of the main findings from this experiment
was that the pupils' school achievements had not matched
their potential. Dr Bridges comments:-

   The children had long since become accustomed to a
   certain level of expectation on the part of their
   teachers and also, probably, of their parents. The
   result was that on the whole their level of aspiration
   or demand on themselves was relatively low.

From this initial experiment, the work in Essex developed. In 1970, Mr George Robb, who was then the Principal County Psychologist, organized a one-day in-service conference on 'Gifted Children and their Needs'. As a result a working party of eight primary and secondary teachers was formed under the chairmanship of Susan Roberts, Educational Psychologist, and was known as 'The Essex Working Party for Exceptionally Bright Children'. The working party brief was to run an annual residential course for a group of 30-40 primary school pupils aged from 8-11 years. The purpose of these courses was not only to give the pupils an opportunity to work together, but also to give the teachers the opportunity to work with the pupils, studying their needs and interests.

The working party decided that if their activities were to be of benefit to other teachers and other exceptionally able pupils, some attempt should be made to disseminate the knowledge acquired as a result of the courses. Accordingly, from 1975, the courses were also used as vehicles through which to develop teaching materials for use in schools. In addition, courses were organized for secondary pupils.

In September 1978, the post of Advisory Teacher for Gifted Children was established. The rôle was outlined as follows:

... to provide an advisory service to schools on matters of identification procedure, curriculum extension materials and organizational strategies

... to extend the work begun by the original working party into each of the eight county divisions

... to organize enrichment courses, extra-curricular activities, Saturday clubs, etc

... to build a supply of resources available to schools

... to monitor the progress of pupils identified as exceptionally able.

Soon after appointment, the Advisory Teacher attended meetings of headteachers in each area of the county to outline aims and objectives, encourage enthusiasm, co-operation and support. This was felt to be necessary for a number of reasons.

First, worthwhile progress in this area of education, perhaps more than in any other area, needs the co-operation of headteachers and teachers so that concern for gifted children is seen to be part of the concern for all children.

Secondly, 'Gifted Child Education' can be a sensitive area since it is often assumed, quite wrongly, that the pupils' 'gifts' provide them with special advantages anyway, and that slow learning or handicapped children have greater priority needs. It was essential to avoid all connotations of 'élitism' and to stress that the philosophy of catering for the individual within the normal school should apply to all children.

Finally, it was equally necessary to base all work firmly in the classroom, involving teachers in the processes of identification and in the devising of curriculum enrichment schemes. It is only when teachers are closely involved in curriculum development that there is genuine, meaningful growth.

The first major effort, therefore, was to promote in-service education throughout the county based mainly in the Teachers' Centres, although often headteachers of large secondary schools requested school-based sessions and groups of small primary schools in rural areas gathered together for after-school meetings.

Accordingly, the first year of office was devoted to an intensive programme of in-service education. It would be appropriate here to outline the content of that in-service education since, in so doing, the broad philosophy underlying the development of the work in Essex will be underlined.

Essential issues raised in In-service Education
A number of questions need to be explored:-

   ... why should we be concerned about gifted children?

   ... what is meant by 'giftedness'?

   ... what are the problems of identification?

   ... what are the special needs of gifted children and their teachers?

   ... what are the possible strategies and techniques for curriculum enrichment?

1.   Why should we be concerned about gifted children?

   From each according to his abilities, to each according to his needs.

                         (Karl Marx)

   First, it is necessary to explode the myth that gifted children will survive despite any difficulty encountered in the school or home environment. Many do overcome considerable problems, emotional, social and intellectual, but many do not.

It is easy to sympathize with the problems of the physically or mentally handicapped child since his handicap is obvious and we are emotionally moved; but a gifted child can also be 'handicapped' because he is different. He is often out of step with his time, his peers and even his own family. He experiences deep frustrations and problems of adjustment; he feels different, but it is human nature to want to identify with the group. He is often acutely sensitive, lonely, intellectually isolated, prematurely aware of problems without the emotional maturity to cope with them.

The following comments were made by individual adolescents aged between 13 and 15 years who attended a residential course for gifted children in June 1978. The comments indicate very poignantly some of the personal problems experienced by these young people.

I have discovered a lot about myself during the last four days ... at last, I don't feel that I am some kind of exceptional freak. Other people have the same problems as I do; being ostracised by classmates seems to be a common problem amongst us, and attempting to be 'one of the crowd' by speaking the same way and acting the same way as others seems a common remedy.

Before I came on this course, I thought I was out on my own. By this, I mean that I would never find a person who could communicate with me. Now I find that a lot of worry and depression has been lifted off my mind and consequently I have changed. Before, I never quite believed in myself or my eventual purpose in life; now I do.

I have discovered that I am not as mad as I thought I was. A lot of people have the same opinions, thoughts and sense of humour as myself ... I prefer to work at my own pace. At school, I get fed up of waiting for others to catch up ... people don't understand this ... At school I don't work to my full ability.

I am a very deep thinker and spend hours pondering over various books on philosophy, sociology and world religions. I have not yet met anyone who thinks along the same lines as I do, although I came nearer to it on this course than previously. I spend far too much time daydreaming, creating whole new worlds and getting totally lost trying to figure out why, what and when, where and how ... As a rule I find I cannot get on with people of my own age ... I sometimes feel a bit of a social outcast ...

Gifted pupils need special provision; few <u>adults</u> can work in isolation without support and encouragement and a young, developing mind requires guidance, stimulus and direction. The influence of the teacher is of paramount importance and many adults owe a great debt to the teacher who inspired further exploration, who extended horizons or opened up new avenues of learning. On the residential course described above, a young person wrote:-

> I think that, on this course, I have been encouraged by the fact that there are a lot of people just like me in Essex and that there are a lot of teachers who care about us and are trying to help us get along. I used to think that most teachers just cared about people who were less bright and always wanted to help them. As for the people who are clever they think we can get along perfectly well without any help. It's been really great knowing they care about us too.

One can also find a paradox in our society in that certain abilities appear to be more socially acceptable than others; an exceptional athlete or footballer often receives more peer group and general acclaim than an outstanding mathematician, thinker, or scientist. Another course member wrote:-

> I enjoy reading, mostly science fiction. I don't like sport. I find that in school too much emphasis is placed on football matches and colours are awarded to children good at sport. Children who are good academically don't get colours or similar awards, and are often called names which give them an inferiority complex.

Equality of opportunity does not mean that all children have the same abilities and talents and can learn the same things in the same way at the same time. Neither does it mean uniformity of attainment and the neglect of the pursuit of excellence in all fields. Equality of opportunity surely means that every child should have the opportunity to develop fully as an individual and as a useful member of the society. Burt (1975) writes:

> It is our duty first and foremost to do the best for the vast mass of the population, who, after all, consist of just ordinary mortals of just average ability. Our next obligation is to provide extra help and extra care for the subnormal and handicapped. Nevertheless, in the interest not only of national survival but the progress of the race as a whole, there is no escaping the obvious conclusion that in the long run it is the highly

intelligent few who can confer the greatest benefits on
the less intelligent many including, it may be, in the
time of crises, the gift of life itself. (p. 190)

2.   What is meant by giftedness?
It is difficult to outline an adequate, all embracing
definition of 'giftedness'. Each child is unique and it is
impossible to list discrete traits or compile a comprehensive
list of abilities and tendencies which would include all
individual differences. One can only build a multi-faceted
mosaic of characteristics which may cluster in any
combination. It is beyond the scope of this chapter to
explore and discuss the relative merits of various
definitions (see Shields, 1969 and Getzels and Dillon, 1973),
but the reader is referred to the discussion in Chapter 1 of
this book.

3.   What are the problems of identification?
Any discussion of 'giftedness' is essentially linked with the
need to develop identification techniques and procedures
which the teacher can use in the classroom for initial
screening. However, there is no laser beam by which the
teacher can be certain she has diagnosed and identified the
abilities, talents, strengths and weaknesses of any child.
     Nevertheless, by a combination of several procedures,
such as careful observation, perception and understanding by
the teacher, objective and subjective assessment, a teacher
can acquire detailed knowledge of a child's abilities. This
assessment must be continuous although some gifted children
manifest certain characteristics very early.
     The most important factor in the process of identifica-
tion must be the quality of the teacher's observation,
perception and understanding. In addition, the methods,
practices and experiences the teacher develops within the
classroom will encourage or inhibit the development of
individual differences. Identification depends on provision
since a child can not demonstrate his abilities until he is
given the opportunity. Gallagher (1964), Tempest (1974) and
Ogilvie (1973) suggest, however, that the teacher's
subjective assessment of pupils is often inaccurate. There
is a tendency for teachers to rate highly pupils who are
persevering, conforming and industrious, ie pupils who fulfil
the teacher's expectations.
     One must also take into account the pre-school
experience of the child. A pupil entering school from a home
where he has experienced love and security, has had
opportunities for enriching, creative, exploratory play, has
had contact with articulate adults who have talked and read
to him, will tend to be a mature, socially well adjusted,

verbally fluent five-year-old. By comparison, a child from
an environment lacking these influences and opportunities for
rich pre-school experience, is obviously disadvantaged,
lacking the skills and achievements of the former.

One can consider three categories of gifted children.
In the first category one finds the high achieving gifted
child who is performing at an exceptional level. He is
overflowing with information and ideas; he converses like a
professor, he astonishes everyone with his erudite opinions,
he learns with astonishing speed. The teacher has no
difficulty in <u>identifying</u> this child as exceptionally able,
but problems may arise in meeting his emotional, social and
intellectual needs.

But one must consider the second category of gifted
children which includes the child whose giftedness may be
masked by behaviour problems such as school refusal,
aggression, emotional maladjustment, daydreaming, withdrawal,
disruptive behaviour, excessive attention seeking (see
Kellmer Pringle, 1970). It is through the investigation of
the cause of the problem that the 'giftedness' is revealed.
Vernon (1977) summarizes the chracteristics of underachievers in a description of collective traits:-

> He sees himself as inadequate, has low aspirations, is
> apathetic and does not enjoy studying; he is poorly
> adjusted or anxious, or sometimes rebellious against
> all that school stands for, often low in popularity.
> Such students tend to come more frequently, though not
> exclusively, from unstable or broken homes, of low
> socio-economic backgrounds, where there is little
> tradition of, or concern for, higher education.

The number of children falling into the third category
can never be known. These are the 'covertly gifted' children
who tolerate the frustrations and limitations of their
learning situations. They are frequently shy, conforming,
reticent children who respond to the demands made upon them
and who do 'the stint' (see Bridges, 1969). Often these
children have the perception and sensitivity to understand
the teacher's dilemma of having a large class of individuals
with diverse social, emotional, physical and intellectual
needs but insufficient time and resources to cope with all
of these needs.

If the subjective assessment of the teacher is fallible,
it would seem necessary to augment this with the use of
objective tests wherever possible.

There is general agreement that certain intellectual
abilities can be indicated by high performance on relevant
tests but whether any test can indicate or measure the sum
total of intelligence is another matter.

Most schools, if they use such intelligence tests,

administer group tests which restrict the opportunity for the
teacher to make a careful, detailed observation of the
individual's reaction to the test. Perhaps the child was
nervous, apprehensive, tired, worried or unwell and so
reacted adversely.

One must also consider whether the objective is to
assess potential or achievement or both. The validity and
reliability of such tests are vital considerations. The
teacher must recognize whether the test is indicating general
or specific abilities, whether it is diagnosing strengths and
weaknesses. Even when all these considerations have been
taken into account, the test result can only be an indication
of the <u>minimum</u> performance of a particular child at a
specific time. The teacher must differentiate between
<u>testing</u> and <u>on-going assessment</u> and must couple the test
result with intuitive understanding of the child. The danger
lies in interpreting the test results rigidly and ignoring
the limitations and crudity of the instrument and the external
variables of the child and the environment.

Nevertheless, used with understanding and correct
interpretation, group intelligence tests can be used to
supplement the teacher's classroom observation. In addition
fluency of reading and quality of comprehension can be
indications of exceptional ability.

Several authorities have compiled check-lists of
characteristics of gifted children, eg Ogilvie (1973), The
Department of Education and Science (1974), Renzulli (1971),
Essex (1979). There is not the space here to compare and
discuss these check-lists. One can merely state that the
purpose of these lists is to define and classify the
characteristics of gifted children and to guide and refine
the teacher's observation of the individual child. Such
lists have obvious inadequacies and limitations but used
with understanding can help to improve the teacher's
subjective observation.

In addition, <u>close liaison with the child's parents</u>
together with detailed knowledge of the child's pre-school
development can reveal certain characteristics which might
indicate giftedness (Waddington, 1961).

It is the policy in Essex to use this broad strategy in
identifying gifted children with the emphasis on continuous
assessment and 'inclusion' rather than 'exclusion'.

4. <u>What are the needs of gifted pupils and their teachers</u>?
The major needs of gifted children are:

   ... recognition

   ... understanding of their emotional, social and
       intellectual needs.

A gifted child of six years old may have the intellectual capacity of a much older child but emotionally he is six years old with the characteristic needs of a vulnerable young child. In some cases, because of heightened perception and sensitivity, such pupils may be emotionally immature when compared with chronological peers. They often absorb and intellectually understand the conflicts and issues in the world around them but lack the maturity to cope with them. A premature awareness of problems can precipitate them into assuming responsibilities before they are ready for them.

When a young child explores questions relating to the meaning of life, the concept of infinity or the idea of immortality, it is impossible to satisfy or even assuage a burning intense desire to know the answer and so give some security to alleviate the bewildered uncertainty of such a child.

It seems unnecessary to state that a gifted child needs a balanced, healthy emotional development if he is to develop into a rounded, mature adult.

Socially, gifted children need to belong to a group, to play and share, to be useful and accepted. They need contact with chronological peers, experience of living in the community, understanding the needs of others as well as themselves. They have the right to develop fully as individuals but they need to recognize that the exercise of rights brings obligations. Society needs the vital contribution of their exceptional talent.

Gifted children may have specific intellectual needs different from those of normal children. To feel normal in a learning situation they need some contact with intellectual peers for the experience of exchanging ideas, mental stimulation and the sharing of interests. They need rapid movement through basic stages to depth. They have exceptional abilities which need to be developed, eg the ability to grasp a concept quickly, to reason abstractly, to relate information, to see unusual relationships, to make conceptual leaps, to solve problems, to anticipate consequences and outcomes, to absorb information rapidly both in depth and breadth.

They need to be challenged to the point of failure and to experience the deep satisfaction of intellectual exercise.

As well as participating in group activities, they need to develop their own specific interests with opportunities for contact with experts in specialist fields.

Frequently, they and their parents need counselling and guidance. Children need the reassurance that they are normal but different; parents need to talk through problems with someone who understands and can offer constructive help and advice.

The specific needs of the exceptionally able child in school are closely interwoven and inter-dependent with those of the teacher. Nevertheless, one can examine the special qualities which, ideally, the teacher should possess.

In addition to having an awareness of and sympathy with the problems of gifted children, the teacher needs the emotional maturity capable of accepting a child with higher potential so that there is acceptance of the rôle of being a learner with the child, the acceptance of uncertainty in new fields.

The teacher also needs to understand the learning patterns of gifted children, to be sufficiently competent to recognize the qualitative differences in children's responses and their levels of conceptualization so that they can plan and guide the child's learning programme accordingly.

The teacher needs to be committed to the educational principle of providing individualized learning programmes whenever possible or necessary. However, pressures on the teacher are constantly increasing as the rôle develops and widens. The organization and philosophy within the school can inhibit or encourage the efforts of the teacher by diminishing or increasing opportunities for creative, innovative, flexible activities and work programmes.

A class of thirty pupils with diverse physical, social, mental and emotional characteristics requires a teacher with infinite patience, extra-ordinary energy and diverse talents if all the needs of the children are to be met.

A plentiful supply of appropriate resources is an essential requirement but, too frequently, resources are limited particularly for gifted children who exacerbate the problem not only in their need for special learning programmes but by devouring materials with an insatiable intellectual appetite.

The primary schoolteacher not only faces the problem of collecting and devizing suitable resources but has the major task of developing the child's basic skills of writing and recording. Frequently, a gifted child is an avid reader, a fluent talker, but a 'reluctant recorder'. The child is thinking and absorbing so rapidly that the laborious task of writing builds up frustration and exasperation. Written work is untidy, careless and superficial. This lack of basic skills and the consequent reluctance to record might be further aggravated if the task is uninteresting or too simple.

Some of the themes of this section are taken up in more detail in the third paper in this booklet.

5. Strategies and techniques for curriculum enrichment
There are two areas which can be explored when discussing provision for gifted children:

        ... the strategies in organization and methods which may

be manipulated to allow greater opportunities for
gifted children to work at appropriate levels; and

... the basic underlying principles which should govern
the teacher's preparation of work for gifted
children.

It is generally accepted as conventional and convenient
to group children according to their chronological age, but
that is the only common factor in any such group, the mental,
emotional, social and physical variables creating enormous
individual differences. Grouping individuals by any criterion
fails to produce a homogeneous group and although various
organizational strategies may alleviate the problems of the
gifted child they certainly will not solve them.

Vertical grouping (mixed age-range) may be seen as one
strategy for coping with exceptionally able pupils.
Certainly in such a situation it is accepted that younger
children work with older ones, but a gifted child could
quickly reach the ceiling of the group and would need extra
and special learning programmes if he is not to stagnate and
under-achieve.

Various degrees of streaming, banding or setting might
reduce the range of abilities in the class, but even in a 'set'
situation the gifted child may be outstanding.

Acceleration, whereby a child is moved permanently into
a class of older children, is another possible strategy; but
acceleration by one year might be inadequate and the child
might not be sufficiently emotionally and socially mature to
cope with older pupils. Moreover having to mark time at the
end of one phase of schooling, eg between Primary and
Secondary, or between Secondary and Tertiary, would obviously
generate further problems.

Occasional or regular withdrawal into a small group can
provide the necessary experience of working with intellectual
peers. Extra-curricular activities can also create
opportunities for gifted children to explore new and
challenging experiences, particularly if the group is small
and the activities unusual or the result of a teacher's
enthusiasm or hobby. Often in this situation there are
opportunities for the exchange of ideas in an informal
atmosphere on a one-to-one basis, the chance to work in
depth and breadth. Saturday morning clubs, 'twilight' groups
at the end of the normal school day or lunchtime activities
can provide that extra, vital time for teachers to give an
individual the opportunity for exploring ideas, talking in
depth or tackling new experiences.

Since many gifted children are capable of independent
work with sustained concentration, it is feasible to
encourage them to do individual work in the school library,
but they need experience in the use of reference, training in

study skills, careful monitoring of their work if it is to be worthwhile and satisfying.

But whatever strategies are adopted the ideal solution lies in striving towards the preparation of individualized learning programmes.

Tempest (1974) stresses that an enriched programme for a gifted pupil should incorporate:

... intellectual challenge through the quality rather than the quantity of work;

... self direction and independence of thought and action;

... opportunities for originality and imagination through problem solving and creativity.

In addition, Havighurst et al (1955) suggest further requirements of an enrichment programme:

... the need for high standards of accomplishment

... opportunities for leadership and communication

... individual attention

... first-hand experiences

... extensive reading.

Many gifted children find joy in 'information gathering' but enrichment should aim at the higher levels of Bloom's taxonomy of educational objectives: comprehension, application, analysis, synthesis and evaluation.

Dehaan and Havighurst (1961) differentiate between 'intensive, vertical, linear or depth enrichment' and 'extensive, horizontal, lateral or breadth enrichment'. Depth enrichment allows a pupil to pursue an activity or develop a skill to a high level of proficiency, to reach saturation point, to feel a sense of completion. Enrichment in breadth demands the preparation of work in new areas not ordinarily explored. It would appear necessary to combine both, utilizing the following avenues:

... building enrichment into the core curriculum

... developing the child's own interests

... widening horizons to include new interests.

Just as slow-learning children need teachers skilled in

remedial education, so gifted children need teachers skilled in 'gifted education'. A teacher with a special post of responsibility for gifted children could develop identification techniques, could organize special activities and build resources, could monitor pupils' progress and counsel pupils and parents.

Follow-up work in Essex

After the introductory in-service education sessions, teachers in Essex were given the opportunity to continue to study the problems and needs of gifted children. Working parties were set up in each area or in individual schools with those teachers who wished to continue. Teachers carried out the broad strategy of identification, in their own schools, analyzing various problems, discussing their findings, talking about their pupils with greater perception and awareness. Many teachers commented that they were observing all their pupils more carefully and sensitively not just the potentially most able ones.

The second year of office of the Advisory Teacher (ie 1979-80), was spent in consolidating the work of the first year. Having carried through the exercise of assessment and identification, the working parties began to prepare curriculum extension materials. Various tasks were undertaken depending on the interests and expertise of the teachers. The work prepared was not meant to be prescriptive but was intended to include collections of ideas, eg reference materials, extension exercises, film strips, slides, cassette tapes, suggestions for visits/exhibitions/outside experts, etc, ideas which a busy teacher could adapt for use in the classroom. Nor was it thought that every project could or should be used in every classroom. The limitation of each project is acknowledged since no 'enrichment kit' can be comprehensive, nor can it anticipate all pupils' questions, nor can it stand without the dynamic interchange of ideas between teacher and pupil, or pupil and pupil (see Chapter 6).

Examples of projects undertaken are:

... reviewing and compiling annotated lists of fiction for very able, fluent readers (both in English and German

... collecting maths puzzles, games, etc, and devising extension activities to supplement conventional maths programmes

... preparing projects on the local environment, history, geography, biology, architecture, etc, in greater depth and breadth than would normally be done.

... gathering together problems and tasks which would
require creative/lateral/divergent thinking

... preparing projects in unusual areas eg mediaeval
studies, classics, law, geology, astronomy

... compiling guides to local resources, both human and
institutional. There are many 'experts' in the
local community willing to help and often resources
in local museums which are neglected through
insufficient information about them

... reviewing reference books and commercial materials
in order to evaluate their usefulness.

Although it is important to gather resources for use in
the normal classroom, it is equally important to create
opportunities for gifted children to work together. Some
schools, without extra staff, are managing to manoeuvre the
organization so that small groups of gifted children can meet
regularly to work on a project together.
Enrichment courses, drawing together pupils from a
number of schools, have been organized so that the teachers
who prepared the projects could have the opportunity to try
them out and evaluate their usefulness and appropriateness.
Although the major work has revolved around the normal
classroom activity, these withdrawal groups have been
beneficial for two reasons. Firstly, not only do they
provide the opportunity for gifted children to communicate
with each other but secondly, they give the teacher <u>first
hand experience</u> of working with exceptionally able children.
The teachers' reaction has been universally one of surprise
at the depth and speed of the pupils' learning capacity. The
exercise of preparing work in greater depth and breadth has
encouraged a general raising of standards, both in the
quality of work presented to <u>all</u> pupils and in the level of
teacher expectation.
Enrichment courses have been organized for pupils
attending schools in a particular administrative or
geographical area. Thirty to forty primary schools may be
invited to nominate pupils who would benefit from a special
day, weekend or week's course. The work is prepared by a
group of teachers in that area who obviously understand the
needs of the pupils and the special characteristics of that
area. This means that history, geography and science projects
for example, can be a direct and relevant outgrowth from the
pupils' environment; and local records offices, industries, or
community resources can be utilized as fully as possible. On
a smaller scale, three or four schools may co-operate and

organize a withdrawal group which meets for half a day each week. Sometimes a teacher from one of the schools who has a particular area of interest and expertise takes the group, eg in mathematics; at other times an outside expert volunteers to guide a series of activities or explorations, eg a local historian, an apiarist, a lepidopterist. Where possible, a pupil or group of pupils may make a series of outside visits, eg to the central library to study its organization, to a local bank manager to discuss fluctuating currency exchange rates or to the telephone exchange to explore the intricacies of telecommunication.

At secondary level, in addition to developing co-operation between schools, close links have been developed with industry so that experts from various industries participate in curriculum extension projects, contributing to courses on science and technology, and management and communication. It has also been possible to 'match' a pupil with an expert in industry so that a specific interest can be shared.

Liaison with Essex University has also been fostered, particularly with the Departments of Science and Electrical Engineering. The tutors not only have the specialist depth of knowledge but the university has equipment and facilities not usually available in schools.

Some schools have appointed a senior teacher to take special responsibility for initiating assessment procedures to identify the exceptional pupils, monitoring their progress, and developing extra-curricular activities to meet their specific needs. Sometimes this responsibility has been incorporated into the rôle of the teacher responsible for developing remedial programmes.

This means that the school has someone who will be the focal point for enquiry, support and activity. This does not mean that individual teachers should not be concerned and responsible for exceptionally able pupils but that a general framework can be built within the school through which information can be received and disseminated, activities developed and collated, policies discussed and expertise shared.

Obviously not every school in the County has participated in these activities, but the general response has been very encouraging and positive. Teachers are concerned to meet individual needs and the curriculum development has been relevant and practical with themselves as the innovators. Quite often the initial task has been to make teachers aware of the problem; once they are aware, their professional dedication takes them further.

Quality of response to the needs of able youngsters varies from one LEA to another. In the next chapter Carolle Kerry undertakes a more wide-ranging survey of the work of those LEAs who take an active rôle in helping able pupils

An LEA initiative

move towards the achievement of their full potential.

FOR FURTHER STUDY

Armstrong, H. G. (1967). 'Wastage of ability among the
            intellectually gifted', Brit. J. Educ.
            Psychol., 37, 2, 257-9.

Blosser, G. H. (1963). 'Group Intelligence Tests as
            screening devices in locating gifted and
            superior students in the ninth grade.
            Exceptional Children, 29, 6, 282-6.

Branch, M. & Cash, A. (1966). Gifted Children. London:
            Souvenir Press.

Bridges, S. A. (1973). I.Q. - 150. Priory Press Ltd.

Gallagher, J. J. (1975). Teaching the Gifted Child,
            Allyn & Bacon Inc.

Hildreth, G. H. (1966). Introduction to the Gifted. New
            York: McGraw-Hill.

Hitchfield, E. M. (1973). In Search of Promise, London:
            Longman.

Hollingworth, L. S. (1942). Children above 180 I.Q.,
            New York: World Book Company.

Hoyle, E. (1969). Gifted Children and Their Education,
            London: D.E.S.

Jacobs, J. C. (1970). Are we being misled by fifty years of
            research on our gifted children? Gifted
            Child Quarterly 14, Summer 120-3.

Jacobs, J. C. (1971). Effectiveness of teacher and parent
            identification of gifted children as a
            function of school levels. Psychology in
            the Schools, 8, 2, 140-142.

Department of Education and Science (1977). Gifted Children
            in Middle and Comprehensive Schools, London:
            HMSO.

Kellmer-Pringle, M. L. (1970). Able Misfits, London:
            Longmans.

Ogilvie, E. (1970). Gifted Children in Primary Schools,
            Schools Council Research Studies, London:
            Macmillan Educ.

Pegnato, C. W. & Birch, J. W. (1959). 'Locating gifted children in junior high schools. A comparison of methods.' Exceptional Children, 25, 7, 300-304.

Povey, R. (ed.) (1980). Educating the Gifted Child, London: Harper and Row.

Rath, J. D. (1971). Teaching without specific objectives. Educ. Leadership. April 714-720.

Renzulli, J. (1971). Scale for Behavioural Characteristics of Superior Students.

Rother, J. & Sussman, S. (1974). Educating Gifted Children, York: Ontario Board of Education.

Shields, J. B. (1968). The Gifted Child, Slough: NFER.

Tempest, N. R. (1974). Teaching Clever Children 7-11, Routledge and Kegan Paul.

Terman, L. M. et al. Genetic Studies of Genius, Stanford
(1925) Vol. I University Press.
(1926) Vol. II
(1930) Vol. III
(1947) Vol. IV
(1959) Vol. V

Toffler, A. (1981). The Third Wave. Penguin Ltd.

Vernon, P. E. (1977). Gifted Children, London: Methuen.

Waddington, M. (1961). Problems of Educating Gifted Young Children with special reference to Britain. Evans.

Wall, W. D. (1960). 'Highly intelligent children, Part I. The psychology of the gifted, Part 2. The education of the gifted' 2, 2, 101-10, 2, 3, 207-17. Educ. Res.

Chapter 9

A SURVEY OF LEA PROVISION FOR ABLE PUPILS

Carolle Kerry

The background

This book set out to survey what had been done and could be
done to improve the lot of able pupils in normal schools.
To this end it has examined a range of strategies and
procedures available in individual classrooms, in schools
and in one LEA. It seemed appropriate to try to pull
together the initiatives taken by LEAs throughout England.
The purpose in so doing was twofold. First, to provide a
platform for debate for LEA advisers and administrators who
might be contemplating how their own authority could respond
to the needs of this group of youngsters. Secondly, to
inform teachers in the various areas of facilities which
were available locally.

A third purpose might be regarded as slightly more
subversive. If the reader, on examining this chapter, finds
his LEA unmentioned, he might well ask himself why this is
so.

A letter explaining the scope of the book and soliciting
information was sent to Chief Education Officers of one
hundred LEAs in England during the early part of January
1982.

In 1977 a similar initiative had been taken by means of
a letter to the same LEAs offering to collate initiatives
and circulate them through the medium of a newsletter
(produced free of charge). This first invitation received
just half a dozen sketchy and unhelpful responses.

Understandably, there was no air of optimism about
obtaining a rounded picture of LEA involvement in the
education of able pupils following the January 1982
invitation. Experience suggested that many LEAs made
peripheral efforts (for example, by mounting the occasional
in-service day); a number claimed to be actively involved in

202

curriculum provision, though their products were never quite polished enough for public view.

Surprisingly, therefore, over thirty replies were received in the period January to May 1982. This at least was a hopeful sign, even though some LEAs admitted to being very little involved in this aspect of educational provision. There does seem to be a national trend to make the education of the able a subject no longer under a taboo.

This chapter looks thematically at the LEA responses. It begins by asking how the respondents set about identifying their more able youngsters.

Identification

Many authorities start their deliberations on provision for the able pupil by asking themselves the question: 'What do we mean by "gifted"?'. There are various definitions and no single one is universally adopted. Most have in common, however, the key notion of giftedness as the possession of some exceptionally high ability in one area, ie a musical, artistic, poetic or athletic talent. Some allow for the possibility of all-round skill or talent.

It is obviously desirable that, in the interests of both the community at large and the individual able pupil, those who are highly gifted should be discovered at the earliest possible age and opportunities given to them so that their abilities may be encouraged and extended.

Identification of the gifted pupil, in an educational context, must come, in the first instance, from someone with a personal knowledge of the child. In some cases this knowledge will be gained by the school from a professional source: pre-school psychological facilities or from specialists in such cases as exceptional musical talent. But more often the knowledge must be generated to the appropriate authority by the class teacher.

However, Suffolk County Council has found that it is possible to identify many very able children on admission to school through a careful parental interview, and one method is described thus:

A perceptive listener may elicit from the parent important clues by the way of open-ended questioning. In relation to other children of the same age, very able children of 4 to 5 years are likely to show some at least of the following characteristics:

... to be very competent in their use of language

... they may have a particular interest which is sustained, have an unusually mature understanding of the rules of various games

... have a mature concept of time

... an ability to enjoy imaginative play

... have good powers of observation

... depending on their home background, they may have an interest in books, and may recognize book titles.

It is suggested that a positive response to a selection of the factors listed above will indicate that a child may be able. Suffolk LEA urges its school staffs to keep careful watch on such children, so that the rate of the child's progress can be carefully monitored.

On the other hand, the City of Newcastle LEA makes specific reference to the difficulties experienced in recognizing the gifted child in pre-school or early school years. In contacts with parents attention of teachers is drawn to differentiating between parental expectation and actuality, distinguishing talkativeness from real linguistic skill, separating passing curiosity from actual deep interest and so on. The attention of Newcastle teachers is then drawn to considering the child's attainment against the characteristics of the able child as shown in a specially formulated checklist, and subsequently cementing the identification by testing, for example, by means of the Schonell 'Draw a man' test. But the warning is given that giftedness does not necessarily show up as a high IQ, and this is where 'instinct' must play a large part in the recognition of the younger gifted child.

But for the teacher who is regarded as the first link in the educational chain of identifying the able child, what tangible assistance does the employing LEA provide to facilitate such identification? It would appear from the returns submitted by a number of replying authorities, that perhaps the most favoured means of identification of the bright pupil is, initially, by supplying the checklist of characteristics. Since the late 1950s a number of checklists have been compiled giving the characteristics of the very able child of given age. These checklists include those characteristics most commonly indicating very high intellectual ability. Very few lists show all possible characteristics, but any very able child will exhibit a cluster of the items cited. Newcastle's 'Teachers' checklist' may be broken down into four distinct sections under the headings:

... acquired learning skills

... interests

... mental processes

... social attitudes.

The City of Newcastle appears to offer its teachers advice in a series of graded steps. Having used the Teachers' Checklist and observed the child over a period of time in the confines of the working classroom, the teacher is then pointed to the advisability of some kind of follow-up procedure by using one of the standardized lists.

At this point it is fair comment that most of the following procedures will be time-consuming, and using such items must, of necessity, impose a burden upon the teacher. Yet most authorities admit it to be a necessary requirement in the process of identifying the able pupil.

If tests are to be used in identification, then it is more appropriate to use several rather than one in isolation, as the end result will be more complete. Newcastle suggests that the following tests may well be used together:

... if one wishes to enquire into the ability of the child to reason clearly without the need to use reading and writing skills, then Raven's Progressive Matrices is very suitable. Also recommended are the non-verbal tests available from the NFER

... a reading test may be sought, and many individual or group tests are available

... teachers can examine their pupils' understanding of what they hear without having to involve them in reading and writing. An age-appropriate version of the English Picture Vocabulary Test is simple to apply, and easy to score

... assessment of number skills can be done by using NFER tests or other appropriate mathematics and number skill tests (Hodder and Stoughton Educational).

The tests mentioned are all readily available for teacher use, and there are, of course, many others. Some skill, however, is required in using and interpreting them. It is not at all clear whether LEAs recommending these techniques provide adequate training for the staff concerned.

In conjunction with the use of checklists and tests as an aid to identifying the bright pupil, some authorities have followed the guidelines implicit in Her Majesty's Inspectorate report Gifted Children in Middle and Comprehensive Secondary Schools. In the report Her Majesty's Inspectors pointed out the various shortcomings of identification procedures, and

they suggested the need for more systematic ways of looking
for extremes of individual ability in the context of
identification of individual differences. They pointed out
that they did not find any one complete model for identifying
giftedness, but they felt that use of some forms of systematic
screening may help.

Harrow LEA has evolved a method of screening whereby
information about pupils' academic attainments is reported in a
standardized form when it is transferred from one school to
another. Objective information available to schools either
from existing records, or from the school's programme of
standardized testing, is made available to all teachers.
Where a suitable climate of opinion has been created, the
Year or House pastoral care system can form a useful
mechanism for receiving and disseminating information
regarding individual pupils. Used in conjunction with test
scores this screening process should help the teacher to
become aware of any substantial discrepancy between scores
and pupil achievement.

In Croydon, the identification process has been taken a
stage further. Checklists are used, followed by staff/head-
teacher consultation. This in turn is followed by visits
from an advisory teacher.

This brief review of some of the LEA approaches to
identification sets out the most commonly adopted methods.
It is interesting that in much of this literature there is
little or no mention of underachievement. Be that as it may,
what happens to those pupils who do get caught by the
identification net? An early pioneer of finding and helping
the able pupil was Devon LEA. The next section looks at
procedures there.

Evolving a policy for the able pupil

In 1977 Devon Local Education Authority published its booklet
'Find the Gifted Child'. The publication has since achieved
both national and international circulation and acclaim, but
primarily it was intended for use within the authority.
Copies of 'Find the Gifted Child' were distributed to all
Devon schools, and each school was detailed to define a
policy for identifying, and making appropriate provision for,
gifted pupils.

Following the introduction and circulation of the
booklet, a number of teachers' centres arranged courses on the
theme of gifted children. These courses served as a forum
for debate and, together with the completion of checklists on
specific pupils, fulfilled a valuable role in in-service
training.

In addition, advisers were enlisted to contribute to a
list of county resources that might be of value to gifted
pupils and their tutors. Such a list was produced, but it

was found that the real need was for local and relevant resources for individual pupils.

After the advent of 'Find the Gifted Child' and the subsequent in-service training there was a marked increase in the number of potentially gifted pupils referred to educational psychologists and advisers.

Having pointed the teachers to looking for bright pupils, provision had to be made for the future enriched schooling of the children. A modest sum was set aside in annual estimates to encourage local initiatives in the provision of gifted children. Projects included innovation in primary, middle and secondary schools. At first these were tentative steps but, as the years progressed, experience gained allowed the projects to become more effective.

In the primary sector, groups of gifted pupils attending several schools in a given area were identified by an educational psychologist. After discussion with both parents and teachers, two tutorial groups of not more than eight pupils to a group began to operate on a weekly basis. A primary school teacher was selected and seconded to this tutorial work for one day a week. The teacher's brief was to identify the particular interests of the individual children, to match these interests to the available local resources, and to feed the information back to the 'parent' schools. The weakness in this method of approach soon became apparent. No one person could possibly have the time to liaise effectively between the tutorial groups and the parent schools.

To overcome this immediate problem, and also to extend the tutorial facilities to other parts of the county, in January 1979 an Advisory Teacher for Gifted Pupils was appointed. Once again, time was the limiting factor, since it seemed obvious that one teacher could not hope to provide direct teaching services to all of the primary school gifted children. The brief given to the Advisory teacher was that, on up to 3 days weekly, he/she should form and work with small tutorial groups; and once again the main emphasis was to be placed upon identifying interests, and feeding this information back to the schools. He/she was also to act as a county 'memory-bank' for the various initiatives taking place both locally and nationally, and to advise the staff on ways in which they might improve their own school provision for gifted pupils.

At the same time initiatives were taking place in middle schools. A small group of gifted pupils was identified in a middle school, and lunchtime club provision was made for these. County support was given to provide a suitably qualified person to undertake these club activities on a weekly basis. The club prospered. The original interest was in electronics and a lecturer from a college of further education assisted, but in time the outlook of the group broadened, and more diverse interests were pursued.

In secondary schools, too, similar attempts were made to cater specifically for the able child. A head teacher of a large comprehensive school offered the services, on a part-time basis, of one member of his staff to ensure that the identification of bright pupils was carried out, and that their subsequent needs were met within the school. Again, the special county fund provided additional staffing to cover the release of this teacher. Approximately 20 pupils were identified, and they have since been involved in a programme of external visits, and many extra-curricular activities including discussions on cultural, political and moral issues. This particular secondary school extended its facilities into the primary school: additional staffing to the school made it possible for a group of eleven bright primary children to attend the comprehensive school on one afternoon a week for a specific programme of activities. Assurances were given to the heads of participating primary schools that the work would neither interfere with the child's primary school education nor would it be repeated when the child transferred to secondary school.

Other comprehensive schools have since followed this example, and in one case links were forged with post-graduate students from Exeter University School of Education.

As well as in-school procedures, other methods have been tried. Workshops for the gifted pupil have been particularly successful in the field of visual arts. In the summer term of 1978 such a workshop was held over a period of four days, and some seventy children attended. The workshop was tutored by advisers and College of Art staff. Subsequently, 25% of the children who attended were deemed to have particular talents in visual arts, and many have been followed up in their individual schools. It was decided to hold a similar venture in following years.

The standards set by the Devon LEA have been copied by other LEAs. In some instances individual items have been expanded and improved upon, but as a totality, Devon must take some credit for the awakening of the awareness of the responsibility which LEAs have towards the gifted pupil.

Another authority who appears to have had a long term commitment to gifted pupils is Berkshire. Berkshire LEA has been working actively for the gifted child since 1975 when a weekend course was led by the Schools' Council 'Gifted Children' Project team. 1979 saw the formation of the County Working Party comprising teachers, advisers and officers of the authority, and in November of that year the County Council recommended to the Education Committee that the Council recognize the needs of specially gifted children in Berkshire and the provision of special educational facilities to meet their needs be made available at an early stage.

The Working Party met regularly during the following

year and focussed its attention on the identification of gifted pupils, a study of the provision currently made, and formulation of specific recommendations towards the implementation of that provision.

The Working Party divided their attention into the three distinct areas of pre-school children, primary and secondary children.

Berkshire working party recognized that both giftedness and general development of children is fed by early appropriate stimulation, a wide range of experiences, encouragement and talk at home. At the time (1979) the Education Committee planned to increase the number of nursery school places available to young children in their area, and this was much welcomed by the working party. These nursery schools, whilst catering for children of differing abilities, would give the talented youngster more opportunity for early learning.

The Berkshire Working Party was very mindful of the gifted child's need to be educated according to his abilities, but at the same time, not to isolate him from his peer-group, as is implicit in the Plowden Report, 1966.

At the same time as the formation of the Working Party, so appeared the publication of the Primary Survey 1978 by HMI. In this HMI draw attention to the necessity for a match between the standards of work and the children's abilities. HMI also drew attention to the failure of some teachers to provide sufficiently stimulating work for the most able pupils. With Plowden and HMI reports very much in mind, the Working Party intimated that sensitive teachers would be able to record the signs of exceptional achievements amongst their children. Similarly, that the teacher will perceive the able youngster who shows skill in talking and reading well beyond his years, and will develop these skills both within a small group and individually. In essence, the onus for stimulating the gifted child fell very firmly upon the individual teacher.

Having established that, then how to make teachers aware of each child's potential was the next consideration. From 1980-2 onwards there appears to be an impressive series of courses designed for both primary and secondary teachers, ranging from 'Extending the able child in the Junior School' to 'Problem-solving for gifted pupils'. Also catered for are the pupils themselves, and activities range from Saturday morning schools to weekend schools, both residential and non-residential. Approximately 24 children take part at each school.

In the normal course of events, by its statement of policy, each Berkshire secondary school has the responsibility of making reference to the established and proposed provision for gifted children. It is anticipated that much of that provision will be within the general curricular and social policies, but special arrangements may complement and supplement the standard procedure and programme. Special provisions for the gifted pupil include acceleration, enrichment programmes, attendance at weekend residential courses, day release sessions at local colleges, Saturday morning school and drawing on specialist skills outside the school for actual tuition.

Strong links are kept between home and school and both the child and its parents are encouraged to go beyond the school environment for means of extension.

The curriculum as a vehicle for special provision

There can be little doubt from the responses received to our request for information that, once able pupils have been identified, the major form of attack on the problem is through some form of curriculum initiative. Those by Croydon and Manchester are typical.

In Croydon heads were consulted on the topic Curriculum and Organization as far back as 1976. In 1979 Primary and Secondary Working Parties were set up to help teachers identify and make suitable provision for the bright pupils. Teachers are advised of the backgrounds to various problems and possibilities for helping able children by means of recommended reading lists and literature published around the topic, eg the Brentwood Experiment and the various DES pamphlets.

In Manchester, teachers have recently undertaken a major review of their curriculum and policy statements. Eight groups have been formed and one of these looked into provision for teaching both children of high all round ability and children with one or more specific talents. Whilst the members of the working group point out that in no way are the recommendations solely concerned with a minority group of privileged children, one of their original concerns was stated as follows:

> Able and talented children deserve as much consideration and resource as any other group. Considerable thought and effort are given to the teaching of those with learning difficulties. It is appropriate to give similar support to the teaching of the most able.

It is also interesting to note that another criterion for special provision was the notion that we, as a country, just cannot afford to waste the talents of our most able pupils. It is surprising that few authorities, or even teachers within an authority, will actually admit to this value judgement, crucial and commonsense though it seems.

The working party offered, as an aid to identification, passage along the well trodden path of checklists and screening, both formal and informal. The group felt that, as schools vary so much in character, the needs and criteria for the identification of talented children would vary, and for this reason the bias on identification techniques should be towards the informal framework.

Teachers are reminded that they should expect able and talented children within their school, and that indications of ability and flair need monitoring, even if children later do not fulfil the expectations. For formal identification through tests, a comprehensive list is given but,as in some other authorities, teachers are reminded that it is impossible to find any one test to measure all things well.

The members of the Manchester working party have recommended, as a source for thought and debate initially, that a person be appointed to lead and co-ordinate work relating to the city's most able pupils. This in turn would lead to in-service training, an advisory service for teachers, and the sensitizing of the staffs of Manchester schools to the needs and problems of very able pupils.

The kinds of initiative just described have a great deal to do with raising the consciousness of teachers. But some authorities go further and provide for specific curriculum enrichment as a matter of policy. The best example of this approach among our respondents was to be found in documents emanating from Suffolk LEA.

Curriculum Enrichment: Suffolk LEA

Early in 1981 a working party was set up to examine the educational needs of very able children within the Suffolk Authority. The working party was chaired by Mr P Jeffery, Chief Educational Psychologist and met on four occasions. Their brief was to consider the identification and needs of the very able children in Suffolk's maintained schools, including children who are exceptionally gifted intellectually, and those with particular gifts, and to make recommendations.

The County Education Officer, in his foreword to the report, urges:

> It is our task as educators to see that the abilities of each child are developed to the fullest possible extent.

It is clear from the report that the working party considered that, wherever possible, the needs of the able child should be met within the context of the child's school. To achieve this it was necessary that there should be a good match between the child and the curriculum offered, ie schools should aim to provide for most of the needs of their very able children within a planned and structured curriculum. Where this was not possible, the child's education could be supplemented by enrichment or withdrawal.

Enrichment involves 'provision of additional experience which supplements regular classroom activity'. Children in enrichment groups are taught to develop high level study skills, and pursue activities which in both depth and breadth are beyond the reach of most children. Enrichment groups should involve extensive reading, give individual attention, provide opportunity for leadership and demand high standards of accomplishment. Children in such an enrichment group find that it provides challenges through quality rather than quantity of work, and involves self-direction, originality, imagination and problem-solving.

Enrichment does not necessarily involve the withdrawal of the pupil from the classroom. It is possible to follow an enrichment programme produced either by the teacher for the individual or by using a commercially produced programme. The working party notes two things of import here:

... enrichment in the classroom may be less divisive than a withdrawal programme, but that

... organization of such a programme may be difficult, and hard work for the teacher.

Enrichment may necessitate the withdrawal of groups of very able children within a school or between schools, to study a subject in depth, or undertake a particular project. These groups enable able children to learn to co-operate and to face stern competition. Such groups must win the support of the other teachers not directly involved so that the work done can co-ordinate with the regular classwork and the ideas generated can spill over into the classroom and involve other, less able, children.

Subject-based work can be extended beyond the normal curriculum by providing separate work within the ordinary class, by acceleration to an older age group or by withdrawal groups. Very able pupils may be asked to learn more about a subject, or how to use the knowledge they have more critically and effectively by learning 'higher order skills' or 'research skills' both of which will have applications within the normal curriculum lessons. Such groups help able children to try out their ideas on their teachers and on each other.

The report then proceeds to consider how teachers may further improve the quality of work given to able pupils within the class. Quite reasonably the report states that the most important resource available to the able pupil, as indeed, throughout education, is the enthusiastic teacher. Several methods of withdrawal are discussed. An interesting idea which emerges is that, if withdrawal takes place at a different time each week, then the lessons missed change from week to week. At this point, the working party put forward the notion that these withdrawal groups might be enhanced if parents and other interested (or perhaps it should be interesting!) members of the public are invited to contribute. (A simple idea, not encouraged by too many LEAs.) Extra-curricular activities are also discussed, lunchtime or after-school clubs providing children of differing ages with an opportunity to meet. Clubs may then progress to a more sophisticated weekend or holiday venture, when children from a much wider area can be brought together. Resources for these sessions can either come from within the educational system, ie secondary schools, or contact can be made with the outside world through industry and higher education.

The information contained within the report of the Working Party gives much food for thought and the whole report is crammed with ideas and observations. As the able pupil progresses through the school and reaches the sixth form it might be reasonable to assume that at this stage his needs will be catered for by the 'A' level syllabus. Suffolk's report suggests we might be doing the sixth former a disservice by giving him four 'A' levels instead of the usual three. Suggestions for the able sixth former, over and above his traditional 'A' level timetable, include a form of general studies programme at an intellectual level well above that traditionally provided for sixth formers; high level links with local industry; and summer school type exercises midway through the course. Many of these initiatives could become a drain on school time and staff, but able sixth form pupils are usually highly motivated and thus require a minimum of supervision.

Suffolk offers practical advice to its teachers to help them develop their bright pupils. The Working Party suggested, among many other ideas:

... the organization of groups of teachers to prepare suitable materials

... the creation of a resources centre

... planning and implementation of in-service courses on the identification of able children.

At the time of writing, February 1982, Suffolk does not have an adviser with special responsibility for the needs of able children and from comments within the report one is led to believe that, if the general financial climate were to improve, then this would be an appropriate moment to consider such an appointment.

The report is a very comprehensive document that must give the authority's teaching staff great heart. Examples are given of individual initiatives with very able children in Suffolk so that 'teachers may know where to turn for further information'. Also listed is helpful information about the work with/for able pupils in other authorities.

If one were allowed room for a personal comment at this point it would be that from Suffolk came the most readable and adventurous document of all the responses to our request for information.

Nevertheless, Suffolk was not alone in suggesting strategies for enrichment for the able pupils, and it is opportune to glance at these other initiatives.

Curriculum Enrichment: a variety of approaches

The London Borough of Croydon set up working parties to consider the provisions for able primary children in the authority's schools. An enrichment course was planned, and the pupils' development monitored. Also monitored was the provision of resources that the able youngster might be expected to use. Lists of resources and their availability are supplied to teachers, and parents' help is sometimes enlisted.

Similar provision is made for secondary pupils.

In Surrey 'enrichment sets' are established in which philosophy and other broader frameworks of the study of human experience are considered. Eminent visiting speakers from all spheres of life cover a further range of subject matter outside the usual range of school concerns.

Oldham Borough Council points its teachers to the 'commercial' packs available, ie individualized Learning Packs for Gifted Children in Primary Schools devised at Nene College, Schools Council Enrichment Packs, eg problem solving, research skills etc. Also available are the sets and packs devised by working groups of teachers. A bank of resources is being built up at the teachers' centre.

Sunderland LEA has been interested and involved in finding and helping the able child since the mid '70s. There is no specialist adviser working on giftedness alone but the advisory team has devised a policy for assisting teachers working with pupils of exceptional ability.

In 1976 a pilot scheme followed these lines: guidelines, after Hoyle and Wilks (1976), were sent to each primary school. In-service courses on 'Identifying possibly gifted children' were mounted throughout the Authority. A group of primary children aged between 8 and 10 were brought together for Saturday morning enrichment classes in art, maths and language. The art classes still operate, mathematics material has been produced, and De Bono's 'Thinking' packs as well as the SCEPS material is available for loan to schools. Other material is available to schools through the advisory staffs and the teachers' centre.

A brief mention must be made of Essex, pioneers in this

field. Readers are directed to the chapters in this book by Belle Wallace, advisory teacher for gifted pupils in Essex County Council.

Some authorities make subject specific provision. Many support able musicians by financing special training. In Surrey pupils gifted in modern languages have the use of individual enrichment programmes in language laboratories, while the less talented in the group receive more conventional tuition as a class. Similarly in other schools, a second modern language (in addition to French and Latin) is frequently offered to many of the most able pupils after their first twelve months in the school.

Manchester Education Authority supports pupils at intensive two day courses for linguists.

In Avon, a group of primary teachers is producing and writing material for upper-aged junior pupils: a series of about 20 tasks which are connected with a study of the industrial revolution. The operation is overseen by a headmaster who has been designated leader of the group and some funding has been received by the Schools Council.

Although good work is done in this field around the country as the work of the Essex LEA (described in Chapter 8) makes clear, there are pitfalls with curriculum enrichment. It is all too easy to point teachers to commercial materials and feel that duty has been done. These materials themselves may need critical appraisal or adaptation; materials are not widespread or readily available; and teachers may need to be trained in their rationale and use. One would want to be slightly suspicious of any LEA which put all its eggs into the curriculum enrichment basket. There is also scope here for a more dynamic approach.

Some of the most successful ventures in dealing with the needs of the able pupil have occurred where the school has been able to call on outside resources. Schools in university towns have much to draw upon, and unique links can be fostered between school and university. Colleges of education, polytechnics and medical schools may also be tapped; but awareness of the value of the gifted (professional) parent should not be overlooked. Competent practitioners of such professionals as law, accountancy and veterinary practice will all yield valuable stimulus material to the able pupil.

Harrow LEA is able to use just this facility, for within its area there is a college of higher education and Brunel University. Suggestions have been put forward that small groups of students in the high schools with similar interests, for example in science and mathematics, might have the opportunity to attend occasional lectures or seminars at one of the institutions.

These last examples lead us to look at the various extra-curricular and out-of-school examples of enrichment quoted by

LEA respondents.

Extra-curricular enrichment
Regular programmes of organized visits to museums and art
galleries are arranged for the most able sixth form students
in Surrey LEA.
In years 4 and 5 of the comprehensive school, select
groups are given the opportunity to specialize in a great
variety of additional subjects which include course modules
in sociology, drama examination courses, school-magazine
production, advanced graphics, additional foreign language
seminars, Latin, statistics, computer studies, electronics,
meteorology and astronomy. Many of these schools run club
activities in the above fields, together with student
participation in the Duke of Edinburgh Award Scheme. This
scheme enables pupils to pursue and develop a great diversity
of special interests and talents, alongside the everyday
school curriculum. Frequent cultural excursions and theatre
visits are incorporated into the activities, and foreign
student exchanges are arranged. Competitive events are
promoted and the raising of personal technical standards is
encouraged in gymnastics and field sports.
The Isle of Man Board of Education is organizing one day
summer school sessions for very able children this year
(1982). The sessions are designed to develop skills in
science, scientific and computer studies, history and
geography, and in mathematics.
Leicestershire has an international reputation for
music, drama and dance. Leicestershire School of Theatre
opened in September 1979. Seven years earlier the Leicester
Youth Theatre was inaugurated by the newly appointed drama
adviser and teachers from the county's schools. In those
seven years a network of youth theatres was established in
all the principal towns in Leicestershire, enabling over 500
young people to meet on a weekly basis to take part in youth
theatre programmes. Leicestershire School of Theatre has
been established to give those young people who are most
committed, an opportunity to work on varied projects at a
high level, and to represent the county at home and abroad.
The school meets every Saturday morning as well as for
residential rehearsal courses during holidays and weekends.
Leicestershire children have taken part in the Summer School
of the National Festival of Youth Theatres, and have visited
Turin with productions of Macbeth (1979) and the Caucasian
Chalk Circle (1980).
The County School of Dance was formed early in 1976
following a blanket mailing to every school in the
Leicestershire Education Authority. The School was
established 'to encourage dance in schools throughout the

Authority and to foster two central dance groups'. The
school is open, through audition, to every child in the
county, whether or not he or she has received previous
dance training. The group usually meets once a week for
training sessions of one to two hours; but when a group
is working towards a production, meetings may well increase
to several evenings a week, with some weekend rehearsals. It
is hoped that the School of Dance will be able to take on a
much wider role, expanding, providing specialist tuition to
particularly able children in the day time as part of the
normal educational curriculum.

The Leicestershire Schools' Symphony Orchestra was
founded in 1948 by Eric Pinkett OBE, the county's first
Musical Adviser. Throughout its existence the LSSO has
featured regularly on radio and television, and has made
several successful recordings. It has performed in many of
the European concert halls, and remains distinctive by
drawing only upon students of school age.

Manchester Education Authority provides a large number
of activities which, even if they are not aimed directly at
the most able, do benefit these children. Examples of such
provision are:

... science summer schools

... the summer school for Advanced Level art students

... dance centres

... support for children in sport at representative
level

... enrichment work in mathematics for abler pupils in
junior Schools

... the work of the Music Centres

... humanities enrichment lectures

... support for field work in Pembrokeshire and
elsewhere

... centre for outdoor pursuits and field studies.

Able pupils in Manchester are also encouraged to attend
the Saturday morning meetings of the Greater Manchester and
Cheshire Branch of the NAGC. Approximately seventy children
attend at any one time, and normally there are seven or eight
separate activities on offer.

The formation of clubs or projects for able pupils is a
common phenomenon around the country. The same kind of

technique has been used for some years by the National Association for Gifted Children. As far as LEAs are concerned use of this form of enrichment may be dictated by funds available over and above the general allocation. However, clubs or projects are formed and do flourish, and when economic times are good more subject areas become available. Most interests are covered from time to time, though some authorities level their support across the board, while others tend to specialize in music or art.

In the Metropolitan borough of Dudley, Saturday clubs have been formed in art, history and geography. In art, two projects were developed, one for 10-12-year-olds, and a major art Summer School for a carefully selected group of 15-18-year-olds. The history format was similar, and children were selected for this from the results of a series of tests given as part of a research project. The geography sessions were for 10-11-year-olds, and here, over a period of two terms, the children studied the River Stour from its source to the Severn. Similar after-school courses were held in literature, languages and science.

Club activities are useful in that they draw together enthusiasts in particular areas from both pupils and staff. Children are therefore able to work with others who have particular skills and often have specific knowledge. Such clubs already exist in some Harrow schools. Harrow has its own Saturday morning music school where talented young musicians come together to develop their own skills.

Hounslow Education Authority provides special Saturday morning clubs for 7-12-year-olds. These Saturday schools are held in local secondary schools, and the 200 or so youngsters are able to call upon the expertise of qualified staff and voluntary students and parents. It is pertinent to note here that Hounslow Authority regard these clubs as virtually self-supporting. It may be worthwhile for any interested teacher to probe more fully into this particular approach in these days of economic stringencies.

Acceleration

If curriculum enrichment is the commonest practice, another widespread method of helping the able is acceleration. This device was used extensively in the United States in the 1960s and 1970s; but it has some inherent drawbacks. Most authorities agree that limited acceleration is desirable; but acceleration by two years or more may produce a mismatch between mental age and emotional age for the able pupil in the peer group. Nevertheless, some LEAs reported examples of its use.

In Surrey it is possible to find accelerated courses in English Language, maths, art and biology which lead to pupils

taking 'O' level one year early. In English this
acceleration is followed by a Novel Workshop during the fifth
year of studies. Here each pupil has to produce a six-
chapter novel by the end of the Spring term, a task designed
to give the able pupil more stimulation than is inherent in
merely following the 'O' level course.

Many Surrey schools offer additional classes or
individual tuition to their most able sixth formers who wish
to compete for prestigious places or scholarships at places
of higher education. 'S' level sessions are available in
all the main subject areas where the calibre and commitment
of the candidate justifies this. Many schools offer
preparation classes and projects to cover all the possible
requirements for the 'Oxbridge' General Studies papers.

There is an occasional acceleration of an individual
pupil to join an older year group in separate subject areas
in which he or she might excel. Able pupils at one school
are encouraged to attend adult education classes, or are
enabled to attend specific course modules at local technical
colleges.

Two or three schools have found corporate membership of
NAGC very useful, as the Association's advice has been
supportive in the school's efforts to extend the abilities
and interests of the brightest pupils.

For secondary school pupils, acceleration is an
opportunity afforded by several high schools in the Harrow
authority. The acceleration programme is basically in
English language and mathematics where, it is felt, most
advantage can be gained. Accelerated mathematics has proved
singularly successful inasmuch as time is then gained by the
pupil which allows him/her to take Additional Mathematics
in the year gained; a useful bridge between 'O' and 'A'
level courses.   Other subjects are available but the
Authority feels that there is little advantage to the able
student since Harrow 11-16 high schools do not offer 'A'
level. Early entry to the 'O' level examination, followed
by a year of inactivity, would hardly be described as
stimulating! Early transfer to sixth form colleges is rare.

Surrey staff take the view that such students in sixth
form colleges are, by definition, capable of taking a wider
number and variety of 'A' and 'S' level courses
simultaneously than is the norm. For this reason, enrichment and extension of the programmes for such individuals
are provided almost exclusively on a subject department
basis. Each head of department decides what additional
opportunities should be offered. These are very often the
results of links with external agencies, or of special
coaching for entries in national competitions and
conferences (eg National Maths Competition and International
Science Fortnight).

Extra curricular activities in Surrey's sixth form

colleges include major dramatic productions, or regular lunchtime musical recitals which give able musicians the opportunity to experience the severer test of performing either individually or in a 'chamber' group framework in front of others.

Individualized learning processes

Some LEAs have opted to provide special resources suitable for use by able pupils. Of these, Surrey is typical.

Surrey LEA established a Media Resources Centre in the late 1970s. Its brief was to provide 'audio-visual' materials which would be particularly useful to exceptionally able children in the Authority's schools. This unit was an outcome of policy-decision to ensure that appropriate provision was available for the able in the same way as it had been for pupils with learning difficulties. Materials used by the unit include Open University packages. Although much Open University material is designed for those following a specific course of study, considerable benefit can be gained by the individual able pupil watching single examples or short series of broadcast programmes.

Subject specific courses are put together by the Media Resources Centre. In science, experiments have been recorded onto video-tape using experienced teachers. The tapes are then copied and become available for loan throughout the county.

In Latin a complete series of tapes was made, designed to support Ecce Romani books. This series emerged as a result of demand from the 12-16 comprehensive schools who were without specialist teachers. The venture was completed by production of a companion volume for use with the Cambridge Classics course. Bright youngsters can also use the series to add a further language to their armoury: particularly useful if previous course option allocations had prevented this.

Along with some in other areas, some Surrey teachers have used individualized approaches simply to restructure work-sheets. They have incorporated questions which can be answered at more than one cognitive level, thus stimulating individual exploration of various topics to greater depths.

These individualized approaches are useful classroom tools; but they must not serve as an excuse for some LEAs to opt out of making more far-reaching policy decisions and provisions.

Training teachers

So far we have surveyed what LEAs advise their teachers to do in order to identify and cope with the needs of able pupils. The one important area so far neglected is that of teacher training, both initial and in-service.

LEAs are involved in, but not directly concerned with, initial training courses. Of our respondents only Harrow saw fit to expand on this theme. Harrow points out that able pupils make heavy demands upon the time, skills and professional judgement of teachers. For many authorities, streaming is no longer viable; setting, banding or mixed ability teaching in the lower school has become the norm. It is therefore imperative that student teachers are aware of the requirements of very able and 'gifted' children, and for tutors to suggest suitable strategies for meeting them should be part of the basic training of all teachers. Harrow LEA suggests this is a matter which needs to be explored and taken up with staffs of training institutions.

Strategies for the training of teachers in-service tend to fall into two main kinds: the production of some form of guideline document, or the use of the advisory service in a stimulus or training capacity.

Buckinghamshire has produced a comprehensive document aimed at both heads and teachers who find themselves with able pupils in their school or class. This document points the way to understanding the child better, and lists libraries, resources, books and booklists that may be helpful to the teacher. A great deal of attention is paid to the Schools Council Curriculum Enrichment packs. Staff are also directed to the national institutions with concern for the gifted: MENSA, NAGC. Much stimulation for the able pupil can be gained from national bodies or from industry, and teachers are encouraged to explore these avenues.

Oldham Borough Council produced a paper outlining the background to the problem, drawing attention to the special educational needs of the able child in the mixed ability class. The paper was intended to stimulate discussion among staffs and to serve as a background to a number of planned in-service courses. Oldham LEA noted that an accepted form of identifying the bright pupil was the use of the checklist (Laycock, 1957 and Ogilvie, 1973). However, as there were difficulties in using these Oldham, in common with a number of other LEAs, plans to use enrichment programmes as a base for its future work. The in-service training will therefore concentrate on enrichment skills.

In several secondary schools Avon LEA is developing strategies for identifying the needs of able children in the first three years. This initiative is guided by the senior adviser for secondary education, and it is hoped that the group will soon be able to produce some guidelines for inclusion in the county's curriculum booklet. A teacher is being seconded for the autumn term (1982) to co-ordinate and produce a first draft of these guidelines.

Newham has recently established a Project for Children of Exceptional Ability. A steering committee was formed in October 1981 to guide and direct the project, and a teacher/

researcher was appointed to work, initially for two days per week, starting January 1982. The aims of the project were to develop ways for teachers to identify children of exceptional ability. This would include the use of checklists and, possibly, simple tests. Once the children have been identified it is intended to offer them some extra provision within the normal classroom setting. The envisaged provision will include some alteration of teaching methods, and the introduction of enrichment materials. A number of Newham schools are interested in forming a pilot group to explore the use of identification methods, and it is hoped to commence the initial work shortly. Depending on what is learnt at this trial stage, it may be possible to introduce the methods throughout the Newham schools.

Suffolk LEA working party came to the conclusion that the LEA should widen its responsibility by in-service training of teachers through courses arranged at teachers' centres and in schools, so that in each school there is at least one member of staff aware of the problems and needs of very able children, including both identification and subsequent curricular provision.

Isle of Man Board of Education is, on its own admission, a relative newcomer to curriculum work in the field of gifted children. The one exception to this is the Board's musical activities which have been carried on for many years. In 1981 a working group of mainly primary teachers was formed, following a visit and course on the Island by a member from Lancaster Curriculum Development Centre. The group felt that a broader area than just material for gifted children should be considered, and a curriculum enrichment programme was decided upon. To this end, a series of curriculum stimulus boxes/materials are planned to come into operation shortly. The Isle of Man Board of Education liaises closely with the Schools Council Gifted Children Project.

In the Leeds City Council area, individual schools take basic responsibility for the needs of pupils, whatever their abilities. However, in some cases a need is felt for more specific guidance, and working parties have therefore been set up to consider the two areas of the identification of pupils of exceptional ability and the provision of special resource materials for them. The groups of teachers have been meeting for some time now, and pilot schemes have been developed in some schools.

Leicestershire has a tradition of commitment to the practice of comprehensive schooling, thus ensuring that opportunities are offered to children of all abilities through the schools. However, there are some aspects of the curriculum which are highly specialized, and therefore supplements are offered in the schools through teachers' centres. Leicestershire has run in-service courses for its teachers to look at the broad issues of identifying and providing for gifted pupils. Also intended was the opportunity for staff to exchange information about gifted pupils and to explore initiatives which might be undertaken in the individual schools.

Derbyshire County Council have reproduced two articles by Y. Gupta, Senior Educational Psychologist at the Centre for Gifted Children, Grays Thorrock, Essex. The articles, in the form of a handout, are given to all teachers and represent the basis of the Council's polity towards able pupils.

Working parties have a habit of concerning only those who are directly involved, and they may or may not result in positive action. Policy statements are subject to the same reservations. Generally, classroom teachers want more tangible help with the thirty pupils who face them at eleven o'clock on Tuesday morning. LEAs often try to provide this through the good offices of the advisory service.

Sometimes an authority appoints a specialist adviser. Essex is an example of such an LEA. Often financial stringencies prevent this; and Suffolk reports itself to be in this situation. Instead, in Suffolk, the LEA working party recommend that one of its advisers should have the responsibility for in-service training of teachers in the identification and subsequent treatment of able pupils. It was also suggested that teachers' groups should be formed, in all curriculum areas, so that these may become the springboard for new ideas, and a place where current practices (including those from other LEAs) and research might be discussed and acted upon. At the same time, resource centres should be created, and these centres, too, should contain examples of both local and national initiatives. Finally it was suggested that collaborative provision for the needs of very able children should be encouraged between schools and groups of schools by the LEAs advisers and psychologists.

In Harrow it is suggested that:

... the advisory service and schools psychological service should offer support and guidance to schools in formulating a policy for identifying intellectually able pupils and implementing such a policy

... to help teachers develop their skills in catering for those of outstanding ability, the advisory service should arrange a programme of seminars and workshops. There may be some value in an introductory conference to increase awareness of the issues.

... the advisory service should produce reports on

specific aspects of giftedness (eg in modern
languages, maths etc) for consideration by the
Schools Sub-Committee and as a basis for wider
discussions.

There is a need for the LEA to undertake in-service
training for teachers on how best to provide for the
intellectually able pupil. The Metropolitan Borough of
Calderdale has recently asked one of its advisers to take a
particular interest in the education of gifted children as
part of the general advisory responsibilities. This adviser
is at present examining the provision and need for in-service
courses, and looking at guidelines and resources available to
teachers and gifted children within the authority. Calderdale
retains a selection system at eleven plus, and children with
high cognitive abilities are generally educated within this
system. Support is given to the schools by the Psychological
Service. Musically talented pupils, and those outstanding in
the area of PE, are catered for in well-established,
successful 'schools' which complement the mainstream
curriculum by providing extra-curricular opportunities in
these two areas. It is expected that courses will be
provided for the authority's teachers during the current
year (1982).

Surrey teachers are always looking out for ways in which
to challenge and stimulate their ablest pupils, and this is
most commonly done in the following ways: staff are encouraged
and enabled to attend courses and conferences arranged by
universities and polytechnics or by certain prestigious
professional bodies. Frequently the school library
facilities and catalogues are being developed with the very
able predominantly in mind. Local links are made with
engineering firms for use of facilities and technical
expertise by pupils to enable them to develop on their own
individual problem solving projects.

Recently, many schools in the Surrey area have devoted
their annual one-day staff training conference to the consideration of how best they might improve and refine their
attempts to cater for the needs of the 'gifted'.

From time to time in Buckinghamshire there are courses
and conferences for teachers concerned with gifted children,
for example, a DES Regional Course entitled 'Making
Provision for Gifted Children'. These courses are
advertised in the Monthly Bulletin, and lists of DES and
other courses circulated to schools.

Oldham, too, runs courses for primary and secondary
teachers at teachers' centres. One forthcoming course is
entitled 'The Able Child in a Mixed Ability Class'.

Similarly, North Tyneside, in their reply, indicated
that some initiatives had been taken in their authority.
Schools provided simple information on pupils regarded as

gifted; one day courses on the needs, identification and teaching of able pupils had been set up; and a collection of resources had been compiled, this for use by teachers. Identification of the gifted was also achieved by LEA assessment procedures. A working group for a Schools Council Project on Gifted Children functioned in 1971, and a headmaster of a junior school has been a member of the Consultative Committee of the continuation project.

The various authors of this book are aware of the existence of other in-service initiatives by individual LEAs. However, where an LEA has elected not to reply to our letter I have elected not to include any details. Reticence on the part of a few LEAs may be explained by what follows.

The place of politics

Nottinghamshire, in common with one hundred other education authorities in England, was asked what provision was made for the gifted pupil. The author (having lived in the county) knew that, in 1979, a Curriculum Development Centre was set up to serve five secondary schools to the west of the city, and a director was appointed to the Unit. Help was enlisted from specialist teachers recruited to the Centre and materials for the most able were produced. These materials have been used both with small tutor groups within the five schools and as resource packs in other Nottinghamshire schools. The tutor groups were all taught within their parent schools but by Centre staff. Saturday clubs were formed, Mathematics Problem-Solving Days were held, usually at the Centre. Weekend-long activities were based at nearby places of interest. The Unit appeared to be serving the needs of the able pupil in the five schools very well. Other pupils of all abilities were benefitting from the various findings. But a change in the control of the Council closed the Centre in the summer of 1981. The Centre just happened to draw some of its clientele from an area of private housing, highly favoured by the University staffs. To the newly formed Council, this was a socially unacceptable form of élitism, and closure of the unit appeared as a priority in the Labour manifesto. The venture disbanded as an aid to able pupils, and now receives pupils of mixed ability, who are in need of any specialist help. Nottinghamshire's reply to the editor of this book merely stated that 'there was an initiative until recently, but that initiative closed since the change of political control of the County Council at the last election in May 1981'.

Over and over again in this book it has been stressed that improvement in a teacher's ability to cope with able pupils' needs is improvement in teaching skills for all pupils. One day, perhaps, educational decisions will cease to be made on political grounds.

EXCUSES, EXCUSES!

So it was that the number of responses to our invitation to contribute information for this chapter was better than expected,but still disappointing. A few replies were unhelpful. Three verbatim quotations give the flavour.

> ... The Advisory Service in Thickford is under considerable pressure because of staffing reduction in the last few years. Mr W Gummidge will let you have some information when he has time.
> /He never did./

> ... I am sorry that we are not able to point to anything in this borough which you might find of particular interest in this respect.

> ... I regret that, because of pressure of work upon the Department, I am unable to help you.

THE SHOW GOES ON

Despite some disappointing responses and a large-scale failure to respond, there is evidence that progress is still being made. We were told, for example:

> ... A Handbook of guidance on the education of gifted children in Hampshire is in the process of being printed and we hope to have this available in the near future.

Cheshire, too, assured us that, following a request from an Education Sub-Committee, an interim report on the 'Education of the Gifted Child' was presented to the sub-committee in 1978. A more detailed report was prepared in the following year for an Inter-Sub-Committee. The latter subsequently resolved to establish a Working Party to study any Government proposals put forward. However, no firm Government proposals have appeared as yet, and consequently the Authority has not moved very far. However, we were comforted that Cheshire is not ignoring the needs of able children, and is very much alive to this particular issue. Perhaps this goodwill prevails among some of the sixty or so non-respondents, too.

Postscript
Perhaps what emerges most clearly from this chapter is the chequer-board nature of provision for the able pupil. The child's chance to gain more or less benefit from the

enormous number of hours he spends in school depends, as always, upon the caprice of the geographical location in which he just happens to live.

For further study

City of Manchester Education Department, undated mimeograph, 'Report of the Manchester Curriculum Group for able and talented children'.

Devon County Council (1977). Find the Gifted Child, Devon Education Department.

Lawrence, D (1980). 'The role of the local education authority' in R Povey (ed) Educating the Gifted Child, Harper & Row.

Ogilvie, E (1973). Gifted Children in Primary Schools, Macmillan (Chapter 6: Provision by LEAs).

Royal Society (1979). Science and the Organization of Schools in England, Royal Society Education Committee.

Rutter, M. (198). Fifteen Thousand Hours

References
Hoyle, E and Wilks, J (1976). Gifted Children and their Education, DES.

Laycock, S R (1957). Gifted children: a handbook for the classroom teacher, Toronto: Copp-Clark.

NOTE:
As we go to press we have received a copy of a survey entitled Teaching Able and Gifted Children (1982) conducted by the NAGC. Following a 50% response rate to a questionnaire this slim booklet of the findings is marginally more optimistic about the extent of provision for able pupils than the present chapter.

Conclusion

Trevor Kerry

I am sitting at my desk enjoying the sunshine and planning a series of individual exercises for the eight-year-olds I have agreed to teach tomorrow. It's just after five. Around the country pupils and teachers have bussed home, and the administrators in education offices are snaking to rail and tube stations. The telephone rings. A secretive and confidential voice asks:

'Are you the one who's writing a book about able pupils?'

'That's right.'

'Good. Whybother's the name. Chief Officer at Snugshire. It's quiet here just now. Just thought I'd call about your letter, old chap.'

'Splendid. Can you tell me what Snugshire is doing for the able pupil?'

'You're not recording this conversation, are you? It is off the record, isn't it?'

'Of course it is. What did you want to tell me? Have you got a new plan to unveil?'

'Well, no. Actually, you see, I really rang to make sure you wouldn't say anything bad about Snugshire, old chap. We're doing our best, against enormous odds.'

'Really. Don't you have any bright youngsters in Snugshire?'

'Yes. Bags of 'em. It's just, well ... there are barriers.'

'Oh, I see. Teaching staff isn't all it might be. Why don't you get your heads together ...'

'No, no. You've got it all wrong, old chap. We've a great bunch of teachers. It's the primary school heads, you see. Claim to a man they haven't got a bright youngster between them, so they don't <u>need</u> to do anything.'

'Well, that <u>could</u> be a barrier. Presumably the secondary heads are keen, though. Even if it's only exam results that they want, they must have some concern to help the most able.'

'You are sure this won't go any further, aren't you? Look, two years ago the secondary heads got together and agreed to put an embargo on the local press. So now they don't make their results public. It's a very equitable system. Does away with competition between schools. Of course, every parent in Snugshire can opt for the secondary school of his or her choice when it comes to transfer time. But by doing away with garbled comparative information through the media - so unreliable, newspapers - we make it easy for them. Do you know, old chap, even with freedom of choice 99.7% of our parents choose to send their children to the nearest school? None of this nonsense about moving house to be in the right catchment area!'

'But do you have a policy statement about the able child?'

'Oh, good Heavens, no. As a matter of fact, old chap, we - I mean the councillors - decided we shouldn't use the word 'able' in Snugshire. It's socially divisive, you see.'

'How about slow learners. You must be doing a lot ...?'

'No, well, actually, we did build a few language laboratories in the 1970s. You have to move with the times. Mostly obsolete now, of course. Sorry? No, must rush. The cleaners want me out of the office. I'd better go. They're on piece-rate ...'

The conversation just reported is a composite of several real dialogues which came the way of the present editor during the making of this book.

Putting together a book composed of individual contributions is a fascinating if somewhat nerve-racking

process. The editor is in the privileged position of being
the first person to learn from his contributors. But his
responsibility to weld the distinctive strands into a logical
whole can be onerus. In the present case, however, they have
welded themselves; for the messages of this book sing out
loud and clear:

... there are many bright youngsters in our schools

... some are easily recognized; others masquerade, are
underachievers

... LEAs need to adopt and implement policies towards
these pupils and to raise the awareness of heads
and teachers

... identification procedures must be used in individual
schools

... once discovered, these pupils <u>can</u> be taught
effectively even in mixed ability classes

... what is needed most is a programme of initial and
in-service education to help teachers fine-tune
their skills

... there are important social and economic reasons for
making sure our recommendations come about

... even at the classroom level, improved teaching
skills will raise the quality of education for
every pupil regardless of ability.

Little remains for this editorial except to ask a
question: will the words of our song fall on empty air?